SURESH KOHLI (b. 1947), a multi-dimensional personality—poet, literary critic, editor, translator, broadcaster, film historian, documentary film maker—has 32 published works (including five volumes of poetry and a novel), and a hundred literary and cultural short films to his credit. His films have been screened not only in India but also in Australia, France, Germany, Spain, Nepal, the UK. He lives and works in New Delhi.

D1723413

STORIES
from
MODERN
INDIA

edited by
Suresh Kohli

Om Books International

First published in 2013 by

OM

Om Books International
Corporate & Editorial Office
A-12, Sector 64, Noida 201 301
Uttar Pradesh, India
Phone: +91 120 477 4100
Email: editorial@ombooks.com
Website: www.ombooksinternational.com

Sales Office
4379/4B, Prakash House, Ansari Road
Darya Ganj, New Delhi 110 002, India
Phone: +91 11 2326 3363, 2326 5303
Fax: +91 11 2327 8091
Email: sales@ombooks.com
Website: www.ombooks.com

ISBN: 978-93-81607-16-9

10 9 8 7 6 5 4 3 2 1

Printed in India

CONTENTS

INTRODUCTION

In many ways, the present selection can be subscribed as a companion volume to my earlier, ever getting reborn, *Modern Indian Short Stories* that was commissioned and published by Heinemann (London) in 1974. Ever since, different foster fathers in India have diligently looked after it. Now it is seeking another one. One of the possible reasons for its success could be the very selection itself that appealed to successive generations of readers.

The urge to make a second attempt germinated soon after the first reprint of the Indian edition sold out the same year. Many reprints followed. Then, in 1991, it was decided to do a revised edition to give the product some more longevity. That also hit the bull's eye, and the same story followed until the imprint went out of circulation.

The book landed in the mortuary until, almost a decade later, another relatively new imprint decided to take a chance. Surprisingly, this edition also went out of circulation within two years. But while the Indian reprint was still alive in the 90s, Heinemann (London) having abandoned the scheme, I decided to not only correct the lapses (though no reviewer really took notice of it, and generally praised the attempt) and give due import to some of the other stories that one had no reason not to include.

The second attempt was stillborn because I changed stream midway and by the time I came to a shore, the original publisher had gone out of business and I realised I needed to start all over again.

More than any other form of writing, the short story has been like an ever-pregnant maiden whose offsprings could be found in various regions, learning and unlearning the idiom in Indian languages. So when one picked up the threads once again it was discovered that there had been many more in the Indian languages in and around the same period that had escaped legitimacy and never really been brought to light. Then came the arduous process of digging and re-digging to try and put together another collection that was not easy because it is like the churning of an ocean. And even though it was not the original plan, one decided to do a little back and forth, in terms of time frame, to make it rewarding. Dovetailing elements that stir the inner turmoil it has been a rewarding experience.

In the last edition of the earlier attempt I emphasised that if *there is a discernible element of continuity in change visible in these stories it is because there was a collective unconscious response to situations and events...the short story in most languages sought to explore the psyche and the mind of the individual* and elements that propel someone to act or react to a situation. So while the basic metaphor remains the same, the location of the particle demands a different perception. *Sometimes the form became more dominant than the story itself. This is largely because of the western influence as the writer as a reader got exposed to a greater variety of narrative skills. But while these skills seemed to enjoy some sort of relevance for the detached individual in a constantly growing alienated milieu, the individual in the Indian society was still an inseparable part of the collective, whether at home or outside.*

Although written in a different context, the brilliant Hindi writer, the late Bhisham Sahni, once observed that no matter what one tries, the smell of the soil continues to revolute in the subconscious, and even though with time the writer as an individual moved to urban settings in search of greener pastures, invariably distanced him from his roots, a recall of the past still echoes and re-echoes in the subconscious prompting him for a revisit. "These writers (talking mainly in the context of Hindi though equally relevant for other languages) had brought with them memories and influences of their small-town or rural life where they had spent their younger days. Sometimes, either nostalgia or a sense of social concern prompted them to write stories based on their earlier experiences and observations," he outlined succinctly.

This element that Bhisham Sahni outlined is still a dominant feature in the works of writers from the southern languages. One reason could be that even if these writers are operating in an urban setting, they are not far from their roots. They still smell and feel and talk of fishes, seas and fishponds as against their contemporaries living in big cities and various metropolis, especially in the northern belt. What is common, however, are the vast spectrums of expressions and emotions that come out in the form of analysis, introspection and nostalgia.

Like in the earlier volume, taking into account the expanse of material available in English translation at any given point of time, making any subject or object-centric selection is out of the question. So one has no option but to rely entirely on translations available, and that too—in the absence of a wider choice of literary journals in English—collections that are language-specific that one can lay ones hands on. Sadly, with the exception of Sahitya Akademi's bio-monthly, *Indian Literature* that on an average publishes three or four stories in a single volume, there is no other source, unless one can lay hands on an occasional language-specific magazine that disappears even before one is able to reach the source.

My process of selection over the years has been limited to these sources. Every time I came across a good story, whether in terms of theme, subject, treatment or the sheer novelty of thought, I would set aside the clipping for better use; later. The selection process for this collection has been the same. Unfortunately, when it comes to the period element, one has been largely restricted to the sixties and the early seventies, and a couple from an earlier phase that could not be included in the earlier volume(s) the quality of translation notwithstanding, and for that one pleads guilty; sourcing the original being another issue.

The English translations of three stories that I selected for this volume—Oh Meghamala, Cock-Fight and Gauthami tells a Story—were thoroughly revised to make them more accessible to the contemporary reader. My editor Ipshita Sengupta Nag proved to be an able ally in that endeavour as also for the rest of this collection.

Despite the visible changes in the post-reforms Indian society made more convincing through satellite images; for most foreigners India is still a big puzzle. Thanks to the impact of the Indian English novel there is an urge in anyone who can afford a trip to visit this land of conflicting images. But then the more palpable, enticing pictures of the Indian English novel, though now representing a much wider spectrum than ever before, is still not enough, and therefore there can be no better way than to present the best of Indian literature—not only to the world, but also to Indians themselves.

In that direction this anthology is a meagre attempt.

1

MRITYUNJAY

Birendra Kumar Bhattacharya

He didn't like to stay in the witches' cave. So Dhanpur told Ahina, "Better take me to the boat, Brother Ahina."

Ahina Konwar was preparing to light a big fire, but Bhibhiram and Dadhi told him not to. Lighting a big fire at a time like this would achieve nothing better than attract the attention of the enemy.

Dhanpur's shin had not stopped bleeding. The heat of a fire would not help. So they were all making arrangements to carry him to the boat.

Bal Bahadur had gone ahead to keep an eye on his boat, which had a canopy. So it would not be difficult to hide Dhanpur in the boat.

Koli had examined the injury and was weeping. Gazing at her rotund, wheat-complexioned face, Dhanpur said, "Koli Bai, why are you inviting misfortune by weeping like this? Take it from me that I am going to die. There is no point weeping over it. You will only get swollen eyes. First tell me how Subhadra is. I would have died in peace if only I had seen her once. Tell me, how is she?"

Koli replied to this in a tone of complaint. "So these fellows haven't given you the news, all this while, have they? Subhadra committed suicide."

Bhibhiram and Dadhi were getting the stretcher ready. In the dim light of the fire, they looked like Messengers of Death to Dhanpur.

Madhu was sitting near the fire to warm his chest and clearing his throat periodically. He was still running a temperature. He felt as if all his joints were about to come apart.

Ahina Konwar alone stood near Dhanpur and observed his reactions to the news very closely. Could the man take this great mental shock in his present condition? But when he saw that the news had not shattered him and Dhanpur seemed to have taken it in his stride, he remarked with a sigh, "By Krishna, it is the others who wouldn't tell you. I had thought..."

"I knew that you had all been hiding something from me," said Dhanpur. "Perhaps it was for the best. But how did she die?" he asked, somehow controlling his emotions.

The agony was now unmistakably manifest on Dhanpur's face. He had been lying face down and now tried to roll over, but all his struggles to turn over were in vain. In a surge of affection, Koli nestled his head on her lap. Dhanpur was now reclining at an awkward sideways angle. Koli narrated everything, in all the terrifying detail.

Then Subhadra must have taken her own life in a state of total helplessness? Dhanpur thought. She didn't even have the patience to wait for him. What if he had survived? Wouldn't he have been heartbroken? She had acted thoughtlessly. How could the silly madcap assume that he was going to die? If that bullet hadn't struck him, he would have survived. But now there was no chance of it, at all. All for the best in a way! He had been worried about her. Now, he had no further worries. He was totally carefree. He had no one to worry about him, either at his Kampur home or at Raha. He could die with his mind at rest.

His burning desire to see his country free was his only unfulfilled wish. Well, you couldn't have all your wishes! The independence movement had received a great setback. It would take some time for it to build up momentum again. Then other people would fight. He wouldn't be there, but his dream would remain.

When people sat around fireplaces, someone somewhere might recall his dark, medium-built appearance. He had liked this body of his, been fond of it. True, he had inherited it from his parents, but the key to it had been entirely in his own hands. He had driven it about like a yoked bull. Well, the ploughing was over now. He could throw off the yoke and go to sleep. And then total peace afterwards.

His lungs were working very fast.

Koli stroked his head and said, "When you get well this time we will find you another Subhadra."

Dhanpur smiled indulgently. "How will you create another Subhadra? Oh yes, another Subhadra is still there. Does anyone know anything about her? Has she come back from town?"

No one had any information.

Then Dhanpur said, "Koli *Baideu,* take me to her place just once. We can certainly elude the police at night and get there. I had promised to rest at her place for a few days. She will probably be waiting for me. But then who will come with me? Do the men have any guts left at all?"

"Why not, in Krishna's name?" Ahina Konwar answered. "He rises and strikes and strikes as he rises; at no time does the true warrior know defeat, they say. In Krishna's name, whether we live or die, you have only to get onto this stretcher. You will meet Dimi and, by Krishna, also get to Guwahati. And there, by Krishna, you have Dr. Barua who will look after you."

"Life will scarcely remain in this body upto Guwahati, brother Ahina. Just take me up to the Garo village. But who will go with you? Madhu? And who else?" asked Dhanpur.

After waiting for a reply for a while, Dhanpur said, "Let Dadhi remain here. Do you hear me, Dadhi teacher?"

Dadhi now came and stood before Dhanpur. "I will remain here till the *Gossain* and Rupnarayan arrive. You better take as much of the stuff as you can. I mean the rifles and the ammunition. You might even need them on the way," he said.

He then added,"Do you hear, Brother Bhibhiram? Upstream, beyond the Garo village is a deserted landing. Tell Bal Bahadur to moor the boat there. Madhu will go and fetch Dimi. Do you hear me, Madhu? Why are you wriggling your torso? Hasn't your fever left you yet? Go to Mayang after you have fetched Dimi.

"I can't make what Lairam is doing. If he has not done anything incriminating then we have to keep the *Gossain* and this group in hiding at his lowland farm. I don't know what Rupnarayan likes about this witches' cave. We cannot remain here, even a moment now. The military has surrounded it on all sides. So the safest place is that lowland farm.

"You are sure to meet Lairam at Dimi's place. When you finish your work there, go to the *Gossain's ashram* at Kamarkuchi. Assess the state of affairs in Mayang from there. Find out about the *Gossain's* wife. I do not know whether she is in the lock-up or elsewhere. She is pregnant, you know. That's why I am worried. The way these butchers go after even the unborn babies, you wouldn't be surprised if they tear out what she is carrying within.

"And yes, you will find the *Shanti Sena* people near the *Gossain's* home. Hand over the rifles to them. I mean, whatever you can."

Madhu stood up and Dadhi noticed that his eyes were red. "How shall I take the rifles from the boat?" he asked. "Is anyone else coming with me?"

Dadhi was in a real fix. "Well, you will have to return the two guns from the Garo village, in any case. Otherwise it would be a breach of faith. You better discuss with Jairam what should be done about the other two."

"Very, well," said Madhu.

Bhibhiram and Madhu helped Dhanpur to the stretcher. Dhanpur winced and cried out in pain once, but then he took hold of himself and said, "Let's go. There is no point in delaying. Koli *Baideu*, please come with me."

Ahina led the group. For once, the old man walked without a word to his companions and they were grateful that he had not crumpled under the weight of fatigue, anxiety and pain.

Bhibhiram and Madhu picked up the stretcher.

"Stand a little to the front of the boulder, Dadhi," said Dhanpur. "The *Gossain* and Rupnarayan will find it easier to identify this place. And tell them that we will not meet again. Say that I have done my share of the work. Let them do what they have to do. It would be better to mobilise the people again, rather than worry about our losses. How does it matter if one Dhanpur has left? There are a hundred Dhanpurs here."

He then groaned in pain and burrowing his head in the blanket covering him, tried to sleep. I am free of all worries now, he thought.

"We shall go as far as the boat takes us," said Bhibhiram and added, "And if the boat cannot advance for some reason, we will start walking. Tell the *Gossain* and Rupnarayan. That it would not be safe to stay in this witches' cave now. Later on, when the military moves away from here, it will make a good hideout. Now, as soon as the train gets derailed, the military will start combing the entire area. Even the witches' cave will not escape their search.

"There is still some strength left in these arms. God willing, there is a whole country of people willing to fight with us. You see, it is not a case of being daunted by defeat in a battle. I shall leave word with Dimi about where and when we shall meet again. If we can reach Guwahati, well and good. Even if we can't, it doesn't really matter anymore." Bhibhiram was panting as he said this and then Madhu and he slowly moved towards the boulder, with the stretcher. Koli *Baideu* was to follow them.

Carrying the stretcher, they then followed Ahina Konwar down the slope, without halting. The moon had appeared in the sky; a bright golden moon.

Koli *Baideu* embraced Dadhi as she bid him farewell. "Don't you be afraid," she said. "Mahatma Gandhi has said that *Swaraj* of the mind is attained the moment you have banished fear. Do you understand? You better wait here."

Dadhi teacher felt a shiver go down his spine after Koli left. There was something in that woman's touch which had truly strengthened his mind and driven away the fear.

Gradually, the stillness of death descended. The fireflies

sought to dispel the darkness with their glow that resembled the thousand eyes in Indra.

Suddenly, Dadhi teacher heard the trumpeting of wild elephants at a distance; somewhere upstream. He was not afraid. Whatever happened, he would have to wait there, like the very boulder he was standing on. He would be relieved of his duty only when the *Gossain* and Rupnarayan arrived.

He gazed at his surroundings. The flora and the fauna, the rocks, the earth and everything around him, in all their hues, followed their prescribed curriculum, learnt well and cleared their examinations. In this school, these elements maintained their own discipline.

Dadhi teacher's mind went back to his primary school at Mayang. It has been closed for four months now; the teacher had absconded and the few children who attended were now no longer interested in lessons.

What is the use of their studying? This was the attitude of the guardians. Some of the children came to school hungry, after ploughing in the morning. Sometimes, they could not come at all. On days, when they sowed paddy or harvested, the whole family, including the children helped, out in the fields. Otherwise they would not get enough to eat for the whole year. Sometimes the boys would just come to school, but not stay for long. This was the fate of even Prince Baneswar and Ahina's sons.

The people had to live hand to mouth, through great want and privation.

And they had not even started sending the girls to school. Age old notions prevailed. *What use did girls have for studies or learning? They were like resting bees. They were there today, would be married off tomorrow and become mothers soon after.*

What would they do with their studies then? That is how their guardians thought.

How many people knew of the efforts of Dadhi teacher and the *Gossain* that had resulted in guardians agreeing to send their children to school?

In uneducated rural societies, the plight of the educated man was akin to that of a white cow. He had to bear on his head the burden of many of the sins of uneducated society.

And the less said about the school, the better. Like the *Namghar*, the village schools had no walls, benches, tables nor cupboards. The teacher's house was the office. The children had to carry a bamboo mat or a dried banana leaf to sit on. The teacher had to depend on some student's kindness for a stiff square of rush matting to sit on.

In a single-teacher school, the teacher had one big responsibility. The stray cattle of the village soiled the school-house as it did not have walls. So the first task of the teacher and the children, every morning, was to clean up the cow dung from the floor. Only then did they begin their studies.

And then the thatched roof leaked during the monsoon, the cold made them shiver in winter and in early March, the winds from the Brahmaputra tormented children, teacher, books and slates alike. On such days the schools got a holiday or a half a day's holiday.

These schools in a village interior also did not see too many inspections by deputy or sub-inspectors. But, on the rare occasions when they did come, the surroundings resonated with fanfare and preparations. When they came on bicycles the excitement was not all that noticeable. However, if they came by car, their reception was even better than what the deputy commissioner received.

Whether it was the deputy or sub-inspector of schools who was visiting, besides the reception with softened rice and creamy curds, there would be prize distributions for the children.

But what was the use? When they got back to their headquarters in town, they forgot the village and its school.

Dadhi teacher had worn out the soles of his feet walking back and forth between the town and the village, in his effort to bring more students and bring about a greater acceptance for the school; this in spite of the fact that he did not get a month's salary on time—sometimes even taking a year. He was the son of a seer; otherwise he would have taken to cultivation as is ordained of the children of cultivators. There was both happiness and tangible result in cultivation, but none of it in Dadhi teacher's work. One simply carried on with work without expecting big results; unless one could work like this, renouncing the desire for results (as extolled in the Gita), it would be impossible to be a teacher in Mayang.

In spite of all this, he still wanted to be a teacher. Everything was useless without education, but even to provide education to the rural populace you wanted a new government—an independent government, Dadhi teacher told himself. That was why you need *Swaraj*, that was why…

Suddenly there was a terrible earth-shattering sound. Dadhi shut his eyes and put his hands on his chest.

Rupnarayan stopped chanting 'Jagabandhu's torn umbrella' and watched as the engine of the prodigiously long train careened rapidly towards the depression. Simultaneously, the wagons and coaches tumbled into the depression one after the other at great speed and this was followed by a thunderous crash.

The whole thing happened in a moment. It was as if a tremendous explosion had taken place somewhere. The depression was about 150 feet deep.

Rupnarayan had personally inspected the depression in the afternoon.

After about 10 wagons and coaches had tumbled down with an earth-shattering crash, an even more terrifying cry filled his ears—the cry of people.

The soul-curdling cry of dying people!

Some of the wagons had fallen beside the railway track. And now some of these caught fire, generating a tremendous amount of heat.

As the clanging and screeching of tortured metal continued unabated, more agonising human cries assailed his ears. The fire of the burning coaches and wagons had, by now, flared up into a tremendous conflagration. The cries of agony continued unabated and the smell of burning human flesh became oppressively nauseating.

Rupnarayan tried to guess the number of dead and half-dead troops and those still fighting for life. Most of the coaches had landed in the depression. Of the few that had turned over just beside the track, two were burning and the passengers in the others must have died even as the coaches turned turtle.

The crash of the derailed train must have been heard in the neighbouring military camps. They were sure to arrive very soon. Then the investigation would begin. No, it wasn't safe to remain there any longer, Rupnarayan said to himself.

He picked up the three rifles and rushed to the *Gossain*, who was still groaning in agony and chewing bits of wild ginger. When he saw the flash of Rupnarayan's light, which was the signal, he stood up with great difficulty, using the rifle as a prop.

"I heard the crash," he said, as he got to his feet. "From what I can make out, things have gone according to plan. Let's go now. You lead the way."

Rupnarayan was labouring under the weight of three rifles, but this was nothing compared to the mental torture that he had suffered at the sight of the train accident. His head had started reeling at the sight. Time and again, the terrible crash of mental and the bloodcurdling cries of agony pierced his heart. The agitation of his mind had left him inarticulate, as he walked ahead of the *Gossain*, who trudged behind him with considerable difficulty.

In the sky, there was the waning light of the moon. Beneath the trees, the darkness was total.

The *Gossain's* hands were still stained with the fresh blood of men—a stain that had become oppressively unbearable to him. After a few steps, his limbs began to tremble uncontrollably. Perhaps long exposure to the cold had brought on a fever and weakened him totally. But the agitation of his distraught mind was even worse.

Unable to contain his mental suffering, he exclaimed, "How wonderful this struggle would have been if we would fight without killing! But, they didn't leave us that option, did they? And the struggle would not have taken such a turn if the Mahatma at least had remained outside jail."

Rupnarayan too had lost his earlier self-assurance. The sight of the accident had saddened him greatly. Not that he thought he had made a mistake, but yet his mind seemed to be drained of all exultation or zeal.

Who could rejoice when men stained their hands with the blood of fellow men? All wars were exceedingly cruel. To have to kill so many people for the cause of independence! They had no inkling of where all these men came from; from London perhaps, or from California or perhaps from Ludhiana or even from distant Peking. They had all come to fight the Japanese here on the soil of India, without the consent of the Indians themselves, almost as mercenaries of the foreign power that reigned here.

That was their crime. And he and his companions were fighting that very power.

Rupnarayan also remembered how some of these troops had committed even worse crimes. They had mowed down non-violent fighters like cats and dogs. And now they had finally received the initial sentence for their crimes.

But then why wasn't his heart exultant? Why did he think of himself as a killer? Why are the fighters for justice also killers? Well, if you fought with guns and rifles and even if your aim was good, could you be anything other than a killer? If one conspired to dismantle tracks and succeeded in derailing trains, did one remain anything short of a killer?

That's right! He was a killer, the *Gossain* was a killer, and Madhu, Dhanpur and the rest of them were all killers.

Yet these were necessary killings. The country would not become independent if one didn't kill like this. What they had done was with exalted goals in mind.

"Courage, my heart!" Rupnarayan said to himself. "This is just the prelude. After this, the rise to the climax, then the denouement, and finally, the resolution."

Even so, his conscience could not be quelled. Perhaps his mind would have found peace if they had been able to achieve their goal through love; without killing anyone. But could they do that? No, it wasn't possible.

Seeking to cover up the weakness of his mind, Rupnarayan

remarked, "Who has ever fought any battle without killing?"

"Why, Gandhi of course!" the *Gossain* countered at once, before he was once again seized by a fit of coughing He tried to muffle the sound as best as he could. This certainly wasn't the time to cough. The military was bound to comb the hillock in search of them.

Rupnarayan made no reply. The very mention of Gandhi's name was like a red rag to him. No doubt he was virtuous, saintly almost divine. But the battle for human liberty could not be fought non-violently. If that were possible, India would have won her freedom by this time. But independence had not come. Was Mahatama Gandhi not the cause of this failure? Subhash Chandra Bose was right. You had to fight. Jayaprakash and Lohia were showing the right path. We had to take up guerilla warfare.

But...

It was this 'but' that was creating all the havoc in his mind. Until he had gone through the traumatic experience of seeing all that destruction and killing, Rupnarayan had been a resolute believer in violence as the only means.

But violence did not give rise to joy. Or else why should he feel this sense of desolation—of heart, mind and soul alike? He would probably fail to find any beauty even in a fresh red rose if someone brought him one just now; would probably see in its redness the stain of the human blood that he had just spilled.

He would never ever exult in the glory of the setting sun with his lost innocence, for the hues would match the glory stains on the soldiers he had killed.

Well, if he couldn't, he couldn't. How did it matter, Rupnarayan told himself. He would perhaps lose his aesthetic sensibilities, but the mind of the future Indian citizens would remain unaffected. They would not experience wars and live with great love and camaraderie. Hadn't Gandhi said the same thing? *Shun violence now, this very moment. Begin the revolution of love from this moment.*

However, Rupnarayan also knew from the history of the world, particularly France, Russia, China, Yugoslavia and Burma, where people had resorted to violent revolutions because it was practically impossible to dislodge the exploiting class in power through a non-violent protest and struggle.

"Gandhi's struggle is too ideal" said Rupnarayan finally, to the *Gossain*. "Look at what is actually happening. It is hardly possible for every individual to acquire the courage of a Gandhi and become a non-violent soldier. So there seems to be no means of achieving independence for India other than the means we have adopted.'

The *Gossain* remained silent. He was not that aware of past political developments around the world. He also had his own inner turmoils. He was a *Vaishnavite* after all, who could not console his conscience for the stains of human blood on his hands. He inherently believed that where there was life, there was goodness. But then this was hardly the time for confessing one's weakness. This was the time to escape and recover physically.

The reality, however, was that a part of his body had died out in the cold, and yet the task of getting through the labyrinth still remained; the labyrinth of the military on the one hand and Saikia, the police inspector's labyrinth, on the other. All discussions would have to wait.

He said, "I refuse to accept that one cannot wage a non-violent war. It can be done. But we haven't been able to. We have sullied our hands with the stain of blood. So we better keep quiet now."

But he did not keep quiet. He kept waging an incessant duel with his conscience as he went along.

The two reached the boulder after a trudge of about half an hour. They found Dadhi sitting on it and shivering, uncontrollably, in the cold. The teacher stood up when he saw the *Gossain* and Rupnarayan.

"The others have left," he said. "What are your plans now?"

Rupnarayan could understand the reason for Dadhi's query. For him it was a question of avoiding a night in the cave.

"I think we better stay here, if you ask me," he replied. "When conditions improve we could go out again. Right now we have no idea of the situation out there. If Saikia and his men have spread out their net, it will be difficult to escape."

"'Can you remain in the cave without food and drink?' Dadhi asked before adding, "There is nothing at all here."

"That is indeed a problem," said Rupnarayan, "but if we have to starve, we shall." And he turned to *Gossain* for his reactions.

By then the *Gossain* was a sorry plight. The irrepressible cough kept tormenting him. He turned to Dadhi and gasped, "It would be a great help if you could light a fire. There is nothing left in this body. The mind is still clinging on somehow. The soul threatens to fly away any moment."

Dadhi looked worried. "Of course I can light a fire, but that would attract the attention of the enemy."

"That is true, but I cannot walk a single step any more. You better leave me here," the *Gossain* offered.

"Why should we go without you?" Rupanarayan protested. "Let us go into the cave and light a fire there. If we stay there…"

Before Rupnarayan could finish, they heard the barking of a large dog, about half a mile away. The three stood still listening to the sound.

Then realisation dawned on Rupnarayan, like a flash of lightning. "I get it now. Saikia has a huge Alsatian dog at the Raha police station. We must now think of fleeing this place."

"There is just that one route to escape," said Dadhi. "Besides…"

"We have to find other routes," Rupnarayan cut in irritably, "Otherwise we will be caught. No more talk now. Let's move.'

"We can get to Kalang if we follow the path of the brook beside the cave," said Dadhi before adding, "Beyond that there is a huge swamp, and the other side is swarming with troops. From there, we must march along to Kalang. But how do we go? I think we have landed ourselves in the net after all.'

Rupnarayan was really alarmed. "Is there no way out then, *Gossain*?"

"There is a way out," the *Gossain* replied.

"What is it?"

"You better leave me here. Get on to Kalang, along the route Dadhi suggests. I can shoot the dog and return if I can. Otherwise this is our last meeting. There is no other alternative. It is better that you two escape rather than have the three of us die here recklessly,'" said *Gossain* as he lowered his rifle from his shoulder.

"What kind of talk is this, *Gossain*?" Dadhi protested. "How many of them could there be, after all? And we have quite a few rifles here, don't we? We can shoot them all and leave."

"What do you say, Rupnarayan?" the *Gossain* queried.

"Dadhi is being immature, I am afraid. They are not just one or two, I tell you. They are coming in great strength; not just the police, but the military as well. And probably Lairam is with them too. Of course, this is only my conjecture. He may not come, for all you know. But they have certainly heard the crash of the train derailing. You are not wrong in his line of thinking. All three of us cannot escape. So we have to choose. I think it would be better for me to remain here. Dadhi and you leave."

The *Gossain* asked Dadhi his opinion. The latter broke out in a cold sweat. What was the right thing to do in such circumstances? No one could question the need for *Gossain* and Rupnarayan to remain alive, in the interest of the revolution. Of the three, his life alone was the least valuable. So, it would be right for him to remain there.

He plucked up the courage and said, "Listen *Gossain*, both your lives are very precious. Let me remain here. Besides, if Lairam is showing them the way, I am the one to blame. So I can at least kill him before I die."

The *Gossain* listened, for a moment, to the barking of the dog and said, "Rupnarayan, Dadhi, listen. Lairam may come or may not. Saikia is not the kind of man to wait for him. I still have faith in Lairam. But the point is that one of us has to die. There is no other way. The responsibility of deciding who it is going to be is also mine as I am the leader. In any case, my time is running out. This asthma has made me very weak. I do not even know if my lungs are working properly. They can stop any minute. But the more important reason is that my soul is dying. This human blood on my hand is something I have not been able to live down.

"I am going through a major moral conflict. There is no point in deluding myself. I only like non-violent battles. Those are real battles. Anyway, there is no point in talking about all this.

"In any case I will not survive this journey; of course, only physically, not morally. You will not understand. I will not break my promise, nor will I slow down the pace of this revolution. And I shall not shirk my duty. I shall carry out the last duty of a leader. You two get along. Save yourselves. Meet the others and tell them of their leader's command: *Carry on the revolution.*

"I do not know whether Dhanpur is alive or not or whether the others are free or have been caught. But, getting caught and staying alive are mundane occurrences. They will take place. But, let them at least be free from the weakness of their leader. Get along now. One mission has been accomplished by the grace of God. Now to wait for the other one.

"By the way, just remember this. If my wife had a baby—that is if they have kept her alive—look after it. And tell Madhu to look after *Satra*. Now get along. No time for words. Go."

Rupanarayan realised that what the *Gossain* had said was both irrefutable and reasonable. And it was their duty to obey their leader. He handed over one of the rifles to Dadhi and then checked the magazine of the *Gossain's* rifle.

"We shall always remember you. We shall not give up the revolution," he said as he was leaving.

Dadhi's eyes filled with tears. "I don't understand why you feel you have to do this."

'I have done what a leader should do. Stay alive, carry on your work and don't grieve for me. I have done my job. Get along now. You will ruin everything if you delay.'

The *Gossain* uttered these words with all the strength in his body and then lay prone with his rifle.

Rupnarayan and Dadhi made their obeisance to the *Gossain* and descended gloomily towards the cave. The waning moon seemed to shiver and drop from the sky. An illusion. Rupnarayan was unable to think straight anymore. The supreme act of the *Gossain's* sacrifice had made it difficult for him to think clearly. Dadhi could not say anything anymore. He knew that Mayang would not have a *Gossain* anymore.

The barking of the dog grew louder. The *Gossain's* body was in its last stages of exhaustion. Suddenly, he seemed to hear the crying of a doe. Was it an illusion? No, he had clearly heard his wife weeping. It wasn't an illusion after all. Why should he have illusions? This was life, after all; so variegated and yet set to a single tune. He had performed his allotted task. He couldn't give his wife anything, but then who gave anything to anyone? All this was *Maya*. In this world, all that one had was duty—Stern, inviolable duty. He had qualified as far as his duty is concerned; duty and also violence. But then that was a pledge in the cause of his country. There was no crime in it. History would forgive him. But then his pious conscience would not. It was sinful to kill people. But no, he had not made a mistake. Even Krishna had been forced to wield the *Sudarshanchakra* now and then. Violence became necessary at time to subdue evildoers but...

The barking of the dog was very near now. The *Gossain* lined up his rifle.

Translated from the Assamese by
DN Bezboruah

2

BURNT TURMERIC

Manik Bandopadhyay

Two murders took place in the village, in close succession, sometime around the middle of *Kartik* that year; one, a middle-aged strong daredevil man, the other, a 17-year-old sickly, timid girl.

To the north of the village, by the side of a silted pond, there stood a *gajari* tree for many years. The place is bare; not covered by trees and bushes. One day Balai Chakravorty was found lying dead under that *gajari* tree. His skull had been cracked open in eight spots, perhaps hit by a number of sticks.

Though there was a hue and cry all around, people were not really surprised. They expected such a violent death of Balai Chakravorty, some even desired it.

On the other hand, there was not much of a ruckus over Shubhra's murder, but people were really astonished and curious at her death. A nondescript girl from an ordinary family, she grew up in front of the eyes of the villagers, along with other girls of her age. She left for her in-law's place after marriage, and, had returned to her parents' home a month ago to give birth to her first child.

Even the women of the neighbouring houses could not imagine that there could be a secret in the girl's life, a dramatic ingredient which would lead to such a horrible end. The village folk could not think of a single reason why, at dusk-fall, when evening lamps had been lit at every household, someone or some people would strangle Shubhra to death near the pond behind her house.

The girl was at her in-law's place for about one and a half years. Village folk now wondered if some development had taken place there that had culminated in this terrible tragedy.

Was there a connection between the two murders?

Nobody in the village had even been seriously injured during the last 20 to 30 years. And suddenly now two persons went to the whole hog of getting killed, in quick succession! A man and a young woman! Everyone was dying to discover some connection between the two murders.

Nobody could even fathom what Balai Chakravorty might have in common with Shubhra. The imagination and speculations of the people could not even take the shape of proper gossip due to the lack of even a germ of fact or connection.

The property of Balai Chakravorty was inherited by his nephew Nabin. He left his rupees-forty-a-month job in town and returned to the village with his family.

He would constantly wipe the glasses of his spectacles, with the end of his *dhoti*, and say to the villagers, "I've declared a reward of ₹50. I would see to it that the villains, who killed my uncle in such a dastardly way are hanged."

At times he would also wipe his own eyes instead of the glasses with the end of the *dhoti*.

One evening, exactly 21 days after they started living in the village, Nabin's wife Damini was crossing the courtyard from the kitchen to the bedroom with a lantern in hand. Just then, a sudden mild gust of wind stirred the leaves of the tamarind tree, at the eastern corner of the house, and touched her body. The lantern flew off from Damini's hand and landed on the verandah of the southern quarter, and Damini fell flat on the courtyard in a fit of seizure, with her teeth clenched, before fainting. The noise emanating from her throat was something like the wailing of the wind at the corners of a concrete house, during a storm.

Shubhra's elder brother, Dhiren, taught in the local school. He was the only practising physician-without-a-degree in the village.

A science graduate, with Physics Honours, he had been teaching geography in the school for the last seven years.

At the beginning of his career, he had been bounding with enthusiasm. He had set up a village library with 47 books and a youth forum with seven boys and started treating people free of cost for common diseases by reading MatriaMedica. After marrying a village girl and becoming the father of four children, his enthusiasm had now considerably flagged.

The number of books in the library had refused to grow beyond 300. The almirah containing the books lay under lock and key at his house. No one paid for a subscription. Occasionally, someone would take an old book for reading. The youth forum hardly met for a couple of times a year.

Dhiren these days charged four annas to eight annas as fees for treatment.

By the time he was called, Damini had gained consciousness; thanks to the pitcher of water poured on her head and face.

But she had a vacant look and was laughing and crying, without any apparent reason. She was also violently trying to break free from those who held her by scratching and biting.

Dhiren's face turned serious on seeing Damini's condition. He said, "It is better to call in Kailash Doctor of Shahpur. I can treat her, but I am not confident of taking the responsibility. After all, I do not have a medical degree, you know."

Pankaj Ghoshal, the old fellow who maintained his family by living off the graciousness of Balai Chakraborty chipped in, "Doctor? What will a doctor do? Listen Nabin, my son, send for Kunja immediately."

Almost all the village folk, who had gathered here, supported the old man's opinion.

Nabin asked, "How much does Kunja charge?"

Dhiren said, "Come on, Nabin, don't get sucked into such a racket. I tell you, this is a disease, nothing else. You are an educated person and have knowledge about the world. How can you invite Kunja for her treatment?"

Nabin muttered apologetically but hesitantly added, "It is their treatment which usually works in such strange maladies."Although Nabin was elder than Dhiren by three-four years, they went to school together and shared the same bench.

Perhaps in deference to that memory Nabin finally sent for both Kailash Doctor and Kunja.

Kunja reached first. Even before Nabin's messenger found him, he had been preparing for the call. The rumour, that the daughter-in-law of the Chakravorty family had been possessed by a supernatural spirit, was fast abounding through the village.

Kunja was a reputed exorcist. People had gathered more to enjoy the thrill of Kunja's battle with an evil spirit.

He first scared everyone by saying, "The spirit has possessed in the mid-evening. He is not going to leave easily," and then immediately reassured them, "But leave he must. No trick will work with Kunja Majhi."

Everybody was asked to clear the terrace and go down to the courtyard.

Kunja sprinkled water on the terrace, muttering some *mantra* all the while. Damini's hair was tied tightly with a pole on the veranda. She was now unable to sit nor was she able to run away. It was no longer necessary for anyone to pin her down. She shrieked in pain at her own slightest movement, as her hair got pulled at the pole.

Kunja teased the so-called spirit, "Oh, you have already started crying! Wait, still a long way to go."

So far, Dhiren had remained quiet. These ignorant villagers would not listen to his advice. But he could not remain a silent spectator anymore.

Turning to Nabin, he burst out, "Have you gone crazy, Nabin? How can you allow such things?

"Brother, please keep silent," responded Nabin.

There were around 30 to 35 men and women with five lanterns in the courtyard. The women were fewer in number and elderly. The younger women were not permitted to come, nor did they dare lest evil cast a glance at them.

All these people stood spellbound looking at the terrace. Nabin did not have the power to deprive them of watching this scene.

The terrace was like a stage, on which a play was being enacted; a play in which mysteries beyond human intelligence had been given a tangible shape. Kunja had made them aware of something extraordinary. Through Damini they had come face to face with the supernatural, but it was so real, and so close.

All fear was forgotten. There was only tremendous excitement accompanied by the thrill of curiosity.

Kunja was sometimes swaying from right to left, sometimes taking one step forward and one step back, all the while chanting obscure *mantras*. A fire has been lit in a small earthen basin, in which he occasionally threw some dried roots and leaves. A stinking smell of burnt leather filled up the air. The crying and fidgeting of Damini was gradually subsiding. At one point, she stood still against the pole, looking straight at Kunja, with drowsy eyes.

This is when Kunja took some raw turmeric and held it at her nostrils.

Damini's drowsy eyes gradually opened wide. Her whole body started shivering.

"Who are you? Tell me, who are you?"

"I am Shubhra. Oh dear! Don't beat me."

"Shubhra of the Chatterjees? The one who has been murdered?"

"Yes, dear, yes. Don't beat me."

Nabin was standing on one side of the veranda. Turning to him, Kunja said, "Do you get the point now?"

From the courtyard, the old Ghoshal gave directions in a muffled voice, "Why don't you find out, who killed her? Hey Kunja, do you hear me? Ask her quickly who killed her."

Kunja did not have to ask anything. Damini herself responded in a whispered tone, "Uncle Balai killed me."

Having said these words Damini fell silent. Many questions were asked about the incident, but she did not utter a word. At one point of time, her teeth got clenched again, indicating perhaps the onset of another seizure. At this point, burnt turmeric at the nose also did not work any more.

Kunja was making arrangements for the next round of occult action, when Kailash Doctor arrived. He had a formidable appearance; huge physique, head-full of salt and pepper hair, thick bushy eyebrows and bristling beard and whiskers all over the face.

He saw the scene before him, shouted at those who stood watching and kicked away the earthen basin of fire towards Kunja and thundered, "You scoundrel, I'm going to send you to the gallows if you have killed her with your occult practice."

The doctor then untied Damini's hair from the pole and took her inside the house. Putting her down on the huge old four-poster bed, that had once belonged to Balai's grandfather, injected some tranquiliser through her arm.

Damini repeated in a doleful voice "Please do not beat me, please. I am Shubhra. Shubhra of the Chatterjees."

Within a few minutes she fell into a deep slumber.

The ignorant village folk were confused by Shubhra's indictment of Balai Chakravorty through Damini, for the former had been killed three days before Shubhra's murder.

But the interpretation of the old Ghoshal cleared their doubt. "Do only living human beings kill others by strangulating? Not some other elements? Who then breaks the neck of wayward travellers near crematoriums, on inauspicious days and moments?

The explanation should have come from Kunja, the exorcist. But old Ghoshal had beaten him to it. He now added to this in a way that even a non-believer would find it difficult to dismiss the possibility.

Balai Chakravorty had certainly killed Shubhra, but not directly. For, no spirit could do so within one year of death, unless his obsequies are not properly performed. He must have possessed someone and through that person killed Shubhra, with flesh and blood fingers.

And the person who had been possessed would not remember anything. That is how the unfathomable mystery of the other world works.

These words reached Dhiren next morning, by travelling through many mouths.

The bright and sweet sunlight of the month *Agrahayan* had pervaded the surroundings. The luxuriant growth of foliage of late monsoon demonstrated God's munificence. The pool of water at the backyard was covered with hyacinths, deep green and juicy leaves and beautiful flowers of a soft and subdued colour.

Dhiren had got the steps especially made this year with the logs of a palm tree so that Shubhra, in the seventh month of pregnancy, did not face any difficulty in climbing up and down.

Now, he was trying to remember, for the umpteenth time, who were the people who went to the steps of the water-pool that fateful evening, and why, and from which side? This thought would make him unmindful and melancholy and indignation would fill up his mind totally.

Some people from the locality came home to tell him about the rumours circulating in the village.

Later, while serving him rice for his meal, his wife Shanti said, "I think there is some truth in it. Otherwise..."

Dhiren glared at her, "Shut up. Whatever you may think, don't burden me with it. I warn you."

On his way to school, he met a number of people but none of whom broached the topic with him, but their eyes silently posed the mocking question, How have you digested the rumour, my boy?

The village priest detained him for a long time to give instructions on the rituals he should perform to neutralise the evil effect of the unnatural death. The priest particularly asked Dhiren to collect, from him, amulets for all members of his family.

The moment he set foot in the school compound, he felt as if he was a distinguished person who had come from outside to inspect the school. Everybody was treating him cautiously; as if he had not existed here for the last seven years.

During his first lesson for the day, half the students sat benumbed, while the other half was whispering among themselves. He read from the book, without once taking his eyes off the pages. He could not look at the boys.

Immediately after his first lesson, the headmaster sent for him.

"Take a month's leave, Dhiren."

"A month's leave! But why?"

"Mathur *babu* came a little while ago and gave the orders. Your leave will be sanctioned, starting from today. You do not have to take any more classes today."

Mathur *babu* was the secretary of the school. His house was within a mile from the school building.

While returning home, Dhiren suddenly felt dizzy. Of late, he had been feeling unwell like this. After resting for a while, under a tree, he again started towards home.

He mulled on whether he should go and meet Mathur *babu* now, but dismissed the thought after remembering that the latter must have just finished his mid-day meal. More importantly, he had, after all, not been dismissed from his services; only asked to proceed on a month's leave. The issue could be taken up with Mathur *babu* later. Moreover, if Mathur *babu* got convinced that Dhiren should not be treated like this just because Damini's declaration had set off a scandal and permit him to join his duties from the next day, it would be a big relief. But it suddenly dawned on Dhiren that it was beyond him to take classes for some time now.

He suddenly realised that, subconsciously, he had taken a path through the field in order to return home, so that he could avoid meeting people.

Reaching home, he flopped on the bed, feeling very weak and tired. He tossed in bed restlessly the whole afternoon.

At dusk he came out to the courtyard, when Shanti was climbing up the steps from the pond, with washed utensils in hand. Dhiren noticed something like a human figure, moving and stirring in the shadows, near the pool.

He shouted, "Who is there? Who?"

The utensils fell from Shanti's hands, with a clattering sound. She rushed to him, trembling in fear and asked, "Where? Who did you see?"

A familiar voice called out from the bamboo-clump, "It's me, Master *babu*. Cutting a bamboo branch."

Shanti said, "I've asked him to do so. Kshenti aunt suggested that a bamboo pole should be cut and after burning its two ends, should be kept horizontally between the pool-steps and the house, every evening. It can be removed in the morning."

These days, Shanti finishes all her cooking and other chores before the dusk. Once it becomes dark she does not even cross the threshold of the house, without Dhiren accompanying her. She keeps the children also confined to the house.

Tied down at home right from the evening Dhiren remains worried with numberless puzzling thoughts crowding pell-mell

into his mind. At times, he just listens in on the conversations
of the children.

Translated from the Bengali by
Nirmal Kanti Bhattacharjee

3

FAREWELL

Samaresh Basu

Shattering the stillness of the night, the military jeep drove past the Victoria Park, in one quick turn.

Section 144 and curfew were in force in the city. The Hindus and Muslims were at each other's throats; with choppers, spears, daggers and wooden rods, the mob had fanned out on every side. It was the night of the long knives!

The marauders were out on the streets, looting. The dark night, torrid with death, lent a strange intensity to their joy. *Basti* after *basti* was aflame. The screams of dying women and children merged with the tension in the air. The noisy Army trucks leapt into the fray, with gunfire spraying in all directions—to preserve, of all things, law and order.

At a crossing, where two lanes merged, a dustbin lay overturned. Using that as a cover, a man crawled out from one of the lanes—on all fours.

He did not dare raise his head and lay inert for a while.

But his ears were keenly glued to the faint sounds coming

from a distance. Nothing could be deciphered; it could as well be *Allah-O-Akbar* or *Bande Mataram*.

Suddenly, the dustbin moved a bit! His every nerve tautened in anticipation. Clenching his teeth, straining his sinews, the man waited; expecting something terrible to happen. A few moments passed. It was still quiet all around.

Perhaps it was a dog, he told himself. To chase it away, he pushed the dustbin gently.

There was silence for a while. Then the bin rattled again.

Curiosity coupled with fear now, the man raised his head slowly. From the other side emerged another head.

A man!

Two men on two sides of the dustbin; both terrified and absolutely still, their heartbeats almost in sync. The look in those two pairs of eyes—scared, suspicious, anxious—slowly grew intense.

Neither could trust the other. Each thought the other man was the enemy. Their eyeballs locked, each waited for the other to strike. But neither did.

Now, an identical question took shape in both their minds; was the other person a Hindu or a Muslim?

The answer to this question would perhaps bring about the final denouement. That's why neither dared ask. Yet, scared, neither could flee. Out of fear that the other might strike!

Dwelling in doubt and discomfort for a while, both became impatient. Finally, one broke the ice. "Are you a Hindu or a Muslim?"

"You answer that question first," the other replied.

But each refused to reveal his identity, suspicious of the other. The first question soon got buried. Another cropped up.

"Where do you come from?"

"From that side of the river. And you?"

"From Chasara—near Narayanganj. And what do you do?"

"I have a boat. I ply it. And you?"

"I work in a mill in Narayanganj."

There was silence once again. In that darkness, where nothing could be seen, each tried to guess what the other looked like. They tried to see each other's attire.

But the darkness and the dustbin in between made it impossible. Suddenly, some trouble erupted nearby. There was an uproar. A medley of different chants broke the stillness of the night.

Terrified, the mill worker and the boatman cringed.

"They are coming close," the terrified worker whispered.

"Yes, come let's get away from here," the boatman replied, equally scared.

The worker stopped him. "No, don't get up. Do you want to die?"

The boatman became suspicious again. What were the other man's intensions? He looked straight into the mill worker's eyes.

The other man was also staring at him and, as soon as their eyes met, he said, "Sit. Don't do anything now."

The boatman became tense instantly. Was the other man threatening him not to go? Suspicion clouded his mind all over again. "Why?" He asked.

"Why!" the mill worker spoke in a harsh whisper. "What do you mean, why? Do you want to die?"

The boatman did not like the way he said this. He tossed around in his mind all the possibilities and willed himself to stay strong. "No, I'll stay here, in this dark, dingy lane for you!" He finally exclaimed, sarcastically.

Sensing his stubbornness, the worker also became suspicious.

"For me? Your intensions don't seem good to me!" He muttered before adding, "You haven't yet told me which community you belong to. What if you get all your people to come and kill me?"

"What are you saying?" Forgetting where they were, the boatman almost screamed out aloud, in hurt and anger.

"I've said the right thing! You don't understand how people behave at times!"

There was something in his voice that put the boatman at ease.

"If you go, will I stay on here alone?"

The tumult in the distance seemed to have died down. Silence returned, like death, once again. The moments seemed to pass in brute terror; the fear of waiting for death.

In the dark lane, on either side of a dustbin, two men thought about the danger they are trapped in and then about their homes, their mothers, wives and children. Would they ever be able to return to them alive? Would those back at home be safe and waiting for them, even if they did?

The riots had struck suddenly, without any warning. Like thunder! Amidst all the laughter, the chatter in the market place, suddenly death had swooped down on everyone; killing, looting, with blood flowing like water down the river! How could people turn so heartless, so cruel—so easily?

What a cursed race! The mill worker sighed. Seeing him, the boatmen felt the same.

"Care for a smoke?" Extracting a *bidi* from his pocket, the worker held it out to the boatman.

By sheer habit, the boatmen caressed the *bidi*, twirled it around near his ear few times and, then placed it tightly between his lips.

The worker, in the meantime, tried to light a match. He hadn't noticed earlier that his *kurta* was wet. The matches were damp. After several attempts, a faltering blue flash appeared but soon died out. Disgusted, he threw the stick away.

"This bloody matchbox has turned soggy!" He mumbled and took out another stick.

Somewhat impatiently, the boatmen got up and came to sit beside the worker. "It will light, don't worry. Give it to me." He almost grabbed the matchbox from the worker's hand.

Striking it a few times, he actually managed to light a match.

"*Allah* be blessed! Come on, light your *bidi* quickly!"

The worker was shocked! He paled as if he had seen a ghost. The *bidi* fell from his lips.

"You...?"

A light breeze snuffed out the matchstick. A pair of eyes widened again, out of mistrust and anxiety, in that dark. A few silent moments passed.

The boatmen stood up suddenly. He said, "Yes, I am a Muslim. So what?"

The weaver replied fearfully, "Nothing, but..." Pointing to the bundle under the boatman's arm, the weaver asked, "What is inside that?"

"A couple of frocks for my daughter and a saree for my wife. Do you know its *Eid* tomorrow?"

"I hope there is nothing else in there!" The worker's fears persisted.

"Are you implying that I am lying? If you don't believe me, check it for yourself." He held out the bundle, for the worker to rummage through.

"No, no, what is there to see, my brother! But you know what the days are like? You tell me, can you trust anybody?"

"That is true brother. I hope you haven't got something on you?"

"I can swear on God that I don't even have a needle on me. I shall be glad to return home, with my life intact." The mill worker offered a body search.

The two sat down again, side by side. Lighting their *bidis*, they smoked intently together, in silence.

"Okay!" the boatman spoke in a manner as if he was addressing a relative or a friend. "So do you know anything regarding these killings?"

The worker read newspapers. He knew a little about what was going on. So he answered testily, "The fault lies with your people! They have started all this."

The boatman objected, "I don't understand all this. I'm only asking what will come about from so much of killing. Some men from your side will die and some from mine. How will the country gain?"

"That's exactly what I am saying. What can happen? Nothing except this!" He shows his thumb to indicate the wasteful loss before adding, "You might die or I and our wives and kids will have to beg. In the last riots, they hacked my brother-in-law into four pieces. My sister was widowed and the responsibility of her children landed on my shoulders!

"We are not human beings. We are like vicious dogs!" The boatman complained in impotent rage.

"True," the worker agreed gravely.

The boatman continued, "Who thinks of us? Amidst all this rioting, how will I earn? Who will give me food? Will I ever get my boat back? They may have sunk her by now. Every month, the *nayab* from the *zamindar's* house would take my boat across the river to attend court. The *zamindar* would give me a tip of five rupees and the *nayab* would pay another five, as fare. That would make 10 rupees! It paid for my monthly expenses. Will the Hindu *babu* come near my boat again, after all this?"

The worker, about to say something, checked himself.

They both heard the sound of heavy boots coming closer. There was no doubt that the sound was approaching from the main road. Alarmed, they looked into each other's eyes.

"What shall we do?" The boatman quickly placed the bundle under his arm.

"Let's run. But which way shall we go? I don't know the roads very well out here."

The boatman suggested, "Let us just move from here. We cannot take police beating just like that. You can't trust these people."

"Yes. You're right. Tell me which way to go. They are almost here!"

"This way!" The boatman indicated the southward end of the lane and said, "Let's go. If only we can reach the *ghats* of Badamtali, we needn't be frightened anymore."

Ducking their heads, they ran breathlessly, finally landing on Patuatuli Road. The deserted road sparkled in the electric lights. Both stood frozen for a while, hopefully, no one was watching them! But they did not have time to waste.

Scanning both ends of the road once again, they ran westward. They had covered some ground when suddenly they heard the sound of hooves. They saw a rider, some distance away, coming towards them. There was no time to think. They hid in a narrow lane, normally used by sweepers.

A little later, an Englishman brandishing a revolver rode past them with great speed. The sound of the hooves seemed to echo in the hearts of the two men in hiding. When the sound faded in the distance, they peeped around and came out of their hiding place.

"Walk along the kerb," the mill worker suggested.

Keeping to the shadows, they quickly walked on.

"Stop!" the boatman said in a low voice. The worker stopped in his tracks, surprised.

"What's happened?" he asked anxiously.

"Come here!" Holding the worker's hand, the boatman led him behind a *paan* shop.

"Look there!"

The worker followed the boatman's gaze and saw a house with the lights on. In the adjoining balcony stood an English officer, saying something and gesticulating through a haze of smoke from his pipe.

Below the balcony, holding on to the reins of a horse, was another policeman. The restless and fidgety horse was continuously tattooing the ground with his hooves.

The boatman said, "That is the Islampur outpost. If we go a little further, we can cross the lane, to the left of the outpost to reach Badamtali *ghat*."

The worker's entire face clouded with fear: "Then what?"

"That is why I'm suggesting you stay here. You'll gain nothing going to the *ghat*," the boatman said. "This is a Hindu area and Islampur belongs to the Muslims. Go home when you wake up in the morning tomorrow."

"And you?"

"I'm going ahead." the boatman's voice turned hoarse with anxiety and fear. "I won't be able to stay on anymore. Today is the eighth day since I last got news of my family. Only *Allah* knows how they are! If only I can enter the lane somehow! If I don't find a boat, I'll swim across."

"What are you saying?" Anxiously, the worker held on to the boatman's *kurta*. "How can you go like that?"

"Don't hold me back, please! Let me go. You don't understand that tomorrow is *Eid*. The children must have sighted the moon today. They must be waiting to wear new clothes and sit on their father's lap. My wife must be crying. I can't brother…I can't…I don't feel happy." The boatman's voice faltered.

The mill worker understood and tried to calm down; the fingers holding the boatman's *kurta* grew weak.

"What if they catch you?" His voice became heavy with fear and concern.

"They won't be able to catch me, don't worry! Stay here, don't get up. I'm going. I'll never forget this night. If fate wills, we'll meet again. Goodbye."

The boatman left, treading carefully.

With a heart full of suspense, the other man stood still. His galloping heartbeat refused to become normal. He remained alert. God, he prayed, let not danger strike again.

The moments passed in bated breath.

As time ticked by, the worker thought about the boatman. It has been a long time now. The boatman must be on his way home now. How happy his children will be to get new clothes for *Eid*! After all, the heart was the heart of a father. He sighed. The wife would break down and cry upon his chest, having got her husband back.

You've returned from the jaws of death, she would say. A smile lit up a corner of the millworker's mouth. And what would the boatman do then? The boatman would…

Halt!

The worker's heart missed a beat. Some men in boots could be heard running. They were shouting and saying something.

"Look who is running away!

Stretching out, the mill worker saw a police officer with a revolver in his hand jump on to the road. Shattering the silence of the entire locality, he fired his revolver twice.

Bang! Bang!

Two blue sparks of fire!

In suspense, the worker almost bit off his finger.

Leaping onto his horse, the officer raced into the lane. He had heard the death cries of his target.

The mill worker knew what had happened.

Before his bewildered eyes swirled a picture of the boatman with his small bundle of clothes, now slowly turning crimson with his blood.

The boatman was saying, *I couldn't make it, brother. My children and wife will weep on a festival day. The enemy stopped me...*

Translated from the Bengali by
Rina Nandy

4

CARE TAKER

Padma Sachdev

*W*hen Sarwar Jan finished feeding *churi* with jaggery to
the newly calved cow and came out, evening shadows
had slowly started spreading their dusky veil over the sky. No
star was visible yet, but Sarwar Jan could notice several holes
in the dust coloured sky.

A stab of severe pain made her heave a sigh and
simultaneously the cow yawned, perhaps in empathetic concern.
Sarwar put the *churi* pot on the ground and caressed the cow's
head with one hand, while the other one was at the animal's
mouth. There was pain in the yellow eyes of the cow and she
was fidgety. Sarwar saw the udders; they were taut and full of
milk, even after the calf had had its fill. Sarwar picked up a
milking pot, pulled out a *peedah* and sitting on it started milking
the cow. Milk squirts fell into the milking pot, like showers of
rain on a mountain rock.

Sarwar had been in this house for 15 years. There had been
several evenings when Sher Khan had been late in returning

home and although it did not happen very often, every evening brought with it moments of anxiety. And she couldn't breathe at ease until he returned.

She could hear some sounds—*Alif* for *Abba*, *Bay* for *Battakh*, *Pay* for *Pani*. It was her younger daughter learning by rote. She hears only *Abba* for *Alif*, thought Sarwar tenderly.

How fondly Shera has given them names—Nili and Lali. Nili is the elder one; her eyes are blue. Lali is the younger one; her hair is red. The eldest is their son, Sawan, who was cutting fodder with a rhythmic movement to impress his father, so that he would be pleased and permit him to go to Sultan Mirasi's house for some time late in the evening. Sawan was very fond of playing on the *dafali*.

Jets of milk were now falling in a rhythm, creating sounds as those created by a music teacher who had practised long hours and they now seemed to be churning Sarwar Jan's heart. This milk, carrying a slight bluish tinge, had come up to the round mouth of the milking pot. Sarwar picked up another milking pot. The sound of jets of milk falling mingled with the sound of fodder being cut by Sawan.

Outside, Bhalu the dog's yelping was becoming more strident. Sarwar Jan sensed something; foot-falls in the lane near the entrance to the house had come to a stop. Perhaps Shera has asked Kataloo to wait for a while.

The sound of a thud, as though something has fallen; this must be the bag full of apples. The sound of something being placed; these must be dry fruits. Then, the footsteps of Shera came towards the courtyard and suddenly stopped, followed by stunning silence. Sarwar's second milk pot by now had also filled. The cow's affectionate gaze rested on her.

A full voice, tinged with annoyance, arose, "Sawan's Amma!"

The milk in the pot spilled over a bit.

Sarwar Jan said to herself. Today, I am merely Sawan's mother! She picked up both the pots and came out, handed over one to each of her daughters, and went up to face Sher Khan. Looking straight into his eyes, the tall fine-limbed sharp-witted Sarwar asked caustically, "Today again?"

"*Allah Qasam*, Saro…" Began Sher Khan, but she turned aside a little and walked away without allowing him to complete the sentence.

When she returned, she had a *lota* in her hand. Sher Khan took the vessel of water from her and without looking at her said, "Kataloo is waiting outside."

"I know," was her brief response.

But her response reassured him. He thought that however apathetic she might be towards him, she would spare no effort to attend to Kataloo. Sher Khan hung his large coat on the peg on the wall and keeping aside the towel soaked in hot water, he began to remove his *peshawari chappals*. He would have to clean his feet himself. Only when Saro was in a loving mood, did she rub his feet clean. It was so soothing!

Just then, Kataloo spoke from outside the door, "Shah, I am leaving. Baaji has sent some sweets, from the city, and a *handi* of milk for Aapaa."

Sher Khan removed his *Karakuli* cap and took out a currency note from the bundle kept under it and placed it on Kataloo's hand.

He took the money, saying, "It wasn't necessary at all, Shah…you give it every time I come." He thrust the note in his waistcoat, offered his *salaams* and left.

Sher Khan pushed the *chappals* to a corner, cleaned his feet, tossed the towel aside and lay on the *satara* spread on the floor.

When a person is all by himself in a room, moments from the past, which usually are hovering somewhere around, start creeping into one's consciousness, like ants. As drowsiness benumbed his eyes, Sher Khan nestled into the bosom of his past.

He saw that his small red feet were numb with cold as he returned from school bare-footed. His shoes had been taken away by somebody. Nur Begum was rubbing a thick, rough, piece of cloth, soaked in hot water, on his feet and he found it very pleasant. Nur Begum drew closer.

Eight to nine years old, Sher Khan, studying in the second grade of his village school, lay still, overcome by shyness. His cold feet did not allow him to move. Nur Begum then rubbed oil on his feet. Then wiping them with the hem of her veil, and taking them close to her breast, wrapped herself with the quilt.

He freed his feet from Nur's hands.

A hot drop of tear fell on his foot; it pierced his heart like a nail.

Now he tells himself, that even after Nur Begum has left, the nail still keeps rankling.

He could hear his mother's voice call out to him. "Sheru, take this, eat this bread with milk. Why do you fight shy of Nuri? She is your wife. Who else is there in this house who she can call her own? You should play with her."

"Amma, let me eat my food in peace. I shall never play with Nuri. She is much older than me," snapped Sher Khan irritably.

His mother said affectionately, "How much older? Only by 10 years, and in four years you will be big enough."

"How big, Amma? As big as Abba is?"

"No, not so big, but sufficiently big; enough to be able to play with Nuri sometimes."

"Then she will become small?"

"Who? Nuri? You are stupid! No one who grows big ever becomes small again."

"But in the school, everyone teases me. Yesterday even the teacher was saying..."

"What did he say?"

"That she is my wife."

"She is your wife, indeed, son. When her *chacha* married your *phuphi*, you were only five. How can you remember?"

"But, Amma, marriage is an occasion when drums are beaten. There was no beating of drums, then how did the marriage take place?"

"Drums were beaten, son. You were sleeping in my lap at that time."

"Amma, I am feeling sleepy. Come and lie beside me. I've finished eating."

"But I've a lot of chores to attend to."

"She will attend to them. You put me to sleep. I feel frightened."

Shera's mother took him in her embrace and wrapping a quilt around began to sing:

*"Darasi de banana bichbinaniyaanloyiyan
Jinhangallaandardisiooaiqallaanhoyiyan
Laggikainchidil noon."*

(I'm wearing woolen blankets in the forest of Darasi.
What I was afraid of, has happened.
It's like a scissor-stab on the heart.)

A thud startled Sher Khan out of his reverie.

He realised that tears were running down his eyes and his daughter Nili was leaving his room with the cup of cold *kahwa* in her hand.

How vivid was that evening of 15 years ago!

He looked around...Nur was nowhere to be seen. Mother had passed away quite some time ago. But Nur was still living— Nur, who had been driven out of the house like a decrepit cow.

Just then, Sawan came in and said, "Abba, come for your meal."

"I don't feel like eating today. You have your meal."

"Abba, the black mare's foot has still not healed."

"I see! Did you ensure that the thorn was completely taken out?"

"Yes, Abba."

"Then, clean it once more with hot water and bandage it with Aak leaves, greased with pure *desi ghee*."

As soon as Sawan went out, Sarwar came in. "What is the matter? Has she fed you lavishly? There are people waiting for you at home also. Both your daughters are sitting at the *dastarkhan*, disconsolate.'

Sher Khan stood up and said, "I'll join you in a while."

As he wrapped the woolen sheet around himself, the *tawiz* tied with a black thread dropped down. Nuri's voice sounded sweet in his ears, *Do tie it on your arm. I had gone to the dargah. I brought it from there. For you.*

Sher Khan picked up the *tawiz*, shoved it in the wooden rafters of the ceiling and went over to join his family for the meals.

Sawan, wiping his hands with the hem of his mother's *dupatta*, said, "Abba, may I ...?"

"Yes, you want to go to Sultan's house? Go. But come back early."

Everyone looked at him in surprise. Sher Khan was allergic to the very mention of Sultan's name.

After washing his hands, Sher Khan went to lie down in his bed. He tumbled into it listlessly.

And then she came back to him…Nur…

The Nur of 18 years of age.

As soon as he returned from school, he would toss aside his satchel and *patti* and start looking out for his mother. Nur would show him the towel soaked in hot water and say, "Come, I'll wipe your feet."

There was an irresistible attraction about getting the feet wiped and he had got used to it. This was the only time when Nur would be with her little beloved; she would wipe his feet and this assured her place in the house. Sheru would ask her to hurry up. She would smile and linger. When his feet were wiped clean, he would feel that he had got rid of the dirt of his school jute matting.

Even now, he greatly relished getting his feet wiped clean.

Nur would bring him maize *rotis* with heaps of cream over them. Sometimes he observed that Nur would be staring at him from the kitchen and sometimes she would sing slowly in a low voice while cooking.

Ajjchhota, kalbadda
Ma ye dinon din jot soayi

(What if he is small today, he'll grow big tomorrow; as the days pass, the flame grows fuller)

He would dart out. In the morning, he would find his *patti* clean, his black inkpot full of ink, his books neatly arranged in his satchel, his *kanni* sharpened fine. He would be pleased, thinking that he was young and this Nur, who was so pretty, who shone like moonlight and whose laughter spangled like sunlight, belonged to him; that she would always live in their house and when he grew big, he would take her to the fair, seating her by his side on his father's favourite horse.

But when he went to school, his friends would start teasing him. "Aha! Your *patti* is so clean! Is there collyrium in your eyes? Your wife must have applied it!" And they would all burst into laughter.

His dreams would be shattered.

The laughter would die down on the arrival of the teacher, but the sullen Sher Khan would remain depressed the whole day.

Seeing him in that mood, his mother would say, "Go and play with other children."

Shera would reply, "No, I won't go, everybody makes fun of me."

The mother's heart would fill with sadness and heave a sigh. The childhood of my son has been smothered. How will it be with his youth? *Ya Allah!* Have mercy! So many ill-matched marriages take place in our community. Then why is it that my son alone feels so sensitive about it?

Nuri's beauty was the talk of the whole village. She was equally well-mannered. When she went to the village well to fetch water, she had no secrets to share with the blooming brides of her own age, who were full of laughter. She would stand aloof, on one side, silent as if suffering from guilt. When someone teased her, she would blush, climb the parapet of the well and fill everybody's pitchers with her own brass vessel. They would bless her. Then, she would pick up her own vessels, find her lonely way home.

Sometimes Shera would throw away the *katora* of milk she would bring him. Nuri would watch the empty *katora* fall on the ground, its sound reverberating in the room and her eyes would fill with tears.

Sher Khan now pulled the quilt a little closer, a sigh rising from his heart and carrying him to his past again. He thought he was only a child, but how cruel could the society be. For him, Nuri was also like his mother. Therefore he would be frightened when his friends teased him or at the mention of the word 'wife'.

He remembered the day when he came from school, with his foot bleeding from a gash with a splinter of glass. His mother was not at home. There was only Nuri. She stood there with the fodder-cutting sickle in her hand, and for a moment he felt as if she would kill him.

Weeping, he had said, "A glass piece got in at school."

Nuri picked him up in her lap, took out the glass with the tip of her sickle. Out of sheer pain, he clung to her.

She caressed his hair and kissed him on the forehead, just as his mother did. Then she burnt a piece of cloth, stuck it on the wound and bandaged it.

After that day, he was not afraid of Nuri anymore.

But then, one day, his mother's brother had come to take him away. It was his mother who had sent for him. His uncle's village was large. It also had a middle school. Uncle had a flourishing business. He had a daughter—Sarwar Jan. Shera was also the only son of his mother. He overheard the conversation between the brother and sister.

Mother was saying, "Shera is too small and Nuri is grown up. You take him away, Vir. I've only one child. I'll manage to live without him, but I cannot see his childhood smothered while he lives here. Send him back when he grows up. In between, I shall come and look him up, every now and then."

His uncle replied, "Khatija, I had told you, even at that time, that there shouldn't be such an age difference between the two."

Mother's reply was choked with tears, "Did Sheru's Abba ever heed my words? And then there was the need for a person to attend to the household chores. I was mostly ill."

Uncle retorted sharply, "You needed a maid servant, not a daughter-in-law. Don't call Sher Khan back until I send him. You can meet him there at my place. But Khatija, take pity on the helpless creature. Set her free."

"She will not leave this house, Vir. Her *chacha* had raised her only to sacrifice her for getting a wife for himself, in exchange. It is four years now. He has never asked her over. Her mother's jewellery now adorns Shera's *phuphi*. But by the grace of God, she is expecting now. Even when we send for her, he does not allow her to come. Nuri has got a home for the first time, Vir. She will not leave it."

"When Shera attains youth, then?" asked Uncle.

Mother was confident. "I'll get him a second wife. But Nuri will continue to be the mistress of the house."

Sher Khan couldn't bear to hear the conversation any more. He felt a storm brewing in his heart. The jubilant feeling, at the idea of living in his uncle's house, disappeared as quickly as it had appeared.

He ran to his room where he found Nuri was weeping and packing his clothes. He wanted to tell her that he wouldn't abandon her for another girl. But seeing her, he lapsed into the usual silence.

Nuri asked him, without wiping her tears, "Should I pack them all, or retain some of them?"

"No. Pack it all, I will never return." He then disappeared from the room briskly.

Nuri smiled a little. Shera did not understand the smile.

He now wondered why he remembered this.

Nuri had grown older now. But she had not changed. The sparkle in her eyes had not dimmed.

Sher Khan wrapped the quilt still tighter.

There was a yellow glow of light in the room. He could even see it with closed eyes. Sarwar Jan blew out the lamp. She tip-toed quietly and lay down beside him. Sher Khan took her into his embrace, mechanically. She was Nuri at this moment... the young Nuri.

Strange, problems that do not get solved in light somehow get resolved in darkness, without any argument!

Next morning, as the sun shone brightly, Sarwar Jan stuffed the children's satchels with apples and almonds sent by Nuri, saying smilingly, "Your elder Amma has sent them."

The girls had run away coyly.

Whenever Sarwar was in a good mood, she referred to Nur as her children's elder Amma. She herself called her *Aapa*. But such occasions were like sunshine in the season of rains.

Nuri was Maulavi Amin's *begum* now and had settled the children of Maulavi's first wife, except the youngest son who now lived with her. It was for this child, who was still a baby, that the Maulavi had wanted a woman or wife, who would rear him alongwith the other children and also look after the household. Nuri had fulfilled all these responsibilities, like a caretaker, and after the Maulavi's death, now lived in the house with his youngest child.

Kataloo managed the orchards, but she could never accept him as someone who she could call her own. There was always a tension between them.

Sher Khan put the harness on his horse. He thought of going out. He had to buy horses. Perhaps this activity would pull him out of his past. Sitting astride the horse, he put it to a trot, and with this, he set his memories also on the trot.

He remembered the night she had stood before him in her fullness. All sorts of women had pushed him into Nuri's room.

Thirty-year-old Nuri did not show any bashfulness on seeing the 20-year-old Sher Khan. She was trembling and looked like a crestfallen yellow leaf. She was weeping.

He had compared Nuri with the apricot tree in the courtyard. Nuri, his first wife, had certainly not been the Taj Mahal of his dreams.

It was Nuri who spoke first. "Sit down, Sher Khan."

Shera was again like the boy who had returned from school, with a glass splinter in his foot. He also began weeping.

Nuri fell silent on seeing him. She took his hand and said, "No, no, Sher Khan, you should not weep. I will weep. I am used to weeping. I will not allow you to spend your nights weeping, the way I passed the nights of my blighted hopes. You are my little beloved and I have also brought you up. You were always my husband. Only I was never your wife. I never felt that I was your wife. It is true that I have seen a husband behind your name, but he is not you. You gave me a home, my own home and I am content with that. I will not let your dreams be shattered. I know your Uncle wants you to get married to Sarwar."

Shera had shrieked, "No, no, I will not marry her."

Nur had said: "You have to marry. I free you, Shera. I exempt you from the payment of the amount of *meher* as well. God will give you happiness. I know because I've always prayed for you. On the night of our marriage, when you were only five, you did not appear to me as a husband; you appeared to me like a home where I could be secure. How one longs for a home! People sometimes leave you but the home never leaves you. Home is also never faithless, Shera."

Nuri had then caressed his head and said, "Don't weep. I'll leave tomorrow morning. It will be a month tomorrow, since Maulavi Sahab's wife died. I shall be able to save his baby son. Maulavi Sahab also needs a woman, not a wife. But I'm not destined to be a wife, it seems. I first got a husband who was 10 years younger to me. Now, I am going to get a second husband, who is 20 years older than me. He also has four daughters who need me." And saying this, she had paused.

A speechless Shera remembered her saying, "This is my home. Do call me here sometimes. The walls of this house are inscribed with the story of 15 years of my life. There is not a single wall of this house which I have not embraced to weave my dreams in the past; not a tree in the backyard of this house in whose blossoms I have not seen the faces of my children; not a rafter of the roof which could stand my stare. Each night of this house I have absorbed in my heart and each day I bequeath to you."

"But do send for me sometimes, Sher Khan. Do not weep. If people see your swollen eyes tomorrow morning, they will say that the elder wife has beaten you."

"Go and sleep on this bed. I have kept water for heating on the fire. I will wipe your feet and then lie down to sleep, till tomorrow morning."

How could Sher Khan forget now that Nuri had kept awake the whole night, with his feet at her breasts? In the morning while he lay fast asleep, she had gone over to the Maulavi's house, like a helpless cow which had been untethered from the tying post but with the rope still tied around its neck.

That morning there had been a lot of commotion in the house, and when a female relation tried to say something about Nuri, Sher Khan had raised his voice. "Be careful, nobody will say anything about Nur Begum. I myself have given her *talaq*. She will be married to Maulavi Sahab today. Amma, today your maid servant has gone and my wife is dead. Nobody in this house speaks a word against her. Otherwise, tomorrow itself I will leave the house and get recruited in the Army."

The whole house had been stunned into silence. Thereafter, if ever there was some whisper pertaining to Nuri, it stopped as soon as Sher Khan was sighted.

Then, the same evening, Shera's marriage with Sarwar had been solemnised.

Sher Khan was like a wayfarer, who had lost his way and who stood at the junction of two roads, staring around. During the night he would call his wife Nuri, and in the morning he felt awkward in facing her.

Nuri was no more than a tale for everybody, but for him, she was a reality.

Whenever his horse, Teerandaz, descended from the hill of Nuri's house, he would observe a swaying shadow behind the walnut tree, and as the horse went down the hill, Nuri would slowly go out of sight; like Anarkali, who had slowly disappeared while being buried alive in a brick wall.

Sher Khan would linger on the hill for a while, at times gazing at the setting sun or searching for Nuri's shadow.

Several years had gone by...

Sawan had arrived in the first year itself and then the two daughters were born; the days slipped from his hands, went on slipping, with the memory of Nuri still there like something stuck in his throat.

Then one day, while passing Nuri's house, Kataloo had caught hold of the bridle of his horse and said, "Shahji, *Aapaa* wants to see you."

Sher Khan got down from the horse and went and stood before Nuri like some thief hauled up before a magistrate.

Nuri broke the ice, "How are you, Sher Khan?"

Sher Khan heaved a sigh and said, "*Salaam-a-lekum*, Begum Sahiba, I am fine. How are you?"

Nuri's eyes filled with tears, but she smiled and said, "You've come this side, after a long time. Maulavi Sahab has been seriously ill. I want him to be taken to the city hospital."

Sher Khan, whose voice sent terror to the hearts of people all around the area, merely nodded his head meekly, like an innocent lamb.

Nuri handed him a basket. "Take this for your children."

Sher Khan said, "I will arrange a *palaki* immediately. I will also go along. You should stay at home."

From then onwards, Sher Khan started visiting the place occasionally. These visits snow-balled into rumours, and reached Sarwar Jan.

One day, she asked, "From where do you bring these fruits for the children now and then""

"Nuri, Nur Begum…from Maulavi Sahab's house."

Sarwar wanted to ask more, but Sher Khan cut her short. "These children could have been Nuri's. Don't raise the subject again."

Sarwar fell silent, and whenever fruits arrived in the house, she told her children, "Your elder Amma has sent these fruits for you."

Sometimes elder Amma was mentioned in light banter also, but sometimes, deep inside, it hurt her. Kataloo called her *Baaji* with a great sense of possessiveness. He brought to her the news of Maulavi Sahab's illness and Nur's dedicated nursing.

And then, when Maulavi Sahab passed away, Shera came to her and said, "Saro, the Maulavi Sahab is no more. I am going to Nuri's place. Will you also come?"

She responded, "No, you go alone."

Shera had mounted his horse and gone. And he had not completely returned home thereafter...

Sarwar had her children. She had a home, but she could not be the mistress. She always found Nuri standing betwixt herself and Sher Khan; Nuri her *saut*, Nuri her mother-in-law, Nuri her enemy, her co-sharer.

Whenever the fruits came, the children enjoyed them with a pleasure that was unbearable to her. Sometimes she felt her husband belonged to Nuri and wondered if the children also... and she was greatly disturbed.

The children had come to accept the existence of their elder Amma, when an event took place that changed the lives of these three protagonists forever; After a long interval, Sarwar became pregnant again. The experienced midwife warned her that it wouldn't be an easy delivery and suggested going to the city.

Sher Khan made the necessary arrangements.

One day, he told Sarwar, "We will go to the city tomorrow. I don't know how long we may have to stay there. If you agree, I will ask Nuri to come and take care of the children and look after the house."

Sarwar was stung and quick to react. "It won't be long before I depart. Bring her after I am gone."

Sher Khan kept quiet, but left Kataloo behind to take care of the children and the house.

No sooner had Sarwar reached the hospital that her labour pains started. In order to save her life, she had to be operated upon and unfortunately had a stillborn.

Outside Sher Khan prayed, *"Allah,* have mercy on me."

Later, Sarwar Jan told him, "I am all right. Arrange a

nurse and go home to be with the children. I'm not having good dreams."

Sher Khan consulted the doctor. He was advised to return after a week when Sarwar would be discharged.

Days went by and Sarwar Jan recovered, now waiting for the stitches to be removed. When she was well enough to take interest in her surroundings, she noticed that every evening someone in the ward below wailed; it was a woman's supplications, her piercing prayers reaching up to the sky, and then trailing and dying voices.

Every evening, Sarwar was seized with an unnamable dread, and trembling, which ceased only after these voices died down.

Where is my baby? Where is my darling? It was born only yesterday. Allah, where have they taken away my baby? The woman downstairs wailed.

Sarwar Jan asked a nurse: "Did this woman also have a stillborn?"

The nurse replied, "No, sister! How can she have a child yet? Her husband is still in primary school. She has lost her mind. Her sister-in-law has been delivering, year after year, and she has been bringing them up. This, she thought, was hers. *Allah* had sent her one at last. She started snatching the infant from the sister-in-law. Her in-laws have brought her here. They do not want to keep her anymore. All these years she had been slaving in their home. Now, when her husband grows up, after another four or five years, some other woman will come to take charge. Women are born ill-fated. But why are you weeping?"

"Will you take me to her?" Sarwar Jan implored, still weeping.

The nurse said, "You are very emotional, *bibi*. Get well enough first. I will take you along later. During daytime, she is absolutely normal. I have talked to her several times."

"In that case, can you call her now?"

"Just now? You seem to be in a hurry. Let the doctor finish his rounds. After that, I will call her."

The girl came during lunch hour, with a plate in her hand.

Sarwar Jan sat up.

Handing over the plate to the nurse, the girl embraced Sarwar. Both started crying; as if they had known each other's sorrow for years.

Sarwar wiped her tears but let the girl cry. Then she told her lovingly, "I am your *Baaji*, come with me. I shall arrange your marriage with someone. And until then, Allah has given us enough."

"No, *Baaji*, I am all right here."

"Nobody can stay in the hospital forever, Begama," she called the girl by her name. "Come, with me."

"No, *Baaji*, there is Rasool in our village. Rasool is my ..."

"All right, I will come to your house. Now banish this illness of the mind," Sarwar said.

After they had eaten, she combed the girl's hair, put collyrium in her eyes, took out her *jugani* and put it round her neck, saying, "From today onwards, I'm your sister."

"All right *Baaji*. May I go now? Some people are coming to see me."

"Is Rasool coming?"

"Yes, *Baaji*," she said shyly.

That evening, there was no sound of wailing downstairs.

The day Sarwar Jan was to leave the hospital, Sher Khan came early in the morning with a *palaki*.

When she saw Begama covering her face with a *ghunghat*, Sarwar forbade her. "No, don't do that. He is your brother."

Begama put oil in Sarwar Jan's long hair and plaited them,

put collyrium in her eyes and made a black spot above her eyebrows, saying: "You will never have a *saut*."

"I don't have a *saut*, I only have an *Aapaa*."

"What did you say?" asked a surprised Begama.

"Nothing. I'm just pining for home."

When Begama embraced Sarwar as she sat in the *palaki* and wept, the nurse rushed to her.

Begama said, "I am no longer out of my mind, sister. I am fully cured today."

Later, when Sarwar surveyed her home, standing in the compound, after a tiring, long journey, she was amazed to see a difference, a familiar newness.

Sher Khan led her to the bed inside. The children stood there, anxious. Sarwar stretched her arms and took them in her embrace.

Then, turning to Sher Khan she said "Shah*ji*, Shah*ji*."

"What is it, Saro?"

"Will you accede to a request?"

"What is it?"

"Please go and bring Nuri *Aapaa* home. She has married off her daughters there. These two are also hers. I have understood, Shah*ji*. This is her house. Please go and get her here. I will not gulp even a drop of water until she comes."

That night it was Saro who lay in Sher Khan's arms...not Nuri.

Translated from the Dogri by
Shivnath

5

A PINCH OF SNUFF

Manohar Malgaonkar

Mother's announcement shook me, "*Nanukaka* is coming," she said.

"Oh, my god!" I said. "Couldn't we send him a wire saying we are leaving and that I have been transferred or something?"

"No, dear," Mother said. 'He must be on the train already. Besides," she added reassuringly, "He says he cannot stay here for more than two or three days."

"What is he coming to Delhi for—in this heat?"

"He wants to see some Minister."

"What? That means he will be here for weeks! Ministers don't see people for weeks...months! Oh, my God!"

"If your *Nanukaka* wants to see a minister, I am sure he will manage to see him." Mother said, "Any time of the day or night."

Mother has always been very loyal to her side of the family, and *Nanukaka*, after all, is her brother.

I, on the other hand, may have something of a complex about ministers. I am an under-secretary, on probation, and as such trained to regard ministers as being two steps higher than God; the secretaries being just one step higher.

I was waiting on the platform when the train came in.

Nanukaka stood in the doorway of a second class carriage; a striking figure, white haired, with an impressive moustache. He still wears the old-fashioned knee-length black coat and the red silk *pugree* of the Deccani Brahmin, and drapes a white *angocha* round his shoulders.

As I went up, he handed me a basket. "Take this out, quick," he whispered. "I will join you outside the station."

I asked no questions, tucked the basket under my arm and turned, only to bump into an enormous Marwari woman who had her head covered in a veil.

But my apologies were drowned by the strange sounds emanating from the basket; the protests of an outraged kitten.

Spitts...strupst...meow...meooow!

I ducked and ran and mingled with the crowd and squeezed through the gate in the wake of a Sikh marriage party.

Nanukaka took a long time. The station yard was nearly empty and the last *tonga* had gone when he emerged, escorted by a fawning ticket checker.

"No room in the third class, and they wouldn't issue second class tickets without reservation." *Nanukaka* explained as he came up to me. "Had to travel second on a third class ticket! But it was all arranged quite amicably. Such a nice young man, the TC. You saw how he even came right out with me, so that there would be no trouble. The kitten, of course, travelled free. How is it?"

"Very quiet," I said. Perhaps it is dead. I thought hopefully.

We got into the car, and even before I had changed into second gear, *Nanukaka* asked, "When have you arranged for the minister to see me? I cannot stay here for more than two days; three at the most."

It was a time for frankness. "Look, Uncle," I said. "I am merely an under-secretary, on probation, and it is more than my job is worth to go asking for interviews with a minister."

"Oh!" *Nanukaka* said, "I had rather hoped...oh, I see. Well, never mind."

He took a pinch of snuff, brushed his fingers delicately on his *angocha*, and sat back, closing his eyes and puckering his eyebrows, as though in deep thought. He also clucked his tongue several times, in a typically *Deccani* way, registering pity.

Mother was waiting at the doorstep, her face wreathed in smiles. She went into squeals of delight over the kitten and made a lot of fuss over *Nanukaka*.

I also found that she had installed him in my bedroom, so that I had to put a *charpoy* for myself in the back verandah.

At mother's insistence, I had taken two days' leave from the office, and in the afternoon, I drove *Nanukaka* to the North Block. He went to see the minister and I waited in the car park. It was two hours before he returned, mumbling colorful Marathi swear words. I didn't dare ask him what had happened, and drove without saying a word.

He cooled down in a little while, though, and said, "Two hours, I spent being transferred from one *chaprasi* to another, tramping through the corridors, and in the end, succeeded in getting a deputy-secretary to give me an appointment—three days from now! Shameful! Shameful!" And there was another series of Marathi expletives.

In a linguistic emergency *Nanukaka* turned to his mother tongue.

A garish yellow sports car flashed past us, blaring its horn, and the young man at the wheel waved his hand at me.

"What a rude man! Who was that?" *Nanukaka* asked.

"Chap called Ratiram, works in the same ministry as I do."

"I see."

"There was some talk about his going as trade commissioner to Hazrat Barket Ali, you know, the Ambassador, but they say it is all off now." I said just to make conversation.

"Why don't you get sent out on one of those foreign assignments?" *Nanukaka* asked.

"To get sent on a foreign assignment is in the same category as getting an interview with a minister, *Nanukaka*." I said, somewhat unkindly. "It takes pull. Ratiram is the son of Sohanlal Ratiram, you know the party boss in Delhi."

Nanukaka sat up with a jerk. "What was that? What did you say? Sohanlal Ratiram's son! How extraordinary! Well, well!" He leaned back in his seat and stared at me for a long time.

"Now let me see. You've got a close-collared Jodhpur coat, haven't you? Good! And can you tie a turban? No? This tie-and-collar business is no good these days. Let's go home. After you have changed, we will go and see him."

"See whom?"

"Why, Lala Sohanlal, of course!"

"Do you know him at all?"

"Of course not." said *Nanukaka*.

I changed into my Jodhpur coat and *Nanukaka* tied a huge orange turban round my head. "Act as though you were my... er...a sort of A.D.C.," he cautioned me as we started for Lala Sohanlal's house.

A secretary, in spotless white clothes, received us and showed us into a cool white room, before he asked our business, very politely.

"Just dropped in," *Nanukaka* said casually. "I had come to Delhi for the *Zamindar's* convention, a rather unofficial gathering you know, since we *zamindars* are not, not exactly, popular, these days…V.P. has also sent a cable, he wants to see me, but he is not coming from Washington until tomorrow. I thought I might as well see Lalaji and tell him what arrangements we, that is, the *zamindars*, have made for the agricultural vote…"

Nanukaka sort of trailed off and I could see that he had not really made an impression on the secretary who was just being polite and playing it safe.

"I have to see whether Lalaji is free," the secretary said. "He seldom sees…er…visitors without a previous appointment."

Lalaji must have been free because from the adjoining room we could hear the unhurried gurgle of the hookah, and then we could hear the haughty secretary talking to him.

"What day is it today?" *Nanukaka* asked me.

I thought he was speaking in an unusually loud voice. "Tuesday," I told him.

"Ooh, only Tuesday, and to think that on Sunday I was in Beirut. Amazing, isn't it?"

I swallowed hard. "Amazing," I agreed.

"And if I had listened to Hazrat, I would still be abroad. Old HB was just dying to drag me to the Foreign Minister."

The steady gurgling of the hookah in the next room had suddenly stopped.

"What did you say?" *Nanukaka* asked, although I had not even opened my mouth. "Why didn't I stay back? You know how it was with HB the last time, when he was in Geneva. He got me involved in the cotton talks. Besides, from Bombay, SK had been sending me cable after cable…"

That was the moment Lala Sohanlal Ratiram came waddling out of the inner room, with the secretary at his heels.

And from then on everything was smothered in the saccharine

courtesy of the seasoned political campaigner. As soon as the introductions were over, the secretary was sent bustling off to order coffee and sweetmeats and *paan*.

They sparred guardedly about *zamindars* and votes and the weather for a few minutes, before coming to brass tacks.

"I hear you know Hazrat Barket Ali well," Sohanlal said with an ingratiating grin.

"Oh! Old HB! How did you know that I know HB? Actually we were at school together, he always regarded me as a sort of elder brother. Rather touching really. Even today, he seldom takes a big decision without consulting me. When the PM offered him the Embassy, who do you think had to make up HB's mind for him?"

"You?"

"That's right, me. Good old HB"

"Ha, ha, ha, ha," laughed Sohanlal, now showing all his *paan*-stained teeth. "In that case, it is a lucky day that you have come to my humble house. Very lucky, because my son—he is in the Balances Ministry here—was going as Trade Commissioner to Hazrat Barkat Ali. But you know how there are wheels within wheels. Someone seems to have poisoned the ambassador's mind about my son; about some transaction concerning evacuee-property. Actually, it was perfectly legitimate…!"

Nanukaka waved away any further explanation. "That should be quite simple," he announced. "I will write and tell HB to do it. No, no. Don't thank me at all. After all, we…er…we men in the public eye must do things for one another, Ha, Ha. One good turn deserves another."

Nanukaka opened his silver snuffbox and took a pinch. Then, flicking on his *angocha*, he casually mentioned the name of the Welfare Minister.

The fixed grin on Sohanlal's face vanished. "Is he a friend of yours?" He asked rather anxiously.

"Well, not exactly." *Nanukaka* admitted, "No, not exactly."

"I am so glad," Sohanlal said, relieved. "So glad! That man, such ingratitude! I gave him a ticket, helped him in every way, and what do I get in return?"

It turned out that the minister and Lala Sohanlal, once the best of friends, were now at daggers drawn since last year when the minister had refused to consider a proposal for his daughter from Lalaji's son.

"He wants a prince!" Sohanlal snorted. 'What is a prince these days? *Faugh!* Keep this confidential. I can tell you that the minister has burnt his boats. I'd be surprised if he is given a ticket for the next elections very surprised. He turns my son down, and finds a prince! Baah! And what is even more funny, I am told that so far they haven't even exchanged horoscopes; even the astrologers on both sides haven't come together to decide whether it would be an auspicious match!"

"Disgraceful!" *Nanukaka* snorted. "Disgraceful! What prince did you say?"

"Some two-penny state called Ninnore."

We left the house soon after that. *Nanukaka* having again promised that he would write to 'Old HB' that very day. As we drove away, both *Lalaji* and his secretary were bowing to him from the porch.

Nanukaka was strangely silent that evening and we went to bed soon after dinner.

But in the morning, he was chirpy again.

"We are going to the Minister's house this morning," he announced.

"Not me, please Uncle," I appealed.

He inhaled some snuff before he spoke, and by that time he seemed to have forgotten what I said. "This car of yours; too old, too small. We will need something much more impressive. You noticed how that secretary treated us coldly at first. If we had gone in a bigger car, he would have been quite different No, not a taxi. A private car, driven by a liveried chauffeur; the bigger, the better."

I remembered that an acquaintance of mine had been trying to sell, for some months, an enormous, stately, outlandish car that would have been built only for a court procession. I told *Nanukaka* about it.

"That's it! We'll take it out for a brief trial," he suggested breezily.

"I am sure we could," I said, "if we looked like genuine buyers. But do we? These motorcar touts can smell a rich man a mile off."

"You leave that to me," *Nanukaka* said. "You just leave the details to me."

"And what about the liveried chauffeur?" I asked.

"You, of course," *Nanukaka* said blandly.

He took his chequebook and wrote a cheque for a thousand rupees. He then folded it neatly and put it into the inner pocket of an old coat of his. "Now call your *dhobi*," he told me.

I called the *dhobi*, and Uncle gave him the coat and took him outside and had a talk with him.

Then we drove over to Sikka Auto Dealers and *Nanukaka* asked if he could try out the car we had in mind.

We had barely got talking to the manager, when *dhobi* rushed into the shop, holding *Nanukaka's* old coat in one hand and the cheque aloft with the other. "Oh, there you are!" He panted. 'Look what you had left in this coat of yours!'

Nanukaka held out the cheque at arm's length and clucked his tongue several times. "'How careless of me!" He said. "I am always doing this sort of thing. Bearer cheque too; anyone could have cashed it. Here, my good man," he said to the *dhobi*, "Here is a reward for you. There is nothing like honesty," and he gave him a two-rupee note and a pat on the back.

After this demonstration of wealth, it was quite easy about the car.

I drove, wearing my white Jodhpur coat and the orange turban, and *Nanukaka* sat regally at the back, looking every inch of what he was supposed to be—a hereditary pundit from a princely state.

We drove to the Minister's house and the servants and the secretary fussed around *Nanukaka*, who refused to state his business but merely called for the visitor's book.

"I have just come to make a formal call," he announced. "I have no wish to disturb the minister. It is just a formality that we in the old princely states still observe. His highness is a great stickler for these courtesies."

They brought the visitor's book and I watched *Nanukaka* in admiration, as he wrote his name with a flourish and added, Hereditary Astrologer to the Maharaja of Ninnore. At the end, he gave his Delhi address; my address.

Without another word, and as though he were in a tearing hurry, he got into the car and said loudly, "Take me to Maharaja Sutkatta's place. I have to return all these horoscopes entrusted to me."

As the car turned out of the gate I glanced backwards and saw a huge, dark, *khaddar*-clad figure peering at us from an upper-storey window.

We had just finished tea, and were trying to house-break

the new kitten, which had just made a puddle on the floor, when a car with a white triangle stopped in front of the house.

Nanukaka went out with folded hands to receive the Welfare Minister who had come to see him.

Our guest left yesterday, his mission accomplished. I never found out what it was that *Nanukaka* wanted to see the Minister about.

Also, I wonder what is going to happen when the Minister discovers that my Uncle has never been within a hundred miles of a place called Ninnore, although I am now convinced that Nanukaka will deal with the situation without allowing a single fold of his *angocha* to fall out of place.

Only, when it happens I want to be somewhere far out of range.

6

GREEN SARI

RK Narayan

In July 1933, I had gone to Coimbatore, escorting my elder sister, and then stayed on in her house. There was no reason why I should ever hurry away from one place to another. I was a freelance writer and I could work wherever I might be at a particular time.

One day, I saw a girl drawing water from the street tap in our street and immediately fell in love with her. Of course, I could not talk to her, I learned later that she had not even noticed me passing and then walking back in front of her while she waited to fill the brass vessels. I craved to get a clear, fixed, mental impression of her features until her vessels filled, when she would carry them off and not come out again until the next water-filling time. I could not really stand and stare; whatever impression I had of her would be through a side-glance while passing the tap. I suffered from a continually melting vision. The only thing I was certain of was that I loved her, and I suffered.

The headmaster, the headmaster's daughter and the school were all within geographical reach and hailing distance, but the restraint imposed by the social code created barriers. I attempted to overcome them by befriending the headmaster. He was a book-lover and interested in literary matters, and we found many common subjects for talk. We got into the habit of meeting at his school, after the school hours, and discussing the world.

During one such talk we were having on political matters, I made a bold announcement of my affection for his daughter.

He was taken aback but did not show it. In answer to my proposal, he just turned to the God in the shrine and shut his eyes in prayer.

No one in our social condition could dare to proceed in the manner I had done. There were formalities to be observed, and any talk for a marriage proposal could proceed only between the elders of the family. What I had done was unheard of. But the headmaster was sporting enough not to shut me up immediately. Our families were known to each other, and the class, community, and caste requirements were all right.

He just said, "If God wills it," and left it at that.

He also said, "Marriages are made in heaven, and who are we to say 'Yes' or 'No'?" After this he explained the difficulties.

His wife and womenfolk at home had to be consulted, and my parents had to approve, and so on and so forth, and then the matching of horoscopes—this last one became a great hurdle at the end.

He came down to a practical level one day by asking me what I proposed to do for a living. Luckily for me, at about that time a small piece that I had written—*How to Write an Indian Novel*, lampooning Western writers who visited India to gather material—had unexpectedly been accepted by *Punch* and brought me six guineas. This was my first prestige publication (the editor rejected everything I sent to him subsequently) and it gave me a talking point with my future father-in-law. I could draw a picture of my freelance writing for London papers and magazines, and explain to him that when my novel was finished it would bring an income all my life and 50 years after.

He listened to me with apparent interest without contradicting me, but off and on suggested, "I'm sure, if your, father used his influence, he could fix you in a government job in Bangalore. Won't he try?"

This always upset me, and I immediately explained my economic philosophy; how I spurned the idea of earning more than was needed, which would be 20 rupees a month or, with a wife, 40 rupees, and I expected my wife to share my philosophy. Not a very politic statement to make to the bewildered and hesitant father of a girl, but I became headstrong in my conviction. However, while it distressed the gentleman it did not materially affect my progress toward matrimony.

What really mattered was not my economic outlook, but my stars. My father-in-law, himself an adept at the study of horoscopes, had consultations with one or two other experts and came to the conclusion that my horoscope and the girl's were incompatible. My horoscope had the Seventh House occupied by Mars, the Seventh house being the one that indicated matrimonial aspect. The astrological texts plainly stated that Mars in the Seventh House indicated nothing but disaster, unless the partner's horoscope also contained the same flaw, a case in which two wrongs make one right.

The next few weeks were a trying period for me.

The headmaster would have none of me. In very gentle terms he expressed his rejection of me, as also his resignation to such a fate, since he seemed to have been secretly in my favour.

I lost the taste for food and company, and lay sulking in a corner of my sister's house, on a gloomy easy-chair. My mood was noticed by others with sympathy. I think I enjoyed a certain amount of self-dramatisation and did all that one does when crossed in hopeless love. I avoided going out in the direction of the street tap. I avoided the headmaster and his school. Late in the evening when it became dark, I went for a brisk walk with my head bowed in thought, looking neither left nor right but totally wrapped up in my own gloomy reflections, just enough initiative left to smoke two Gold Flake cigarettes and return home.

My sister, being my hostess, tried to cheer me up in various ways. My pensive pose got on her nerves.

At this period, I remember writing a play. It kept me busy all the afternoon. The play was called *The Home of Thunder*—a frightful tragedy in which all the principle characters are struck dead by lightning, on a tower open to the skies. The play ended with a clap of thunder. It was a highly philosophical play examining the ideas of love, resignation, and death, the writing of which diverted my mind a great deal. I had great hopes for its future, and in due course, sent it round to all kinds of producers and directors in every part of the civilised world. I had forgotten all about its existence till a few months ago, when David Higham's office discovered and returned the manuscript while clearing out old papers.

The evil of my stars soon became a matter of discussion among the headmaster's astrological group.

He sought me out, sent me here and there to meet his colleagues, talk it over with them and bring him their opinions and conclusions. Finally, he sent me along to meet an old man living not far from us in the back of a coconut garden. His name was, strangely, Chellappa-sir. I don't know why—perhaps he was a retired teacher he was said to be an expert, I went to his house and explained my mission.

He snapped at me, "What do you want me to do? Am I Brahma to change your stars?" He looked angry for some inexplicable reason. "Go tell the headmaster one thing. I don't care whether his daughter gets married or not; I'll hold on to my views. I have spoken to that man again and again, but still he is full of doubts. If he knows better astrology than I do, he should not trouble me like this. If he listens to reason, he should go ahead and fix a date for the wedding, that's all. I see no harm in it. He hasn't noticed the moon's position in his daughter's horoscope, which neutralises Mars. But that man expects me to give him a guarantee that Mars will not harm his daughter's life. I can give no such guarantee. I am not Brahma." He raised his voice to a shrieking pitch and repeated, "I do not care whether that man's daughter is married or not..."

In spite of all these fluctuations and hurdles, my marriage took place in a few months, celebrated with all the pomp, show, festivity, exchange of gifts, and the overcrowding that my parents desired and expected.

Soon after my marriage, my father became bedridden with a paralytic stroke, and most of my mother's time was spent at his side, upstairs. The new entrant into the family, my wife, Rajam, was her deputy downstairs, managing my three younger brothers, who were still at school, a cook in the kitchen, a general servant, and a gigantic black-and-white Great Dane, acquired by my elder brother who was a dog-lover. She kept an eye on the stores, replenishing the food-stuff and guarding them from being squandered or stolen by the cook. Rajam was less than 20, but managed the housekeeping expertly and earned my mother's praise. She got on excellently with my brothers.

This was one advantage of a joint family system—one had plenty of company at home. Yet, with all the group life, there was still enough privacy for me and my wife. We had a room for ourselves and when we retired into it, we were in an idyllic world of our own.

Within six months, she proved so adept at housekeeping that my mother left her in complete charge, and we found the time to exchange pleasantries and intimacies only when she took a little time off during the day and came to my room, or at night after everyone had retired and the kitchen door was shut. Presently, I did not find too much time to spend at home either.

In order to stabilise my income, I became a newspaper reporter. My business would be to gather Mysore city news and send it daily to a newspaper published in Madras called *The Justice*. The daily was intended to promote the cause of the non-Brahmin, who suffered from the domination of the minority Brahmin class in public life, government service, and education. Though *The Justice* was a propagandist paper against the Brahmin class, it somehow did not mind having me as its correspondent in Mysore.

I left home at about nine in the morning and went out news-hunting through the bazaar and market-place—all on foot. I hung about law courts, police stations and the municipal building, and tried to make up at least 10 inches of news each day before lunchtime. I returned home at one o'clock, bolted down a lunch, sat down at my typewriter, and typed the news items with appropriate headings. I now had an old Remington portable (the double barreled one having been given away for

20 rupees, off-setting the bill for cigarettes and sweets at a shop), which was a present from my younger sister. It took me an hour or more to type the items, and then I signed and sealed the report in an envelope and rushed it to the Chamarajapuram post office before the postal clearance at 2.20 p.m.

If my youngest brother Laxman (now a famous cartoonist) was available, he would be ready, with one foot on the pedal of his bicycle, to ride off to the post office, for a tiny fee of a copper for each trip; but when he wasn't there, I practically sprinted along with my press copy. There was really no need to rush like that since most of the news items could wait or need not be published at all but we were in a competitive society; I feared that other Madras papers like *The Mail* or *The Hindu,* whose correspondents had telephone and telegraph facilities, might get ahead of me. But those correspondents were lofty and did not care for the items I valued.

After the dispatch of the copy, I relaxed in my room; that was also the time when my wife would give me company. I described to her the day's events, such as traffic accidents, suicides, or crimes, which were the grist for my mill; then I sank into a siesta for an hour and was ready to go out again, at four o'clock, after a cup of coffee.

This time it would be a visit to the magistrate's court before closing time, to take down the judgment in a counterfeit case or murder conspiracy.

On Saturday afternoons, I sat at the municipal meetings, watching the city fathers wrangle over their obscure issues— all through the evening it would go on. In those days, there were always a couple of lawyers in the council, and they never permitted the business to proceed beyond the examination of the procedure and the by-laws. No more than a couple of items in the voluminous agenda would be covered at the end of two hours. After a coffee break, I would suddenly clutch the agenda papers and leave, afflicted with a headache.

Some days, there would be academic matters to cover; a distinguished visitor's lecture at the university or a senate meeting.

In those days, there was a local League of Nations Union, which strove to establish peace in this world in its own way. The secretary of this union, who was a history professor, decreed that our reports should be scrutinised by him before we filed them. I resisted his order as an encroachment on the freedom of the press, and he threatened to discredit me as a correspondent (which would, in effect, only mean denying luncheon facilities), whereupon I declared that I would report him to our Journalists' Association, pass a resolution against him, and syndicate it to all the world's press and denounce him as an autocrat and enemy of freedom.

He responded with, "Do you know that I have powers to smash you and your papers..." I walked out of the union meeting in protest, and so did a couple of my colleagues. I began to ignore its activities and boycotted its functions. I realised soon that this did not affect the prospect of world peace either way, or provoke my news editor to question why I was not covering the League of Nations Union.

Murders were my stand by. From Nanjangud or Chamarajnagar, at the extreme south of Mysore District, the police brought in a steady stream of murder cases. On such occasions, I let myself go. I hung about the mortuary for the post-mortem verdict and the first police report. As long as I used the expression 'alleged' liberally, there was no danger of being hauled up for false reporting or contempt of court. I knew a lot of police officers, plain-clothes men, and informers, apart from presidents and secretaries of various public bodies (including Pinjarapole, a home for aged or disabled animals) who craved publicity and sought my favor.

Quite a number of wedding invitations came to me, from fond parents hoping for a report and a photograph of the bridal pair in the paper. I could have gladly given all the space available to whoever wanted it, but my news editor, when he did not reject it outright, mutilated and decimated my copy. He compressed my most eloquent descriptions into two lines.

What did I make out of it all? Our contract was that I would be paid three rupees and eight annas per column of 21 inches. I fancied that the news I sent would cover at least 15 inches each day and fetch me at least 75 rupees each month, but thanks to the news editor's talent for abridgement, I had to crawl up each day by fractions of an inch. I measured my total "incharge" with a scale at the end of each month and sent my bill; and they would invariably doubt and disallow my measurements and send me some arbitrary amount, never more than 30 rupees, often less.

But I enjoyed this occupation, as I came in close contact with a variety of men and their activities, which was educative. It lasted about one year, and might have gone on, perhaps indefinitely, but for a letter I sent to the editor, which soured our relationship. They had withheld my payment for three months, and I wrote to say, *I am a writer in contact with many newspapers and periodicals in America and England who make their payments on precise dates; I am not used to delays in payments...*

To which the editor replied. *If you are as eminent as you claim to be, you should not mind a slight delay on our part; if, on the other hand, you could realise that after all you are a correspondent eking out your income with such contributions as we choose to publish, your tone is unwarranted by your circumstances.* I resented the tone of their reply, and decided to give up this work as soon as I could afford it.

Money was a big worry. When a cheque was delayed, it caused all kinds of embarrassment for me. My budget was precisely framed. I had to find money to pay for my share of the expenses at home, also for face powder or soap that my wife would ask for. I grandly promised her even a sari, and bought her a green one on credit, costing about 60 rupees, the shopkeeper agreeing to take instalments, of 10 rupees, on the fourth of every month.

If I delayed, a bill collector would appear on the morning of the sixth at our gate, demanding the instalment. He was a tall, gaunt man, with sunken cheeks and the expressionless face of a corpse. When I heard the clicking of the gate latch, I would tell myself, *Here it cometh, my lord*, echoing Hamlet. I rushed forward to stop him before my wife or anyone else could see him, and turned him back with soft words, promises, and a small tip of coffee; until I liquidated this debt, I felt guilty whenever I saw my wife in the green sari, as if I had given her a stolen present.

I continued to send in my reports of the turbulent city of Mysore, and off and on, I received a cheque from *The Justice*. But I voluntarily stopped this work on the day I received a cable from my friend Purna, who was now at Oxford. It read, *Novel taken, Graham Greene responsible.*

My friend and neighbour Purna, who used to hop over the wall and come to listen to my reading of *Swami and Friends*, had left in August 1981 for Oxford, promising to find a publisher for my book, while he was there.

When I had completed the novel, I had faithfully dispatched it to Allen and Unwin and when it was returned, to another publisher and then another. I had got used to getting back my manuscript with unfailing regularity once every six weeks—two weeks onward journey, two weeks sojourn on the publisher's desk and two weeks homeward journey with a rejection slip pinned to it—all in all, it provided me with six weeks of hope! I had got used to this as an almost mechanical process and had shed all emotions surrounding rejection. The last publisher to return it to me was Dent, and I had advised them in my covering letter to forward the manuscript, when rejected, to Purna at Exeter College, Oxford. I sent a parallel letter to Purna advising him to weigh the manuscript with stone and drown it in the Thames.

Purna, however, seems to have spent much of his time visiting London and carrying the manuscript from publisher to publisher. After trying them all, he wrote to me, *To the Thames? No need to hurry. Maybe never. Do not despair.*

This went on while I was spinning out measurable news for *The Justice*. Graham Greene was living in Oxford at that time. Purna, by some instinct, approached him, and gave him my manuscript. An introduction thus begun established a personal interest and a friendship between us that continues to this day. Graham Greene recommended my novel to Hamish Hamilton, who accepted it immediately.

Purna's cable made me gasp with joy and surprise. I saw myself in a new role as a novelist. I could see the relief in my wife's face, although she did not want to be demonstrative about it. The first thing I did on receiving the cable was to write to *The Justice* that I would not be able to supply them any more news from Mysore, although the advance from the novel was 20 pounds (less 50 percent tax).

Swami and Friends was published in October of 1935. A few reviews were enthusiastic but it had no sales; it appeared in the company of record-breaking best-sellers such as *Man the Unknown* and *Inside Europe* and was simply flushed out of sight in the deluge. So much so that Hamish Hamilton rejected my next novel, *The Bachelor of Arts*, with the words *Swami and Friends was a sad failure. I don't think Chandran [The Bachelor of Arts] is going to do any better.* I hope someone will prove me wrong some day.

Twenty years later, I met Hamish Hamilton in London at a party in the office of *The Spectator*, where Graham Greene had taken me. It was a very interesting and cordial meeting. Egged on by Greene, Hamilton remembered his comments on my literary future, joked at his own expense, and then remarked, "Remember, I was your first publisher, and I always feel happy at the thought of it." Next morning, he sent me a copy of his *Majority*, which had extracts to celebrate 30 years of his publishing firm, generously inscribed for me.

Thanks again to Graham Greene's recommendation, *The Bachelor of Arts* was published by Nelson, fulfilling a fancy I had entertained several years ago, when a Nelson representative had come from Edinburgh to see my father about the supply of books for our high-school library, I had confided to this salesman, "If I write a book, will you ask your company to publish it?" *"Undoubtedly,"* he had said and given me his card.

My father lived up to the last day of February 1937, as if to satisfy a technical need, and died leaving us to draw his pension for the full month. That was all the resources we were left with. My father had never believed in savings, property, and such things.

Now we feared a total economic collapse. But we managed.

My elder brother, now back from Madras, as an experiment, had opened a small shop in a new extension and called it National Provision Stores. My brother Seenu had a Government job and moved off to Bangalore.

Mine was still a pure gamble. Sometimes I wished that I had not given up *The Justice*, but I was sustained by the gambler's inexhaustible hope and a Micawberish anticipation of something turning up. With a second novel published and a daughter added to the family, life seemed to be "not so bad".

Short stories were being accepted in India as well as abroad—Graham Greene helping me in London. So after all, my claim to the editor of *The Justice* about contacts with London editors, was being fulfilled, although it had, perhaps, been premature. The great Gods who could view the past, present, and the future, as one block, would have realised I had not been false!

My brother and I shared the household expenses. He looked after the supplies and the miscellaneous items of expenditure, and I had to see that the house rent was paid; all aspects of the shelter were to be my responsibility. 'Rama Villas', in which we lived, was to be retained at my cost; there could be no question of our moving to another house.

Fortunately, our house-owner lived in Bangalore and only came down to Mysore once a month to collect the rent. I told him once, The rent is my responsibility, I have no fixed income. If my books sell, the royalty will come in only December and June. So please permit me to settle the rent once every six months, although I will pay into your bank account what I'm able to earn meanwhile.

He was good enough to accept this arrangement. Now I had a scrappy, fitful income from various sources. In addition to other items I had to find money for baby-food, gripe-water and toys. I did a variety of writing: a humorous article every week for a *Merry Magazine* at ten rupees a week; a most taxing experience for me—to perform a thousand-word literary clowning, week after week. I had also begun my third novel, *The Dark Room*.

I took a pad and pen and disappeared every morning for three hours. I found it impossible to write at home now—there were far too many worrying distractions, and also the baby. She was just a little over a year old, and I found it impossible to remain at my desk when she was around, since my wife often left her in my care when she was busy in the kitchen or in the garden gathering flowers for my mother's daily worship.

I had also a routine duty; to carry my daughter to let her watch the pink bougainvillea flowers over the compound wall of Reverend Sawday's bungalow at the corner. She would gaze at the bunch of flowers for about 10 minutes with rapt attention, and then I would have to lift her up to give her a glimpse of the white terrier that barked and frisked about inside the Reverend's compound. Only then would I be free to deposit her at home and leave.

Before sending me out, my wife would give me a cup of coffee and sometimes whisper a warning: "Don't make a fuss. Not enough coffee powder at home. Get some at the store when you return."

I set out to do my writing at the College Union, where the secretary had given me a room. I shut myself in for three hours, gazed on at the green football field outside, across the street, and spun out the fate of Savitri—the heroine of *The Dark Room*. I was somehow obsessed with the philosophy of woman as opposed to man; her constant oppressor. This must have been an early testament of the 'Women's Lib' movement.

Man assigned her a secondary place and kept her there with such subtlety and cunning that she herself began to lose all notions of her independence, individuality, stature, and strength. A wife in an orthodox milieu of Indian society was an ideal victim of such circumstances. My novel dealt with her, with this philosophy broadly in the background. I wrote nearly a thousand words, then went back home for lunch, exhausted, but also feeling triumphant at having done my quota of work for the day.

The Dark Room, once again read and approved by Graham Greene, was published by Macmillan in 1938. I had the unique experience of having a new publisher for each book. One book, one publisher—and then perhaps he said to himself, *Hands off this writer*; Hamish Hamilton, then Nelson, now Macmillan.

Macmillan had produced *The Dark Room* attractively. The reviews were favourable. I was buoyed up by them, but my wife did not share my optimism. She preferred to await the royalty statement, and when it did arrive, it revealed an 'Unearned Advance' (the advance was 40 pound less tax) rather than a cheque. I dashed off a letter to Macmillan, suggesting that they should have made the existence of the book better known to the public. Their depots in India had no copies, and the literary pages of the newspapers and magazines carried no advertisements. I had naively expected the publishers to seize upon the reviews and splash the quotes all over.

Macmillan replied that they had advertised the book as best as they could under the circumstances (what did it mean?) Their message typed in purple copying ink, and pressed out, possibly, on a wet sheet of paper, looked jittery and cheerless.

Presently, I had to set aside my principles and settle down to hackwork. At this time, my friend Purna, who had introduced my *Swami and Friends* to Graham Greene at Oxford, was on the personal staff of Sir Mirza Ismail, the Prime Minister of Mysore, and was in touch with the 'state guests' coming to Mysore.

At this time, Mr. Somerset, Maharaja's private secretary. Sir Charles Todhunter, an encrusted British administrator who had made it his mission in life to keep Indians properly occupied and out of mischief. It was his belief that what the Indians urgently needed was not political freedom but social graces. With this aim, he patronised Child Welfare, the Society for Prevention of Cruelty to Animals, the Good Manners League, and other innocuous institutions calculated to wean away the natives from mischief. The names Gandhi or Nehru were taboo in his presence. Sir Charles believed that, properly handled, Indians could shape into useful citizens, as proved by the terrified and efficient clerks he had in his establishment.

Seenu was one of them, having been spotted by Sir Charles at Bangalore and roped in.

While Sir Charles kept his dogs, cats and ducks sheltered in the main building, he housed his clerks in a derelict, unventilated barnyard under a smoky, verminous tile roof at the furthest corner of the compound, and summoned them to his presence with a buzzer. He glared at them over his narrow spectacles, thumped his huge fist on the desk and drove them to slave for him, 12 hours a day, by sheer bullying. His main job was to see to it that the Maharaja did not lose his loyalty to the British Crown or establish any industry which might affect British interests.

To question this man on literary matters would seem incongruous at any time. Yet Somerset Maugham seems to have done so. At a banquet arranged in his honour (although I cannot believe that either the Maharaja or his private secretary would have seen a novel by Maugham or anyone), Maugham asked, "How is it that I haven't seen anywhere the famous writer living in this city—Narayan?"

Sir Charles turned to his assistant in consternation, "Find out if there is a famous writer in Mysore. Consult the university vice-chancellor, if necessary."

After due investigation, Maugham was told, "There is no novelist in Mysore. We may, however, find you one in Bangalore" (at a safe distance of 100 miles). The honoured guest looked displeased and declared that his entire trip now seemed to him a waste.

Although I don't fully believe this story (imagined by someone and passed on from person to person), I suspect that Purna may have asked Somerset Maugham on some occasion, "Have you read The Dark Room?"

"I shall look for it in London when I go back."

"Would you like to meet Narayan?"

"I am afraid there is no time now, but do give him my compliments." (Later Maugham read The Dark Room and did write to me.)

Then Purna may have told this story to someone, with a slight exaggeration, and, passing the round in official circles, it developed into a full-fledged apocryphal and eventually reached Sir Mirza Ismail's ears. He, perhaps not wishing to share Todhunter's reputation, invited me to meet him at his Mysore residence called 'Lake View', overlooking Kukanahalli Tank. This was an unexpected offshoot of Maugham's visit.

As if to substantiate my theory, that fiction outlasts fact, the original story is still current after nearly 40 years! Occasionally, I came across some ancient raconteur retailing his own version— It seems PG Woodhouse when he came to Mysore, as a state guest demanded to meet RK Narayan and lost his temper when Todhunter said there was no such person in the city! And he left in a huff, declaring that he could not accept the hospitality of such an ignorant host. Or sometimes another name may be substituted for Maugham's: HG Wells, Bernard Shaw or John Gunther. Sir Mirza's call made me extremely uncomfortable, I had got on so far without meeting a minister or a Maharaja, and I hated the very idea. I did not even possess the right clothes for visiting a *dewan*. A *dhoti* and a cotton jacket over it was my main outfit, and I had resisted the Western style of dressing for many years. My normal wear was stylish enough for my encounters along Sayyaji Rao Road.

Nowadays, young people, hippies and non-hippies alike, have accustomed us to indifferent clothes and styles, but those were times when any doorman would turn you back if you were not properly dressed. I attempted to back out of this engagement, but Purna would not hear of it. He almost bound, gagged, and dragged me on to the presence of Sir Mirza, tutoring me all the way on how to impress him. "Don't fail to explain how the Indo-Saracenic traditions seem to be continued in the present-day buildings of Mysore, of course tempered and modified by contemporary needs."

He came up to the threshold of Sir Mirza's chamber talking in whispers, adding, "Also explain how the Chamundi Hill, presiding over this city, reminds one of the ancient Greek cities." Sir Mirza loved Mysore City, had remodelled its buildings, boulevards, and avenues, and liked to hear a good word about it.

I walked into his room in my *dhoti*, cotton coat and a muffler around my neck, feeling uneasy, as if I had gone wrapped in a bath towel. In contrast to me, he was impeccably dressed in a silk suit and a black fur cap. He offered me a seat and put me at ease, enquiring about my literary activities in a general way without going into details. My prepared speech beginning, The Indo-Saracenic...etc...was in a mess, delivered piece-meal in irrelevant fragments whenever a pause occurred in Sir Mirza's own speech. He was too polished to show any surprise, but gently assured me, in the course of our conversation, that if I wished to join the publicity department he would take me in. I declined the offer and expressed a wish only to write on Mysore.

Purna innocently believed that any magazine or newspaper editor in India would commission me to write on the Indo-Saracenic theme, if ordered by Sir Mirza, who lost no time in writing his proposal to several editors, who, in their turn, politely welcomed his suggestion (Mysore Government being the biggest advertisers of sandalwood soap and silk), but when approached, put me off unceremoniously.

Finally, the Government of Mysore commissioned me to write a travel book on Mysore. I was given a railway pass for travelling within the state, a cash advance for expenses, and letters of introduction to various district officials asking them to give me "all facilities."

Mysore State, extending up to Bombay in the north, Madras in the south-east, and Kerala in the South, offered inexhaustible material for a travel writer; rich in rivers, mountain ranges, forests, and wild life, not to mention temples, monuments, and battle-scarred fortresses and ruins. By bus and train, I explored every nook and corner, listened attentively to the claims of the local enthusiasts, in any obscure mountain retreat or village lost in a bamboo jungle, that here was to be found the earliest sculpture or civilisation or the highest waterfall in the world, or that these footprints on a forest track were Rama's, or that the golden tint to that lily pond was imparted by Sita when she plunged in for a cool bath.

In every place, people found a token of a legendary hero, or a mark left by the Gods during a brief sojourn. Belur and Halebid temples, with their 12th-century carvings, or the dungeons of Srirangapatnam, where in the 17th century Tipu Sultan had kept his British prisoners, seemed modern in comparison. I climbed a peak of the Western Ghat to view the Arabian Sea coast, visible as a vibrant string of silver far off. And also I went down eight thousand feet underground to see a gold field in Kolar, where the heat and pressure choked one's breath out.

I accomplished the full range of travel, leaving my wife and child back in Mysore City, and all through racked with anxiety about their welfare. Now and then, I found an excuse to cut short my tour program and return home unexpectedly, to satisfy myself that all accumulation of notes and data was in order, and settled down to write my book. I was supposed to make good use of gazetteers and bluebooks, but I found such reference work tedious and impossible, with the result that though my legendary tales and descriptions might beguile, the factual portions turned out to be unreliable.

A friend in the Mysore Civil Service who knew all the parts of the state marked in red the inaccuracies in my manuscript, and declared that the book be kept away from any unwary traveller setting out to see the state. I believe I tried to save myself by appending 'about' or 'approximately', before every date or distance; with all that, I don't think my book has seriously misguided anyone. When the manuscript was ready, the *dewan* ordered the government press to print an edition under my direct supervision: paper, type, and binding to be chosen by me. The superintendent of the press seemed overwhelmed by the authority vested in me and became so attentive whenever I opened my mouth to say something, that I found it embarrassing. It was becoming a difficult situation for me, since I knew nothing about the printing of books, but those who placed me in control of the government press must have assumed that an author of three novels published in England must, of course, be an expert in printing.

Every afternoon, sitting there as an advisor to the superintendent, I had to manage a difficult conversation across his table.

"Do you approve of these types—Plantin 12 point or Baskerville 10 point?" placing specimens reverently before me.

I looked at them casually and said, "Well...this one seems possible..."

"Shall I order the matrices for this series?"

"Surely, go ahead, but you must see that they don't delay..." I had to advise, approve, and at the same time try to learn what on earth it was all about.

"These are samples of the binding cloth. Walthamstow is the best of course, but we shall order whatever you choose, and this is thirty-six-pound featherweight paper ..."

I looked through the offerings gravely, disapproved a few on principle, and approved others. I also threw in a hint. "Let us keep as close to the get-up of *The Dark Room* as possible; the *dewan* liked it."

At once, the superintendent secured a copy of *The Dark Room* and went at it with a measuring scale, calipers, and magnifying glass, after stripping off its jacket, binding and spine. Cables were sent to England to ship the materials immediately. Not a moment to lose. No one paused to consider if there was any need for all this desperate rush. However, working at fever pitch, the press was able to deliver 1,000 copies of my journey through Mysore within six weeks.

I carried the first copy to Bangalore and presented it to the *Dewan* at his office at the red secretariat. I had thought that my financial troubles were now at an end. Not only the writing of the book, but the production of it in convincing form, struck me as an achievement, although it was a responsibility undertaken ahead of experience. Sir Mirza glanced through a couple of pages of the book and murmured a thanks.

He extended his hand across the table, and said, "Thank you again. It was good of you...," which seemed to mean now...Be off young man, I have so much to do now...I was aghast. I had expected a cheque to be held out to me rather than a bare hand.

When I left home I had budgeted so many items for the ₹1,200 I was to get. I had asked my wife, Do you want anything from Bangalore?" She was more realistic. "Let us first see the cash, and then we will decide how to spend it, she said. Whereupon I lost my temper and cried, "Always doubting! So much like your dear father!" She immediately protested, "Why talk of my father now?" "Why not?" I cried wildly, and added, "I have discussed it all with Purna, and he has spoken to the *dewan*. 1200 is not a big sum. Some foreign journalists demanded ten times that for the same proposition, but the *dewan* was keen on giving it to an Indian writer, and that is that." She would not share my optimism, and it angered me and led to arguments when I left. I promised my daughter when she followed me up to the gate, "If you are good, I will get you ..."

Now in the *dewan's* office, I respectfully stood up and said, "Yes, sir, thank you. May I know when I may expect payment?"

"Oh!" he exclaimed, suppressing his astonishment at a writer sullying his thoughts with monetary notions. "What do you expect?"

"Twelve hundred," I said. Purna had advised me to be specific while mentioning a figure.

"Very well," said the *dewan*. "As you go down, see the chief secretary and tell him. He will help you."

I walked into the chief secretary's room with assurance. He was busy over the telephone and looked through me, without either welcome or rejection. I stood at the edge of his table and, when he put down the telephone, proclaimed, "The *dewan* has sent me to see you." I explained my mission.

He motioned me to a chair and asked, "Is there any paper about your demand? Did the *dewan* give you anything in writing?"

While I was wondering how best to answer, the chief secretary lost track of my case owing to the interruptions caused by the telephone, visitors, and his factotums bringing in papers. After an hour, he looked at me again and said, "Please give a written requisition, otherwise we won't be able to proceed."

He pushed across a sheet of paper on which I wrote, *As promised by the dewan, I shall be glad to accept ... etc...*

The chief secretary studied my paper. "Did the *dewan* actually promise or promise to consider?"

I did not understand the subtle distinction, and merely said, "He promised that you would arrange the payment. Please make it urgent as I would like to go back to Mysore this evening."

"Yes, yes, of course, by all means; you may go if you like, and you will hear from us in due course."

He apparently dismissed me from his thoughts, but I stuck to my seat in the hope that he might still produce a cheque somehow. He left at lunch time without any further word. I followed him out and asked, "Should I see you again?"

"Why not?" he replied vaguely, and was off. (I never saw him again, neither that afternoon, nor next day nor ever in my lifetime; he was always away or at a meeting and could not be approached.)

After waiting all that afternoon I thought that I might see Sir Mirza again and complain of his order not being carried out, but when I reached his office, I found the door shut. I was told that the *dewan* had left for a conference at Simla, 1,000 miles away.

I sought out Purna. He merely said, "Don't worry," and sent me on to see the publicity officer next morning, explaining, "Your payment will have to come only from the publicity department."

I sat all day in front of the publicity officer. Attendants were fetching stacks of paper and dumping them on his table. He rummaged through them every time to say, "Your file has not yet come …"

"Where from?" I asked.

"From the finance section," he replied.

At six o'clock my papers arrived. By then, I was exhausted watching the traffic of people and papers across his room. The publicity officer glanced through my file and pushed it across for my edification. My recent application was on top of a pile of letters, its margin marked by a variety of inks and handwritings, and all the preceding correspondence between me and the government were below. I read with a sort of poignant interest the marginal notes on my application for payment.

Financially unacceptable, the finance department had said. Someone had queried, *Was there a contract?* It was answered by the legal section. *None, Government's commitment limited to providing facilities for writing the book, vide D.O. dated* ...A further query was, *Were quotations invited from other authors? What was the basis on which this particular author was selected for this commission?'*

I could not resist adding, on the marginal space available, my own reply to this particular question, *A bogus story arising from Mr. Somerset Maugham's visit. You may ask, if you please, who was Somerset Maugham and if his name is also in the approved list of contractors.*

We cannot console ourselves with the thought that this happened three and a half decades ago. Bureaucracy is the same, even today, the world over. If I should make the mistake of accepting a government commission to write a book today, I am sure it would go through the same process of elucidation and final liquidation through self-defeating procedures.

7
OH, MEGHAMALA

Gulabdas Broker

*B*aba was dead. Mother had died long ago. Meghamala was left alone.

Not quite alone, though. She had a young brother, much younger than her. Meghamala was extremely fond of him. But what could he do? He was very young. How old was she herself? Barely fourteen.

She was brilliant in her studies; perhaps not very beautiful to look at but elegant no doubt—very elegant. Charming and courteous. Having studied in an English medium school, she spoke English very fluently. And what a winsome smile she had; she could win anybody's heart.

But what was the use of all that now? Baba was gone. There was the house, of course. But who would maintain it? Her brother was too young! What about his education?

Big thoughts full of anxiety surged in Meghamala's young mind.

But before those thoughts could take possession of her

mind, her uncle arrived. He had come from faraway Calcutta, where he lived. He took Meghamala, and of course her younger brother, back with him.

Here Meghamala found shelter, but not peace.

Her Baba was like a flowing brook that made soft, gurgling sounds. He would laugh and make her laugh and play and make her play. He would get her anything she fancied. He had put her in the best school of the city, no matter how expensive it was. He would dance with delight at Meghamala's progress at school and would say: "Had your mother been alive!"

But he would not let Meghamala become sad by reminding her of her mother. He would burst out laughing and say: "Why do you need a mother, Meghamala? Am I not a mother to you?" And he would give an utterly sweet smile.

Meghamala would no longer miss her mother. She would forget her fourteen years and cling to her Baba.

"You...you...you are everything to me, Baba!"

There would be such a glow in Baba's eyes.

But now Baba was gone! Suddenly, like a fruit dropped off a tree!

They had still been talking about Meghamala's performance in her school function. And Baba had got up in great excitement. "I am going to give you a new surprise today, Meghamala! I have brought it in advance only for such an occasion." He laughed and almost ran to the other room in excitement. And then, he fell...

Meghamala rushed up to him. She thought his foot must have got caught in his *dhoti* and he must have stumbled.

She laughed, "Now that's enough, Baba! I know everything. Yes! Your daughter, after all!" She said.

She shook him. And then broke down into tears.

Her Baba never got up!

As her Baba's eyes closed, the glow in Meghamala's eyes also vanished.

She did not regain that glow, even at her uncle's house.

Her uncle was not a bad man. But looking at him, one would not think of a flowing brook; one would only think of a huge, immovable mountain without any greenery!

As for her aunt, she was a difficult person to live with. She would fire her for anything and everything.

Meghamala, who had nothing but love in her father's house, now had everything but love in her uncle's house: Strict discipline without any affection to compensate; a good school but not one with the atmosphere of her earlier English medium school. The teachers were good, but not tolerant enough to put up with mistakes Meghamala committed, because of her unfamiliarity with the Bengali language.

Her uncle was always ready with words of advice and the oft-repeated comment, "My brother did not bring you up well."

Her aunt, eternally grumbling, said scathingly, "This wretched girl has grown so big, but is good for nothing."

How could one live in an atmosphere so devoid of affection?

Meghamala would remember her Baba and cry. Her young mind would long for love, so characteristic of her father.

But she did not get love. What she got was advice and words of rebuke.

Meghamala would constantly look around. Could she not get even a semblance of love from somewhere? If she could, she would willingly pour the vast resources of her love bottled up inside her.

But ultimately, when she was eighteen and fully convinced that she could never have anything like love in her life, she came across someone who gave her not just a little bit of love, but spread before her the entire universe of love.

The young man was as sweet, as he was cunning! He used to hover around the school where Meghamala studied. He noticed Meghamala's large eyes, restless, as though always searching for something. He looked at the many graceful curves of her body, gifted to her by her youthfulness and realised the nature of her hunger.

He mingled his special type of hunger with Meghmala's hunger. She was not yet grown up enough to distinguish between different types of hunger. Nor did she have enough experience to make a distinction between the underlying motives of love. So she completely surrendered herself to the allurements of love Narayan spread before her.

Her uncle was suspicious and her aunt was convinced about Narayan's ulterior motives.

As such, the atmosphere in the house was unpleasant. Now it became unbearable. Narayan held before her, golden dreams. Finally, taking with her whatever gold she possessed, Meghamala eloped with Narayan in search of the gold of her dreams.

Only one thing made her sad and miserable. Her poor younger brother! What would happen to him in that atmosphere? And how would she live without him?

But she also found consolation; the moment she settled down she would send for him. Narayan had promised her that.

Things were fine in Delhi, as long as Meghamala's gold lasted. But as her stock started decreasing, Narayan's love declined in the same proportion.

By the time Meghamala reached the end of her gold, Narayan's love for her died. One morning, Narayan vanished as suddenly as he had appeared in her life, without as much as bidding her good bye.

What remained behind was only young Meghamala, and the vast city of Delhi. And an overpowering bitterness squeezing tightly the bits of Meghamala's broken heart—contempt for Narayan, her uncle and aunt, and perhaps the whole world, exception for her little brother. He was the gift of her father and resembled her mother. Now the poor child was being roasted in the hell of her uncle's unpleasant household. She told herself that once she settled down, she would pull him out of that hell.

But how could she settle down? She had come to Delhi completely closing behind her the doors of her uncle's house. But how long could she pull on in this great city with a broken heart and the little gold she had saved with great difficulty? There was no alternative other than getting a job somewhere. But who would give a job to a girl like her, with insufficient education and no experience?

Even If Delhi did not offer a job to Meghamala, it did give her certain understanding. She noticed that a large number of men, who did not give her a job, offered her a ready smile—a smile that was sweet and tempting, a smile that would guarantee both food and a roof overhead.

That aggravated the bitterness in her heart. For, by now, Meghamala had learnt to realise the implications of those smiles. She had matured into an experienced adult woman. Her failure to get a job had brought home to her the point that she should not give loud expression to her contempt for those smiles. She should only offer her own smile in response. It did not matter if that smile was unreal or if her whole existence rose in revolt as she smiled back.

What her pleading for a job could not do for her was attained by that smile, which while spreading itself around at last settled in the heart of an elderly gentleman. He promised to house Meghamala in a posh, well-furnished flat.

Meghamala listened to that proposal with a smile on her face.

Only when she was alone did she shed tears over it. And in that lonely moment, she asked forgiveness of her Baba and of her mother, who she now remembered faintly.

And thus, Meghamala became one of those young women of Delhi who supported themselves on the strength of their physical charms.

Gradually, her mind became attuned to that situation. The elderly man may not have been a man of morals, but he was certainly sensible. He saw to it that she was not left wanting for anything. He went on adding to the elegance of her flat. He put up, with great understanding, even the anger and annoyance she occasionally directed against him.

On such occasions, even Meghamala would smother him with "affection", and surrender with great ardour her body to him as this is what had made her comfortable life possible.

Perhaps her physical ardour was too much for his ageing body. One day, he too deserted her, like Narayan; however not secretly like him, but carried away on the shoulders of four persons, covered with garlands of flowers.

But Meghamala did not weep too bitterly over his death for now she had her own flat with a telephone in her own name, which the elderly gentlemen had so lovingly installed. And she had her energetic young body, which, by now, she had learnt very well to use to her own advantage. In that body now resided a woman who could not feel love, particularly for impudent and brazen men; still, that body was youthful.

Meghamala decided to utilise her body to the fullest extent. Ever since she had started earning, she had known nothing else;

Now she rarely remembered her Baba. Even when she did remember him, she tried to forget him. She had a very faint memory of her mother. She only thought of her younger brother, who she intended to call some day, to bring him over to stay with her.

She now made a resolve to hasten that time. She decided that she would not confine herself to any single person. Rather, she would find her own men, or so plan that those men would come searching for her. The plan would be facilitated by the telephone, which still remained in the flat like a secret functionary.

And so, Meghamala started building up contacts with different types of people As she smiled to herself at the stupid babble of love and pretended to be delighted by it, she went on piling her bank balance and continued to be in greater demand.

The most expensive alcoholic beverages started flowing in her flat. *Sarees* of different varieties were added to her wardrobe and her pliable body sent out innumerable invitations. She started going to clubs and was seen at stage performances and cinema shows. The number of her friends grew day by day.

Meghamala became a full-fledged "society woman!"

She no longer had to worry about her daily meals. She was not bothered about the problem of how she was going to keep up her standard of living. She had even ceased to worry about the future, when she would not have her youthful body any longer. Meghamala, who was poorly educated, had learnt to feel safe and secure so that she could make her own calculations and remain calm and happy in her situation.

When Meghamala felt completely secure about herself, her original intention to call her brother, which she had buried somewhere deep within her, stirred again.

Gradually, the more she thought about it, the more determined she became with her intention. She told herself, that she remembered her Baba and mother's love. Her brother had been too young then. He would definitely not remember anything. And he had been forced to grow up in the loveless, wretched atmosphere of their aunt and uncle's home. How would he have lived in that restricted environment? Probably he had not been able to study much and could not do anything worthwhile to earn a living.

She remembered how even as a child he had loved her a lot and trusted her. He would keep hovering around her calling, *Didi! Didi!*, Whenever he was even slightly puzzled, he would fix his large eyes on her with utter faith and confidence. Meghamala remembered how she would feel a surge of affection for him during such moments!

But perhaps, the greatest reason was that Meghamala needed somebody to love her for her own sake, and not for any extraneous reasons. For tears came to her eyes at the very thought that ever since Baba's passing away, she did not remember anyone showing her the slightest amount of genuine affection. Narayan also had ulterior motives for expressing his love. And now, love was not showered on her; it was love showered only on her golden body. And maybe love only for the gold she possessed.

After Narayan's disappearance, several men had pretended to love Meghamala. But she knew that they loved her eyes and lips, her cheeks and hair and her youthful body. But they had no love for Meghamala as a person.

Meghamala also longed to love someone truly. Rather than a man's wealth and his cheque-book, his flat and telephone and his relationship with her, she was eager to love a man for his own sake—love him without restraint and restriction.

But, she had no such man in her life. She had only one feeling for every man who came to her—contempt. At times, her contempt mingled with compassion, at times with generosity, but basically, her feeling was of utter contempt.

Perhaps her brother, who she knew was now called Nirmal, was the only person who would be able to love her for what she was. He was probably the only man who would be able to give her affection, without any selfish motive,

She decided to call Nirmal to Delhi.

It did not take long to implement that decision. A few letters were exchanged, and after some initial reluctance, Nirmal decided to join his sister. She had assured him that she was completely on her own. She earned sufficiently well in Delhi to look after her dear ones.

In preparation for Nirmal's arrival, Meghamala brought about some major changes in her life; as a first step, she changed her residence. She took an equally posh-looking flat in an area where good people lived, so that there could be no grounds for any objection. Moreover, she also changed her manner of functioning. She no longer invited her 'friends' to her flat. Instead, she went wherever they called her. She did organise parties at her place. But on such occasions, she invited respectable men and women from her neighbourhood, apart from her own colleagues. She began to dress up so well that it would become difficult for any stranger to mark her out as different from the innumerable high society women of Delhi.

At last Nirmal arrived. It became a day for great celebration. He was no longer a little boy. He had grown into a young man. Meghamala embraced him and cried a lot. Nirmal was wonderstruck to see his sister's prosperity.

Tears welled up in his eyes as he talked about his times with their uncle and the difficult period when he was growing up. Both of them spoke about whatever little they each remembered of the old days. Essentially, these were Meghamala's memories. Nevertheless, Meghamala's description of Nirmal as a *Khoka* delighted both of them. Meghamala assured him that he would never have to face any hardship, as she was well settled.

Nirmal was curious to know what she had done that had enabled her to live in such comfort. Meghamala evaded the question by referring to her knack of getting things done by her influence with various institutions and government offices. And, for the first time in so many years, they were able to eat and rest peacefully without a care in the world.

But the happiness did not continue for long. Nirmal could not understand why his *Didi* received telephone calls at odd hours of day or night after which she went off saying, "I've got some work."

She had no office to attend to and no fixed hours of work, yet she never seemed to have any leisure. She became alert the moment the telephone rang and her demeanour changed and she would become "all sweetness" on the phone.

He noticed that whenever she went out, she did not wear ordinary working clothes; instead, even if it was in the afternoon, she would dress herself as though going to a party. Nirmal wondered.

He often expressed his curiosity. But Meghamala evaded his question by telling with a smile, "Oh, Nirmal, you have moved among small town people. How would you understand big people and the ways of this capital city?"

At times she would get annoyed and ask, "Why do you have to know all that?"

There were occasions when Meghamala had reasons to feel annoyed. However much she tried, Nirmal could not find any gainful employment. Even if he was called by somebody for a job, he was without a job again in just a couple of days.

That was because he was adept at nothing. He had not studied much. And he was not used to doing just any odd thing. At such times Meghamala would say, "Do you know, my dear, what all I have done so that you could get such a job?"

"But *Didi*, how can I help if I can't do it?" Nirmal would reply, fixing his big eyes on Meghamala with a sorry expression on his face.

With that there would be a surge of tenderness in Meghamala's heart. Poor *Khoka*! How can he do these jobs when uncle had not given him much education? And why should he do such jobs, in any case? Is she not there to earn money?

But Meghamala had another reason to worry; Nirmal was developing a taste for all the expensive liquor easily available at home.

Meghamala did not throw too many parties, but whenever she did, liquor was inevitably served. She served expensive brands, as was customary in such circles in Delhi. When all the guests were offered drinks, how could Nirmal be left out?

In the beginning, he used to protest. He did not even like alcohol. He would ask Meghamala, "Why do you serve such things in our house, *Didi*?"

"Everything must be served, my dear, if you want to live in comfort."

He often wondered what she meant by "serving everything".

In course of time, that too became evident.

In the meanwhile, the telephone calls came even when Meghamala was away. Nirmal began to notice the attitude of the neighbours towards him. They never failed to be courteous. But they preferred to avoid him as far as possible. And even with regard to Meghamala, except in response to the invitation to her parties, none of them ever dropped in to meet her.

Nirmal was not so young that would not be able to read some meaning in all this. The exchange of looks and the barely perceptible smile on the faces of their neighbours were things that Nirmal noticed and they conveyed a lot to him.

He finally understood why things were always plentiful in the house even though he was not earning anything and his *Didi* also was not doing any job.

But that realisation did not make him happy. He started drinking a lot; he would resent it earlier, but now he had developed a fondness for it.

The more he drank, the greater was Meghamala's worry about him.

One day when she found that Nirmal had had a drink too many, her anger rose into a flame. She shrieked, "What is this, Nirmal? Do you want to become an alcoholic?"

Nirmal stared at Meghamala. He remembered the faint smile of the neighbour. He resented the memory of that smile. At his moment, he also resented Meghamala.

He blurted out whatever came to his mind, "Even if I become an alcoholic, the responsibility won't be mine."

"What do you mean?" Meghamala's temper rose.

"I had never seen liquor before," Nirmal said calmly.

"You are taunting me, is it? And you are answering back to me, you slothful, indolent fellow!"

"Precisely because I do not want to talk back...I.... I..." Nirmal stammered.

"You will go on gulping glass after glass, is that so?" Meghamala's voice was clearly contemptuous.

Nirmal echoed her tone, "Yes, I shall go on gulping drink after drink, *Didi*, I shall. That is the only way I can live in this house."

"The great man refuses to do any work and wants to boss over!"

"You are there to do the work. Then ..." Nirmal blurted out.

"Are you not ashamed to say whatever enters your head?" Meghamala's anger had crossed all limits. She gave a thundering slap on Nirmal's face.

Nirmal said nothing. He merely stared at her.

When Meghamala looked at his eyes, she noticed that those eyes did not overflow with faith and trust, like they used to in the younger days. Instead, there was only dark contempt, just contempt.

Meghamala was startled. Was all that she had built going to crumble down?

She mellowed.

"*Khoka!*" She could finally say with great difficulty.

"My name is Nirmal Kumar," he said and went inside without another word.

Meghamala remained seated; stunned and stupefied.

After a while, the telephone rang. Meghamala's voice once again acquired the sweetness of honey.

"Yes, I shall certainly reach there. On the dot of seven, isn't it? No, no, nothing is the matter. Only a little cold. But you...yes, yes, definitely. At seven. It would be exciting," she said over the phone.

As she put down the receiver, she found Nirmal standing at the door. He had obviously been listening.

Meghamala gave a shadowed smile. "I'm going out in the evening, Nirmal. I may be coming late."

Nirmal made no comment.

Meghamala continued, "And forget the whole thing, my dear." There was tenderness in her voice.

"I'm also very sorry, very sorry," Nirmal said in a hoarse voice.

Meghamala returned late at night. She opened the front door, using her keys and turned on the light.

On a table, in the drawing room, there was an empty glass and a bottle of rum, half empty.

She noticed that the glass was serving as a paperweight. She picked up the sheet. She panicked even before she could read the content. It read:

Didi, don't you see? I would be just like this if I stay here. I am leaving. Forget me.

Meghamala slumped on the ground. She allowed her surging tears to flow freely. "Affection and love! Can I ever hope to have them? And can I ever give affection and love to anyone?" she asked herself. "You're a fool, a fool!" she muttered and in the midst of her flowing tears, smiled bitterly.

She might have been able to bear her tears, but she could not bear her smile. She held her head with both hands and cried out loud, "Meghamala! Oh, Meghamala!"

And gulped the liquor straight from the bottle.

Translated from the Gujarati by
Sarala Jag Mohan

8

THE STICK THAT BROKE

Aabid Surti

$\mathcal{S}$he came out of the room with the help of a walking stick. The snow-capped mountain peaks in the east had just about started to fade into the darkness.

Every now and then, the tired Nepali coolies at the bus terminus tried penetrating into the stretched out fading light. But nothing except the snow-covered road, house-tops, and towering trees were visible. There was no sign yet of the awaited bus from Almorah. So there was nothing better for them to do except puff at the *bidis* and pretend not to feel the cold.

Sabana *Bi* slowly walked onto the concrete road, and went past the bus terminus.

She had an old bond with these streets. The numerous marks on them still bore their faint imprint on her vision despite the 80 years gone by; which road went to Bhawali and Mukteshwar, and from which side she had entered the town as a coy bride. It was as easy for her to tell, as a young woman pointing out the moon to her beloved!

Marking her steps on the snow, she turned towards the dusty road. She thought that she could count the 200-odd steps that would lead her to her husband's grave. But the trembling, the palpitation in the chest, made it virtually impossible. She resorted to prayers. Each new step seemed like a long walk. In that dark night, her voice seemed like a companion; like Sharafat Ali.

She recalled the day she had first visited the graveyard following her husband's death; the sea of tears that had burst out of her eyes, the endless hours when she sat quietly on the wet grass with a flushed face. There had been no one around to share her grief; no one except old Sharafat Ali, who sat solemnly, at a little distance, by the grave of his wife. His body seemed to have outlived its term; the wrinkled face, the rough and dry skin that resembled a worn-out paper, the body bent with the onslaught of the weathered storms.

"Sister," Sharafat Ali said with a sympathetic look, "Man has failed to resolve the two greatest mysteries—birth and death. Both are divine miracles. He brings you into this world, and when the time comes, when you have played your innings, he calls you back into the pavilion."

Sabana *Bi* stared at the old man and noticed the tears. She could anticipate how he must have loved his wife. He wiped the tears away and recited some couplets from the Holy Quran. She could not understand until he translated them, explaining the philosophy in simple words; Sharafat Ali had been talking about the purity of spirit, the meaning of life and a human being's duties in the world.

She couldn't sleep a wink that night. She got up to place a lighted *chulah* in the middle of the room to keep her body warm and was then comfortable. The light of the burning coal shone in her eyes. Then she suddenly started feeling restless. Sharafat Ali's words started echoing in her ears and this went on till late into the night.

At dawn, Mamdu brought in a cup of tea. Sabana *Bi* got up with an effort. Then remembering the moments at the graveyard, she smiled to herself. Mamdu noticed the shine in her eyes and said, "Amma I've brought some tea."

Taking the cup from him, and putting it down on the floor, Sabana *Bi* said, "Tea is fine, son. But bring me some work too."

It took Mamdu some time to comprehend. There was a look of surprise on his face, as he stared at her.

"Son, get me a sewing machine. Jumman needs stitched cotton bags for his shop. It will not only help me while away my time, but also be productive for the house."

"Isn't my salary of ₹200 enough that you want to torture yourself at this age?"

Sabana *Bi* intercepted and retorted angrily, "Who ever said I am old?"

Her gaze was fixed, her body started to tremble. Then regaining composure, she continued, "I still have enough strength and I will do some work, whatever be its nature."

Mamdu continued to stare at her silently. The change in Sabana's attitude was beyond his comprehension.

The following week there was a sewing machine in Sabana *Bi*'s room. She spread a mattress on the floor and set to work. Her long hands began to move briskly at the small wheel, her nimble fingers started to play at the lifting and falling needle. The noise of the machine overpowered the still atmosphere of the room.

Mamdu tried his best to dissuade her, but she stuck to her resolve.

Whenever Mamdu pointed to her age, she would first get angry at her son, and then would smilingly say: "I haven't aged yet son, look at my hands, they work faster than anyone else's."

She would start working early and, by dusk, a big bundle of bags would reach Jumman's shop.

"You work very hard, sister," Jumman would say, teasingly, while counting the bags. And she would smilingly note down the order, then slowly walk towards her husband's grave.

She would, invariably, run into Sharafat Ali on the way. Gradually, the two would reach the graveyard, read prayers in memory of their loved ones and then stretch out on the green grass to ease their tired limbs. Then Sharafat Ali would offer her some cardamom.

The gesture would briefly send her down her memory lane…returning, she would pick up a piece and start chewing it.

"How does it taste?"

Sabana *Bi* would nod approvingly a couple of times, enjoying the taste, then pull out a little packet that she had concealed in her clothes, offer it to Sharafat Ali and say, "Okay, you taste this."

He would draw the packet close to his eyes, and sniffing at it, would enquire: "Is it…?"

"You often said your wife made it for you in this weather. So I made it for you today," she would reply.

Sharafat Ali would break the delicacy into pieces, and lingeringly savour the sweetness. In moments such as those, Sabana *Bi* would gaze at him fixedly. The sight of him savouring the delicacy made her feel as delighted as a child.

Now, she stopped at the first lamp-post and heaved a deep sigh. She was out of breath and this was apparent from her weather-beaten face. She pulled the stick out of the snow and started to move ahead, leaving slender marks behind on the snow, crushing the flakes under her feet. After reaching the dust road, she started going down.

This was her routine every Friday. There had been no change in it over the past 15 years, except on the days the rains washed the familiar paths or heavy snowflakes lowered the branches of the trees. But the moment the weather was favourable, she would embark on her mission again.

As she walked on, she remembered the day Sharafat Ali had asked: "Where is your stick today?"

"Can't find it. I have forgotten where I left it. But whatever happened to your stick? Have you also lost it?"

"No. It broke. It was an old one, wasn't it," Sharafat Ali spoke, making his face a lot more solemn than was necessary.

Sabana *Bi* smiled at the answer. Seeing the smile on her face, Sharafat Ali's face also brightened.

By the time she arrived at the second lamp-post, she felt a restlessness she hadn't experienced before. With one hand she pressed at the stick and bent low, holding the post with the other. Her breathing had quickened. With a blurring vision, she looked in the direction of the graveyard, her face turning ashen.

Only one more lamp-post separated her from the graveyard. Her feet began to move. She had the feeling that her husband's grave had moved further—miles away.

In Sharafat Ali's company, the same distance was easily covered. But now he wasn't alive to give her company. He had suddenly abandoned the world; had suddenly disappeared like a broken star.

Covering the distance, she finally entered the graveyard.

Today, two graves stretched out in front of her; one in which her husband lay in peace, the other, newly laid, accommodated the mortal remains of Sharafat Ali. Both were now covered by a thick layer of snow. She stared at them quietly.

There was no one to console her today. All the strength seemed to have left her body. Her limbs were tired and they hurt. She felt weak and was on the verge of collapsing. But, she suddenly got up and with renewed will, began walking towards home.

An anxious Mamdu was waiting for her in the room. The moment he saw his mother enter, he enquired, "Amma, did you meet Jumman Uncle today?"

She did not answer. Instead, she went and sat beside the *chulah*.

Mamdu lay down close to her, and muttered, "All the work is lying undone for the past four days. Jumman uncle said…"

Without lifting her head, Sabana *Bi* said, "I can do no more work, son. I have aged!"

Translated from the Gujarati by
the author and Suresh Kohli

9

LAST SUMMER

Nirmal Verma

He climbed down two steps and hesitated on the final step; touching the water with his big toe. A lukewarm tingle spread through his bare body. He felt the desire to let himself go, but he held back. His gaze settled on the pool, which lay silent and unmoving in the bright, white sunshine; somewhat lazy as well, in the way that still water sometimes becomes in the summer.

He couldn't restrain himself much longer. Only an instant later his body disappeared into the white-blue water.

In those last days of summer he often came here. He stayed below all afternoon in the blue and cold darkness of the water. For some time he forgot his city, even his home. Inside the water he felt as though he was sleeping.

When he came out, Mahip was beckoning to him, waving his hand in the air. He lay on the grass near the pool. Behind him, the sunshine on the white clubhouse was fading.

"That's enough...come, let's go in," Mahip said.

"You won't swim?"

"Not today. Hurry up, I've been holding back my thirst because of you."

He wanted to lie in the water for some more time; he wanted to lie in the water all night. The electric globes all around the pool had lit up. On the other side, a small girl stood on the diving board. Maybe she is afraid of jumping, he thought. He scrubbed his body with a towel.

"Don't you get bored?"

"Of what?"

"I can't stay more than five minutes in the water."

He took off his wet trunks.

Mahip's face became red and he turned to look the other way. "You're completely primitive!" he said, somewhat angrily

He laughed. He felt a strong desire to go into the pool again—this time without his trunks. What a difference it makes if your body is completely naked in the water.

After a while, they walked into the club lounge. Nothing like beer after a long swim, he thought; if it was cold and there was nothing to do. For the past few days, he had had nothing to do. Coming from Vienna he could not bring anything at all with him. He had been very uncertain about what to take home. He had returned after three years and this was his first long holiday in all that time.

"Any letters from Keshi?" Mahip asked.

"No," he said. "He may not be able to come."

"You'll see him before you leave, won't you?"

"Nothing's decided yet. I might not have that much time," he said.

He watched Mahip. He was drinking his beer silently. He knew many of Keshi's friends, but after coming back he had been able to meet only Mahip. He had had very few friends of his own, and even the ones he did have, had grown so close to Keshi over these years that on the infrequent occasions when he met them, it seemed to him as though he were meeting not his own friends but Keshi's. As they drank their beer and all other talk came to an end, they would settle down with Keshi.

"Have you booked your seat?" Mahip asked, somewhat indifferently. He had probably asked this question 300 times…each time his indifference increased a little.

"Not yet." He poured the rest of the beer from the bottle into his glass. "There's plenty of time," he said. He had stopped counting a while ago. At first he used to think—this day, this night. They shone like smooth pebbles, sharp and clear under water. They must still be there, but now he didn't count them. They were not for him now.

"I'll have another beer. You?" Mahip asked.

"You get one, I'll take a bit of that."

"I've heard they have 'beer gardens' in Vienna. Have you been to one?"

"I haven't… but they're open this time of year. These days there is also an orchestra outdoors…" he said. He knew that Mahip had no interest in this. If Keshi had been here, they would have been able to talk with each other. And he would listen quietly to the two of them. That was how it was before. But these days Keshi was not here, and Mahip felt it was his responsibility to talk to him. He had tried several times to tell Mahip that he wouldn't feel bad if they stayed quiet. But this was impossible.

"Don't you get bored at home?" Mahip asked. The beer had finished and darkness had fallen in the lounge.

"No," he said. "I like it."

"You must feel strange here...after so many years!"

"Not very." He lit a cigarette. His voice sounded a little strange to him. He felt a slight pleasure that in the dark Mahip could not see his face.

"You haven't thought about staying here? You could find a job very easily."

"I haven't thought about it," he said. He had thought about it sometimes in the beginning, when he came; he had been very enthusiastic then. Now, sometimes he felt like laughing at that enthusiasm he had.

When they went outside after a while, he felt his wet hair drying slowly in the breeze. He had always liked the days of August in Delhi. They did not weigh upon you, and during these days you could think about other days; those that had passed or were to come. August is the only month of the whole year that is like a bridge: you can pass over it, but in itself it is nothing at all.

They emerged from Willingdon Crescent onto Kushak Road. A gust of hot air blew, and the dust flew off the street onto the footpath, flew off the footpath and, filtering through the *jamun* trees, settled on the brown bushes outside the bungalows. A long time ago, they used to live in this part of the city. Babu had not retired then. And Keshi had not gone into the Army. Those days they slept out on the lawn and at night the badminton net would flutter a long time in the breeze. Those nights Neeta (his sister) would always keep crying and they would not know whether she had had a bad dream or was scared by the fluttering of the net in the breeze. He thought of telling Mahip this. But then something occurred to him and he stayed quiet. Mahip would think he was saying all this because he'd drunk too much beer. At moments like these Keshi always stayed quiet. He would say that if you started thinking about the past after a few drinks, you didn't have any deeper feeling.

I don't have that, he thought. Maybe I had it when I was a child. One night he had said to Keshi, "Look, I'm dying." He was very young then. Keshi was impressed by this. Later he had said to him, "If you'd really died that day, nothing much would have happened. I would only have been sad. But you only said it and didn't die—that's deep feeling. That's really very deep feeling."

They reached the Secretariat building and stopped in front of it. Several buses stood there. But there was a lot of time. They stood in silence. Mahip took a deep breath.

"Have you met Aruna?" he asked.

"Not yet. I'll go there one day."

"Why did you need to come this far if all you're going to do is sit at home?"

"There's lots of time still," he said. He felt Mahip was looking at him. He felt a slight uncertainty and looked the other way, where the old barracks were. That summer he had had the suspicion several times that after being with him for a while people would still look at him, astonished. They said nothing at all. Maybe it was only an illusion, and in fact nothing at all. Maybe he was feeling this way after drinking, and afterwards he wouldn't think of it at all.

Mahip's bus had arrived, and he climbed in and sat down. "Will you come tomorrow?" he asked.

"Yes. I'll be near the pool," he replied.

He wanted to say something else to Mahip, but the bus moved off and he stood there alone.

On those summer nights he often reached home late. His father never felt bad about this; he knew that he had nothing to do those days. He was only concerned that he might be bored at home. He wanted to reassure him that he was very happy. Now whenever he thinks about those days, he feels he was truly happy then. But he could not say this. To say that you are happy—that is laughable. Even if you do say it no one will believe you.

Those summer days he had nothing at all to do. His younger brother Keshi had gone into the Army, and when he grew bored alone in his room he would go to the swimming pool. He felt better there than at home. He felt good at home too, but Ma and Babu were there and they were very alone and he could do nothing for them.

After they had gone to sleep at night he would drink cognac. Sometimes Ma would see him, and she wouldn't say anything at all. Her saying nothing bothered him and he felt the desire to go for a swim again, but you couldn't go into the pool at night.

That night, climbing up the stairs, he stopped suddenly, startled to hear Ma's voice in Babu's room. She rarely went to Babu's room.

"I don't know where he stays all day. Has he ever told you anything?" It was Babu's voice.

"You always worry uselessly," Ma said. "He's come back after three years. You think he'll stay the same as before?"

"No...no, where did I say that?" Babu's voice had become strangely abashed.

He didn't listen any longer and began to climb the stairs silently.

Reaching the terrace, he would find a strange calm. There he had gathered many cans of paint, whitewash and several brushes. He would lean the wooden ladder against the wall and tie a can of paint to the ladder with a rope. When the moonlight shone brighter, everything could be seen; even at night. He kept plying the brush in the plaster-covered corners of the wall for a long time. He would forget that Ma was waiting downstairs with his dinner. He remained stuck to the wall like a bat. On those moonlit nights his hazy shadow would fall on the wall like a misshapen animal.

During those warm August nights he had plastered and painted the terrace and walls systematically and cleanly. Sometimes he felt strange standing high on the ladder. All around was air and endless openness. Then he would feel that to be able to cover oneself with something, to be able to surround oneself, brought so much consolation. Only someone who has ever climbed up against a naked wall on an open roof could know this. Then he would feel about the same as he did during the day in the blue dark of the swimming pool; very calm, very empty.

When he came down after a while, he found Ma standing there in the dark. Seeing him, she became slightly self-conscious.

"How long have you been waiting here?" he asked.

"Oh, it's nothing. You weren't in your room, so I came here. I was just looking at you."

Ma was a very small woman. She had kept on shrinking with age.

"Won't you eat your food? It's been lying there a long time!" she said.

Disconcerted, he busied himself with putting away the brush, wet with lime, and the can in a corner. Laying the ladder down he said, "You go ahead, I'm coming."

His mother's behaviour had seemed a little strange to him since he had come. In the beginning, she would talk to him.

But now that his departure was drawing near, she had begun to stay quiet. Now too, she spoke in an apprehensive manner, and she repeated the same things. When he had left, three years ago, she had said nothing. Now he was leaving again, and she hadn't raised the subject at all.

When she came to his room, it was with careful steps. Once his eyes had opened in the middle of the night and he had the slight impression that someone was standing there in the dark, near the head of the bed. He did not even have the courage to turn over. Afterwards, recognising Ma, he felt quite angry, but the next day he couldn't say anything to her.

They had dinner together; Ma would sit on the mat, Babu on the divan next to the radio. Next to the table, two chairs would stand empty—one Neeta's, the other Keshi's. Neeta stayed at her in-laws'; Keshi was in the Army. Whenever he saw these chairs, the whole house seemed empty.

Babu stayed in the room a long time on the pretext of listening to the radio. This would irritate Ma. Also, she didn't understand Babu's questions very well. She would look sometimes at her son, sometimes at Babu, wondering.

They could never understand how they might converse again after this interval of three years.

"You do not get all this to eat there?" Babu would glance at Ma, smile.

Instead of responding, he just wanted to finish his meal quickly and go upstairs; but he sat there.

Hearing this talk of food, Ma said, "Yes, Neeta said you can't get anything other than meat and fish over there...really?"

Before he could answer her, Babu said, "And yes, it must get very cold there?"

"Yes, but the houses have central heating. You don't feel the cold inside," he said slowly.

"I had written asking you to buy an overcoat."

Ma got up and went to her room. A laden silence fell in the house. He waited. It seemed to him that Babu would say something to him. Outside, the heat of August and the bright night gathered around. Babu said nothing and stared at him unblinking. His shirt became wet with sweat at his armpits. He kept praying in his mind that Babu would say something that would break this strange tension that had drawn tight over the years. But at the last moment Babu suddenly changed his mind.

Going near the door, he stopped, said, "Can't you prolong your holidays?"

He looked at him with a questioning gaze. When Babu didn't understand, he asked, "Is there some work to be done?"

"No, what work would there be!" That same abashed smile came to Babu's face. "I was thinking, this time you could have Diwali here. Keshi too will be here then."

He stayed quiet. He knew that was impossible. But he didn't say anything.

He went up to the room on the rooftop. At this time the entire house was quiet. The light in the verandah had been turned off. Only the light in Ma's room stayed on for a long time. She didn't sleep much at all. She would go to her room after dinner and sit there alone.

He felt a slight happiness. Now no one would come. He sat down on his bed. In one corner of the room lay a bundle on which the dust and grime of the past years had slowly accumulated. Before going to Vienna he had packed all his school and college books in this bundle. On the wall hung a Juan Gris print, which he had sent to Keshi from Leipzig. Keshi had always been interested in many things: old paintings, records, first editions. Buying things for him in Vienna was always troublesome. He himself had never been interested in these things. During these holidays too, when he had nothing at all to do, he wasn't able to read even one of those books.

That night when Ma came to give him his glass of milk, she stood for a while in his room.

He sat down on the bed. He felt that Ma wanted to say something but was shrinking from saying it.

"Sit here for a while, Ma!" he said.

"No, I have work to do," she said. "Did you meet Aruna?"

"No, not yet," he said. Then he felt a slight regret at his lie.

"Go see her one of these days. When you weren't here, she often asked about you."

"I'll go there one of these days," he said. "Ma, how long will you stand there?"

"I'm all right. I'm just going," Ma said. But still she stood there. Perhaps she had understood he was lying. She always understood.

"I think if you go and spend a few days with Keshi, you might like it there."

"I like it here too... and then there are not too many days left now!" he said.

"Yes, not too many days left now," Ma said.

He started at her tone. He looked at her, but there was nothing in her expression that he could catch.

Ma went over to the door and stopped at the threshold.

"Neeta will come next Sunday, will you be at home?"

"If Neeta comes I'll stay home," he said.

Ma left, and he came and stood near the window. His eyes began searching for something in the empty compound beyond the house, beyond the bushes, above the shadows of the lane, where the hot night of August lay spread. You are still afraid, but for what? You'll leave after a few days and no one will know anything at all.

No one will know that some girl lives with you in Vienna, about whom neither Ma nor Aruna know. You should have told them right away, he chided himself. If you had told them right away, then maybe nothing at all would have happened.

But it wouldn't make any difference...he'd leave after a few days and no one would know anything at all. And when they did find out, it wouldn't make any difference even then.

In the end...right at the end, it never makes any difference—if your parents are very old, he thought.

He felt a slight happiness that Keshi was not at home. Seeing him after three years, he would certainly have suspected something. Perhaps he would have asked nothing at all, but something like a wall would have come up.

A breeze arose outside the window. He turned back and lay down on the bed and turned out the light. For a long time that night he kept thinking about his childhood. Those days people would jokingly call Keshi the Chinese Mandarin. He was always very quiet. Neeta and he always made fun of him behind his back. But in front of him they became somewhat apprehensive. He recalled a very old event and laughed out loud in the dark.

They were very young then. In those days they lived at a hill station. It was the summer holidays. One day Keshi, Neeta, and he had gone into a garden behind the cottage. It was an old, neglected garden, and no one came there. They had the fantastic idea that many precious objects often lay hidden in such deserted places. They began to dig. They kept digging for a long time. Neeta grew bored. At last the hoe clashed against some hard object. It was a large rock. The three of them lifted it together. With pounding hearts they looked into the hole below and kept staring, motionless.

In the hole lay the branch of a tree, a long bone, and a broken piece of glass.

They touched each object in turn—the branch, the bone, the piece of glass. Then suddenly Neeta, crying, ran away towards the house. They left the things right there and returned quietly.

That night before he slept Keshi asked, without turning his head towards him, while looking at the ceiling, "Do you know why Neeta began to cry?"

"Maybe she was scared."

"No, it's we who were scared. She's very sensitive."

"So?" He looked at Keshi. He was still looking at the ceiling.

"When you were touching them, didn't it seem to you as though they were resisting?" He was silent for a while, then said in a very low voice, "It's a big thing to be able to resist." Keshi took a deep breath and, turning on his side, fell asleep.

Keshi had been exactly like that, since his childhood.

He couldn't sleep for a long time. He began thinking about his apartment in Vienna where he had spent the past three years. From there the canal that ran from the Danube could be seen. The leaves must have begun to fall over there, he thought. Then he heard the sound of Babu coughing. When he poured water from the pot the sound came all the way upstairs. Ma must have put the chain on the staircase door, he thought, hearing light footsteps on the stairs. The entire house became silent again.

Only the shadow of the curtain would sway on the Juan Gris still life when the breeze blew.

One evening when he came back from the swimming pool, Neeta was waiting for him. He kissed Bulu. Her eyelashes were very long and when he kissed her they tickled his cheek.

"I've collected lots of things for you." He smelt her hair. He recalled a strange smell from long ago, which used to come from Neeta's hair.

"What things?" Bulu looked at him.

"They're in the cupboard."

"Mama, you said you'd teach me the Charleston." Bulu looked at him, questioningly.

"When you learn it you'll dance only with me; not with any other friend of yours," he said.

"Even when I grow up?" A slight disappointment lay in Bulu's voice.

"Only when you grow up! Right now you're nothing."

When she grew up, Bulu would look like some 19th century Russian princess, he thought; exactly as beautiful, exactly as decadent.

They went upstairs. When Neeta visited, everyone would sit in Keshi's room. They all drank tea together. A special cup of chocolate was prepared for Bulu. Neeta dragged Babu's easy-chair from his room. He lay on it with his eyes closed. In front of Babu he and Neeta felt a strange constraint, even today. This constraint disappeared when Keshi was around. But in his absence, a silence lay between them. He himself could never begin a conversation the right way.

"You didn't come. Your *Jija-ji* really wanted to meet you." Neeta looked at him. "What do you do all day?"

He laughed. "Sometimes I go swimming...at Mahip's club," he said.

Neeta looked at him with some slight curiosity.

"I learnt it there," he said quickly. "Neeta, you should learn too. Lots of girls go swimming there."

"At this age? You're crazy!" Laughing, she looked at Babu. He still lay with his eyes shut.

"Your age is nothing," he said. When Neeta laughed that way, he really could not believe she was Bulu's mother. The two of them looked like sisters.

In that house there was only Neeta who the years in between had left untouched. Or maybe the word untouched wasn't right, they had touched her, the way we touch a book. The cover outside becomes old, but everything inside stays just the way it was before.

Slowly the evening light began to pale. The three of them sat in silence around the tea table. Bulu had gone out onto the terrace.

"You should have gone somewhere in the summer," Neeta said, looking at Babu. "Sitting here alone you must get very bored?"

"Yes, Keshi wrote, in fact," Babu said, leaning forward a little. "But we no longer feel up to travelling back and forth." He laughed as though he was embarrassed.

"I can write to Keshi if you'd like me to. He can come and take you there," Neeta said.

Babu looked ahead with a vacant gaze, then said slowly, "I would have gone, but then your mother will be alone. When he leaves, the house is going to be empty anyway. We'll go somewhere afterwards."

Neeta's eyes lifted to him. He looked out of the window. He felt the urge to take a cigarette out of his pocket but then his hand hesitated and stayed in his pocket. Even now he felt a strange reluctance to smoke in front of Babu. He doesn't say anything, but still the desire dies on its own.

The yellowness of the evening spread in the room. The glow of the final sunshine had gathered on the teacups. Sometimes a bird would fly off the ventilator and circle around the room, and its shadow would wander across the heads of the three of them and then dissolve into the air.

That summer was the first time he had felt that Babu was so alone.

Bulu came down from the terrace and into the room. The atmosphere in the room suddenly eased.

"Mama, where are my things?" She came and stood in front of him.

"What things?" Neeta asked.

He rose and walked over to the almirah. From a low drawer he took out a long leather bag, which he had bought in Vienna just before he came.

But where did Bulu have the patience to wait! With a swoop of her hand she snatched the bag and, setting it on the table, opened it. The very next moment, a multitude of coins, small and large, lay scattered on the table.

For a moment Bulu could not believe it.

"All these are mine?" Her voice did not hold a question so much as the astonished belief that all these could be hers.

He pulled his chair up to the table. Slowly he began to explain to her—an Austrian Shilling, one Crown from the Faroe Islands, Italian Lire—each of the countries he had gone to, its coins had stayed with him. Showing her a German Mark, his hand suddenly hesitated—all at once he recalled the night he had spent on the streets of Berlin. But, touching the other coins, he did not recall anything in particular. It felt as though he too were seeing them for the first time along with Bulu.

"You went to the Faroe Islands too?" Neeta asked with some slight surprise. "You never mentioned it in any letter."

"We stayed there just one night," he said.

"Are they as small as they seem on a map?" Bulu asked, curious.

He pressed Bulu's palm against his cheek. "They're smaller than your palms," he said.

"Mama, shall we start?" She clung to him.

He looked at Neeta. She sat in one corner against the wall. Babu had gone to his room a long time ago. The August haziness had settled on everything like earth-coloured sand—warm and gritty.

He pushed the table away from the centre. Bulu quickly gathered up the coins. Her brown hair had come loose and fallen on her shoulder.

Even today he remembered that August evening. For some moments he had forgotten that he was in his own home in Delhi.

It didn't take long to teach Bulu the Charleston. After much back-and-forth on the radio dial he found a station from which a little music emerged in staccato fashion. It bore not even a distant relationship to the Charleston; the tune sounded as though someone had fashioned it at the time of the First World War. But even that much was enough for them.

Even that much was enough, because after a while they forgot the radio. When Bulu spun and looked his way, he felt somewhat alone. Then they drew close. Bulu came into his arms. A small, flying smile touched her lips, and they parted. This smile was not for him. This smile of girls her age, dancing the Charleston for the first time, was not for anyone—this he had found out long ago, in Vienna.

"Mama, faster!" Bulu whispered softly into his ear. Her face had become pale; she seemed excited. As she danced, her eyes became very bright; this he had noticed before as well. Every time he became a little nervous. To bear any girl's eyes, when they were right in front of your face and as bright as Bulu's often became, had always been a torment for him.

"Okay, now stop it... that's enough." Neeta's voice was heard from a dark corner of the room. They had completely forgotten her.

"Mama...not yet," Bulu said.

He wiped the sweat from his forehead. It seemed to him that in the past months he had completely lost the habit of dancing.

"Not now, Bulu, some other day," he said.

"Then when?" Suddenly Bulu's eyes brimmed. "You'll leave and I'll forget everything." Then she felt slightly ashamed at her own tears. Laughing, she said, "First of all you taught me the waltz, remember?"

He looked in her eyes and his own voice seemed strange to him, "Bulu, let us have a waltz."

Bulu glanced towards Neeta and smiled. Bulu had a thing for the waltz that he had never understood—not Keshi's deep feeling but rather a particular kind of attachment that always made him somewhat apprehensive when he saw it. But this evening they were very happy. Neeta too slid forward on the divan and watched them with a smile. Once they tried to pull her up to join them, but she laughingly extricated herself. A pale darkness had fallen across the room. Their steps were so slow that sometimes he felt that they were standing in one place. The rumbling of the tune on the radio could still be heard; the same tune that someone had fashioned at the time of the First World War. Its notes were concentrated, like the flame of a burning matchstick, within a handful of space; when it rose up even slightly, it seemed as though cupping hands had been removed from the matchstick and it was fluttering, naked, in the dark room. In that haze, Bulu seemed quite grown-up. She leaned her head on his shoulder. But from her breathing it was clear that she was still very young. That familiar smell came from her hair; that smell of summer holidays and hill stations long ago, which used to come from Neeta's or Ma's hair when he was a child.

They stopped. The tune from the radio had suddenly gone out. Neeta stood up and turned on the light.

"You look like an expert," Neeta said, laughing.

He was almost out of breath. He lit a cigarette and sat down in the easy chair where Babu had just sat for a while.

"Mama, over there you must go dancing every evening?" Bulu looked enviously at him. She had gathered her hair behind her.

A fevered light had gathered in her large eyes.

The lamp-post outside the window had come on. Beyond it was the Delhi sky sad and empty looking in the fading August light.

Bulu, tired, now lay on the divan. Ma called Neeta into the kitchen for some work. He sat alone in the room for some time, waiting for Neeta. Bulu's eyes had begun to close with the weight of sleep, but even now her cheeks were burning. He took off Bulu's shoes gently and put them in a corner.

"Mama!" Bulu opened her eyes.

"What's the matter, Bulu?"

"Are you going?"

"I'm not going anywhere."

Bulu shut her eyes again and turned on her side to face the wall. He put out the large light in the room keeping only the table lamp lit. For some time he kept watching Bulu. He felt as though she were some Turgenev heroine. Then with slow, careful steps he left the room.

There was no one upstairs; there was only the pale moolight which on those humid, hot August nights lay on every rooftop like a torn, dirty rag.

In front were many buildings—stuck to one another. The rectangular stretches of wall between water pipes looked like dilapidated cinema screens across which some misshapen shadow would crawl sometimes.

Now no one will come—he thought. He went into the *barsati*. He turned the light on, then opened his suitcase. Some books on archeology, which he had brought with him from Vienna, lay on top of his clothes. He moved them aside and took out the bottle of cognac, wrapped in a towel, which he had brought with him.

In the beginning, sitting here alone and drinking seemed quite wretched to him. Even when he felt the urge, he would ignore it. But on some nights when he couldn't sleep for a long time, he would drink a little. He couldn't drink a lot of cognac at once anyway.

In fact, even today, he felt a slight hesitation drinking at home. Comfort would come to him, but later. After drinking a little he always started thinking about Vienna. But that came later; in the beginning he felt a strange fear. But when he lay down in bed after drinking, then he neither felt fear nor thought about Vienna. Then he only wanted to sleep.

But now he knew that sleep would come. He was very tired. But he wanted to put it off for some time. He wished to be surrounded by sleep at his own will, the way he slowly became lost in the darkness in the depths of the swimming pool.

He poured a careful measure of cognac from the bottle into a glass. That moment a shadow fell on the wall. His hand stopped. But he was not in a hurry. Before turning around he took a long swallow from the glass. It felt very good to him. Cognac always felt good to him.

He turned around and looked. Neeta was standing at the threshold.

"I thought you'd fallen alseep." She came in and sat down at the foot of the bed. Gently he pushed the bottle of cognac under the bed. He had thought that seeing him drinking, she would go away. If she had gone away he would have felt no particular remorse.

"Has Bulu fallen asleep?" he asked.

"She gets excited very quickly. You shouldn't have danced with her for so long."

"She's okay. She's just like you when you were young," he said.

"You haven't come to our house. Your *Jija-ji* asked me several times."

There was something in her voice, not reproach, but still something that had been between them for years. He often forgot that she was older than him—and not only in age. She had her own past, which he could not ever touch.

"Neeta, you won't feel bad if I…"

"No… no," she said, somewhat hesitantly, "but do you… every night…"

"Every night, not at all!" He took the cognac out from under the bed. This time, telling the lie, he felt a small pleasure.

How indifferent cognac can make us! We begin to play with ourselves too.

"Nindi!" Neeta began to say something and stopped. He looked towards her. Her eyes had suddenly become bright—like Bulu's.

"What, Neeta?" he asked.

She kept staring at him for a long moment.

"You've sort of changed." Her voice was low, uncertain.

"You really think so?" he asked, joking.

"You don't?"

"I think about it," he said. "When I was there, it never occurred to me."

For some time they sat silently.

"Do you come home often?"

Neeta looked surprised. "Not the way I used to. When Keshi was here I used to come very often."

For some time their thoughts dwelt on Keshi, who had gone into the Army. His books, his photographs, his albums, his prints were all still kept in an upper drawer.

He poured a little more cognac into the glass. A faint warmth had slowly begun to enclose him within itself.

"I had something to say to you...that was why I came here today." In the silence of the room, Neeta's voice sounded somewhat alien to him.

He was playing with his glass. His hands stopped. It seemed to him as though he had been waiting for this moment a long time.

"Can't you stay?" Neeta's voice had become dispassionate.

"What's the point of that?"

"Ma and Babu are very lonely. When Keshi was here, I didn't worry about it."

"Nothing to be gained from that," he said. "Even if I try, the home will stay this way."

"You don't even want it any other way."

After drinking, everything seemed very light to him. "Yes, maybe I don't," he said.

For some time the two looked at each other.

"Keshi told me, is it true?" Neeta's voice was dry.

"Is what true?" he asked.

"You don't live there alone...'

He kept looking at her.

"Yes, we live together."

"You haven't married her?"

"No, we only live together," he said.

"Have you told Aruna anything about this?"

"No." He took a long swallow of the cognac and set the glass down. "There's no use doing that."

For some time the two, brother and sister, sat quietly. Now they had nothing more they could say to each other. For a moment he had a strange desire to say something to Neeta—all those things that had taken place over these years away from home. But he stayed quiet.

It won't make any difference at all, he thought.

"I should go now." Neeta stood up from the bed. Then she looked all around the room. "Did you paint the room yourself?"

"How do you like it?" he asked, laughing, and said in the same breath, "I've done the outside too."

"When Keshi comes, he won't be able to recognise it." Neeta was still staring at the walls, astonished. They walked slowly up to the long wooden bookshelf and stopped. Keshi and Neeta had built this shelf a long time ago.

"Your books are still here," he said to Neeta. Sometimes he felt amazed that Neeta had not taken a single book with her after her marriage.

Neeta looked at the titles in a preoccupied manner, then suddenly looked at him. He felt as though some ancient memory had wrenched loose inside her.

"Have you seen Zweig's house in Vienna?" she asked.

"Zweig? No. Where do I have so much time!" he said. He had never been interested in books and writers.

"Nindi, don't you find it a little strange?" She turned her face away from the shelf and looked at him.

"A little strange how?"

"This night... this night we're all at home...after such a long time...except for Keshi."

Her voice had choked and he looked away. Suddenly it seemed to him as though the two of them were standing in front of a piece of land that was completely unfamiliar, unknown. Between them—the brother and the sister—they made a silent agreement that they would not walk on it. Their increasing years lay there. They would leave it just the way it was.

There they were alone.

Then the days of September came. The colour of the sky began to stay blue all day. The leaves kept falling in the streets. In the days of August they were very shiny and bright. Now their colours began to grow dark. A dry crispness came into the air. But now it was very white and clear. The town that had seemed to shrink in the summer now began to seem open and spacious.

Those days he often stayed at home. Ma didn't come to him much. Babu mostly stayed in his room. He had gone to Neeta's house once. Bulu's school had opened and she was able to see him only for a very short time. But she would come to the airport the day he left—even if she had to come alone. But these days she didn't have much time at all.

When he stayed at home, he was always afraid that Babu might think that he wasn't enjoying himself. So as soon as it was evening, he would change, so that he would understand that he was going out to meet his friends. He would buy cigarettes and go and sit in some restaurant nearby, and when he was certain that Babu must have left for his walk, he would go back into his room.

The day before he left, he had gone to the swimming pool. Mahip had told him to come in the evening; he couldn't restrain himself and went very early. It was a day in early September. There was a moist lightness in the weather. The sun was quite hot even those days, but its sharp edges had withered away.

He swam in the pool all day. When he grew tired, he would let his limbs go lax and lie in the sunshine. Now there was no longer the black oppressiveness under the water that he had felt in July. The delicate roof of the water slipped over him, and above it the sun kept trembling like a melting candle.

Once he heard a faint rustle that was neither the sound of the water nor of the air. He felt as though somewhere very far down—in the dark of the water—someone was tapping, *khat-khat-khat*, the way we might hear the sound of a tree being cut in the forest. When he came up to the surface of the pool, there was no sound anywhere. The sun had begun to sink, and his teeth chattered in the cold.

He changed his clothes and came out to the clubhouse terrace.

Chairs lay empty on the terrace. Only Mahip sat in one corner.

"You're a strange fellow!" Mahip said.

"Am I very late?" He pulled a chair over to the table.

"Will you drink something?" Mahip asked.

Today he wasn't very sure about drinking. All the things he needed to pack lay scattered about at home.

"Drink something…your lips are turning blue. No use dying of cold before you leave!" said Mahip.

He asked for a glass of grog, tea laced with rum. Mahip stuck with his beer. He recalled something and laughed.

"Today I heard a strange sound in the pool," he said to Mahip.

"What kind of sound?" Mahip asked.

"I can't recall it now," he said, laughing.

"Now you've started hearing sounds too?"

But he paid no attention to Mahip's jokes. He could still hear a soft *khat-khat at* his temples.

"Is it definite for tomorrow?" Mahip asked.

"Yes," he said. "Tomorrow morning."

There was no one on the terrace apart from them. The bar of the club was downstairs and right next to it the dance floor. Once in a while they could hear fragments of conversation or the sounds of laughter. For a moment he could not believe that at this time the next day he would not be here.

The opening bars of a Quadrille rose up from the dance floor below—so high and ear-piercing that their glasses on the table began to ring softly. He had never imagined that they might dance the Quadrille here in this day and age.

After drinking the grog he felt a pleasant fluidity in his blood.

"Did you meet Aruna?" Mahip asked.

"No...I couldn't make it there,' he said.

Mahip looked at him over his glass of beer. "You used to go to her house often, before."

He looked at Mahip and stayed quiet. Three years ago... he tried to remember. He felt a slight surprise that he had no regrets about those days. He felt happy that he had not seen Aruna. You could not see someone whom you had loved very much at one time and did not love anymore. But he didn't want to tell Mahip that. It would truly sadden him.

For the first time in Mahip's company he felt a sense of loneliness. If there had been some other friends with them, it might have been all right. Then there would have been no possibility of finding himself so vulnerable.

"I heard you went hiking last year?" he asked Mahip.

"Yes, last summer," Mahip said with some eagerness. Going hiking had always been a kind of fashion for Mahip. To this day he hasn't been able to understand this strange craze of his.

"We went to Rohtang Pass." Mahip moved the beer glass aside. "Keshi was with us. If you'd stayed longer this year we could have planned a trip together," Mahip said.

Some boys and girls walked onto the terrace in pairs. They talked in loud voices. Maybe they had come from the dance floor. They held bottles of Coca-Cola in their hands; they pulled some chairs together and sat down in another corner.

The dancing had ended. Now there was silence in the bar downstairs. The lights of the swimming pool sparkled; the distant lawn lay dark.

"What are you thinking?" Mahip asked.

He laughed and said, "Nothing."

"Listen," Mahip began to laugh too "I used to think you'd marry Aruna. All of us used to think that."

He looked at Mahip. Maybe he's drunk a lot, maybe he's been drinking since the afternoon, he thought.

Beyond the terrace was the Delhi sky—soundless and unlimited. Somewhere, from some corner, the broad beam of a searchlight would rise up, cut across the smoky September dark, and vanish. For a moment, he couldn't believe that this had been his own city for years. Smoke had risen from the buildings nearby and now hung in the air. Seen from afar, it seemed as though the entire city was surrounded by a light, blue fog.

And then he thought; I can stay if I want. If nothing else this is the age when every man begins to get a little worried.

He realises this is his land, he stands right here. He had never thought about this until that day. Keshi had known this and he went into the Army. But that had never been possible for him.

From the bar below, the very old melody of *The Blue Danube* rose up to the terrace. The boys and girls sitting on the terrace went down the steps to the dance floor.

"You must have seen it?" Mahip asked.

"What?"

"The Danube. Is its colour really blue?"

He began to laugh. He recalled the days in Vienna that he had forgotten a long time ago.

Blue is a very sad colour, he thought; Blue Period, Negro Blues. It's a colour you create; in itself it's nothing.

"It must be a lot of fun over there," Mahip said, drinking his beer.

"Yes, a lot," he said. "You should come there sometime. There are two sofas in my apartment...I've put them there for you and Keshi," he said. After drinking the grog, he felt a little warm. He felt the desire to go again into the swimming pool, but he stayed where he was. He told Mahip about the Ringstrasse, about their beer halls, which were so large that 500 people could sit there at once. And then the Stadtpark was there too—the largest park. He used to go there on Sundays. These days, leaves would be falling there too, day and night. In the evenings the orchestra played there and you could send in your requests too; after playing your piece, the conductor would turn towards you and bow.

He stopped. Mahip's eyes had begun to drift shut.

"We should go," he said.

The bar downstairs had closed. They were the only people left on the terrace.

"If you want, you can come to my room for a bit...I have some port," Mahip said, yawning.

"I'll head home now...I haven't packed anything at all yet.

They came out. The September night lay spread all around them. There wasn't a single cloud in the sky. There were only stars, which shone like polished brass buttons.

Before taking a taxi, they stood silently on the footpath.

"What time will you leave in the morning?"

"Very early...you'll be in bed," he said.

"I'll try," Mahip said after he sat down in the taxi. He leaned his head back on the seat and slept off.

He reached home quite late that night. Ma had come to undo the door chain. She stood aside to let him enter. He was afraid that he was not stepping straight. Whistling very casually, he began to climb up the stairs.

First he went into the bathroom. Even after washing his hands and face for a long time, he felt that the smell of grog still clung to him. Ma would know. He shouldn't have drunk this night, he thought. He felt that his head was spinning slowly. He was happy that his head would keep spinning this way until he fell asleep.

He came to his room. Ma had gathered up his things from different corners and put them by his suitcase. She had washed his socks and handkerchiefs and set them apart. He didn't have too many things to pack. A few days ago he had bought the necessary things—a woollen muffler for winter, gloves, a pair of shoes; the two detective novels that he always bought to pass the time on a journey. He had never been interested in Neeta's and Keshi's books. During this holiday he had tried several times to read them but every time he grew bored.

After a while Ma came into the room. In her hand was

a small label. It bore his name in large letters, written with a neem twig dipped in ink. Below his name were the names of the two cities, the one from where he was going and the one where he would get off.

"Babu gave this," Ma said. "Put it on your suitcase...it won't get lost."

"There was no need for that," he said.

"You've kept your ticket out?" Ma asked.

"Yes, it's in my pocket," he said.

"You should have bought a wallet, you put everything in your pocket," Ma said.

He began to put his things into the suitcase. He wanted to throw the bottle of cognac away outside, but he couldn't take it out in front of Ma. He let it remain in the suitcase.

"You've told Neeta and Bulu?" Ma asked.

"They know," he said.

Ma sat with him even as he ate. He wasn't hungry, but that night he couldn't get up quickly.

"Can't you stop with Keshi for one day?" Ma asked.

"Let's see...I'll try," he said. He knew this was impossible. But to tell Ma; that seemed meaningless to him.

For sometime it was quiet in the room. Ma's silence seemed somewhat strange to him. When he lifted his head and looked, she was sitting with her face turned to the wall—immobile and unspeaking.

For the first time he looked at Ma with some attention. He had been looking at her from the beginning, but for the first time it seemed to him that she looked thinner, more wasted, more faded than before. She sat shrivelled up, as though she was embarrassed by her own worthlessness. The thing that had been in her years ago had now slipped so far back, so far away, that it seemed impossible even to be able to see it.

Suddenly he started. Ma had spoken, and her voice had become very soft. "I wanted to say something...you won't feel bad, will you?"

He looked at Ma.

"Write a letter to Aruna once in a while. She has great regard for you and Keshi."

He did not say anything. A suppressed anger welled up within him. For a long time he could not understand at whom this anger was directed. But he couldn't stay there very long. He was comforted by the fact that Ma did not know anything at all yet.

He went upstairs. Last night's moonlight was still scattered over the rooftop—a pale white, as though somewhat doused. When the breeze blew, the neem tree would sway above the wall.

He tied the old prints and records that he had brought from Vienna for Keshi in a bundle and put them in a corner. Maybe he'll come during Christmas, he thought.

The Juan Gris still life hung on the wall even now. Don't know why Keshi didn't take it with him, he wondered. The way Keshi and Neeta's things were kept in the room, it seemed as though they had gone out for a little while. He felt reluctant even to touch them. He left them there the way he'd seen them the first time.

He turned out the light and lay down on the bed. He began to think about the summers that he had spent at home. But he could not recall anything about them at all. His attention was constantly diverted by small, insignificant things. Whenever he could not fall asleep he used to recall, one by one, all the houses they had lived in long ago. When the houses ended, he would count the cities in Europe that he had visited; last summer and the summers before that...

Suddenly he felt he heard a slight rustle in the room. Maybe he was asleep, and dreaming, he thought. But he could not be sure. He sat up on the bed. For a long moment he stared unblinking into the dark. It seemed to him that a whitish shape had moved in front of him.

"Babu...is it you?"

"Turn the light on, won't you, I can't see anything here." He heard Babu's voice in the dark.

He was so frightened that for some time he was unable to find the switch. Even when there was light in the room, he kept thinking for a small moment that this was an illusion; he would open his eyes and there would be no one in the room.

But the very next moment his eyes fell on Babu.

"What...what are you doing here?" Even though he didn't want it, anger was apparent in his voice.

"I thought you would still be awake," Babu said. A meek expression of abashment had gathered on his face.

But he didn't believe it. He felt that before waking him he had stood for a long time in the dark. He realised that Babu was still standing.

"Do sit down!" he said, rising from the bed. His voice was still filled with irritation.

"No...no, you sit. I only came to show you this. Take a look...how would this be?"

His glance went suddenly to the chair hidden behind Babu. An old overcoat lay on the arm of the chair. He could not understand why he had brought this here.

"Try it on and see. If it fits, take it with you...I don't use it at all," he said.

"I have a coat already, I told you that before."

"You have one, there's no harm in having a second. You have to stay there another three or four years...you can't get such overcoats nowadays. It'll serve as a raincoat too", he said.

"Where will I find the room for it in the suitcase?" he said, but his voice sounded uncertain even to himself.

"Carry it on your arm," Babu said. "Nowadays people on planes carry so many things on their arms."

He remained silent. In place of irritation now there was only emptiness.

"Try it and see...."

"No. It's fine the way it is. I'll take it with me."

For some time Babu looked around, somewhat distracted; in that time he didn't look at the overcoat even once, as someone never looks again at the place where he has committed a crime.

Babu did not stay in his room for long.

Afterwards he felt a slight regret. If he had tried on the overcoat in front of him, maybe he would have been quite happy. But he did not think a lot about that and lay down on the bed.

For a long time he could not find the courage to turn out the light. His heart still beat rapidly. It occurred to him that if he had not woken, perhaps Babu would have left the coat on the chair and gone out quietly. Even today Babu seemed to find it difficult to give him something face to face. When he was young, he would leave his pocket-money on his desk; he never gave it to him in his hand.

He turned over. For a long time he kept listening to the sounds of the house. Ma went down to put the chain on the door. From one rooftop somewhere, the sound of a radio came floating on the air to rest on another rooftop. Once in a while the sound of a cough would be heard from Babu's room.

After sometime everything became silent. He turned out the light. The door was open. The moonlight outside, spreading slowly, had slipped inside the threshold. He tried to fall asleep again.

Very late, when much of the night had passed, it seemed to him as though he and Keshi had gone to Kufri to ski. Snow lay all around. He was slipping down very rapidly. After going some distance he felt the point of his ski strike something hard. He was slightly surprised. He sat down on the snow right there and began to dig into it with the bent nose of the ski. A lot of snow came up and he threw it aside. Then suddenly his hands stopped...below, far below the snow, a hole was visible, and it seemed to him as though someone was crying inside it. He bent down and looked into the hole but there was nothing there; only a bone, a branch of a tree and a piece of glass.

His eyes flew open. The house lay desolate. There was no one anywhere; only the moonlight from the terrace had jumped across the threshold and onto his bed. He turned over and fell asleep again.

Translated from the Hindi by
Prasenjit Ranjan Gupta

10

THE BOSS CAME TO DINNER

Bhisham Sahni

Mr. Shamnath had invited his boss to dinner. Neither he nor his wife could pause even to wipe the perspiration from their faces. The wife, in a dressing gown, her tangled hair tied in a knot, her make-up all smudged, and he, pencil and paper in hand and smoking cigarette after cigarette, ran from room to room, ticking off items in a long list.

By five, they had succeeded in putting some kind of order into the arrangements. Chairs, tables, side tables, napkins, flowers; they were all there on the verandah, neatly arranged. A bar had been improvised in the drawing room. Now, they turned their attention to the bric-a-brac in the room, either shifting them behind the almirahs or shoving them under the bedsteads.

Suddenly, a problem reared up before Shamnath. "What about mother?"

Till now, neither he nor his wife had thought of it. Shamnath turned on his heels and asked his wife again in English, "What about mother?"

The wife, interrupting her work, did some hard thinking. "We'll send her to the neighbours. She can stay there for the night. We'll bring her back tomorrow."

Shamnath, cigarette dangling between his lips, screwed up his eyes and looked at her thoughtfully. "No, that won't do. I want to give a wide berth to that next-door hag. If mother stays the night with her, she will again start coming to our house. I tell you what. We will tell mother to finish her meal early and retire to her room. The guests won't start coming before eight."

The proposition sounded right.

But suddenly the wife said, "But if she falls asleep and starts snoring! Then? Her room is next to where dinner will be served."

"We'll ask her to close the door and I'll lock it from the outside. Or, better still, I'll ask mother not to fall asleep. She must keep awake and sitting."

"But suppose she does fall asleep. You never know how long dinner will last. In any case, you can't leave the bar before eleven."

Shamnath threw up his hands in irritation. "She was going to visit her brother and you stuck your nose in. You wanted to keep up appearances before your friends. Now what do we do?"

"Tchah! Why should I earn a bad name by coming between mother and son? I wash my hands of this affair. Do as you please."

Shamnath held his peace. This was no time for bandying words, but for cool thinking. He turned around and looked at mother's room. Her room opened onto the verandah. As his gaze swept over the verandah, a thought flashed through his mind. "I've got it!," he said.

Promptly, he strode towards his mother's room.

With her back against the wall, mother was sitting on a low wooden *chowki*, her face almost covered with the *dupatta*. She was counting her prayer beads. Since morning, she had been nervously watching the goings-on in the house. The big boss from her son's office was coming to their house, and she was anxious that everything should go well.

'Mother, finish your meal early this evening. The guests will be here at seven-thirty."

Mother slowly uncovered her face and looked at her son. "Son, I won't take my meal today. You know very well that I don't eat when meat is cooked in the house."

"Anyway, anyway, retire to your room early."

"All right, son."

"And mother, I will receive the guests in the drawing room; till then you stay in the verandah. When we move into the verandah, you will quietly slip into the drawing room through the bathroom."

For an instant, the mother looked at her son. Then she said, faintly, "All right, son."

"One thing more, mother. Do not go to sleep early, as you do. Your snores carry far."

"I can't help it son," she said, ashamed. "I have difficulty in breathing since my last illness."

Shamnath had fixed everything. But still he felt anxious. The arrangement did not seem fool-proof. What if the boss took it into his head to step into the verandah? There would be about 10 guests, mostly his Indian colleagues and their wives. Any one of them might like to use the bathroom. Oh, what a nuisance!

He brought up a chair and placing it by the door said, "Mother, let's see how you look in this chair."

Mother nervously fingered her beads, adjusted her *dupatta* over her head and sat down on the chair.

"*Hey Bhagwan*! No, mother, no not like this. Not with your feet up. It's not a cot. It's a chair."

Mother now dangled her feet.

"And please, please, mother, don't walk about barefoot. And don't wear those wooden sandals of yours. One day I'll throw them away."

Mother was silent.

"And what will you wear mother?"

"I'll wear what I have. I'll wear what you ask me to."

The cigarette still dangling from his lips, Shamnath inspected his mother with half-closed eyes, trying to decide what his mother should be made to wear for the occasion. He was a stickler for discipline in the house; he had the final say in everything—where the pegs should be fixed in the walls, in what corner the bedsteads should be placed, what should be the colour of the curtains, which *saree* his wife should wear, what should be the design of the tables. Mr. Shamnath was meticulous about the smallest detail.

"Better wear white *kameez* and *salwar*. Just go and dress up. Let's see how you look in them," Mother got up slowly and went into her room.

Shamnath turned to his wife and said in English, "Mother is a problem! There's no end to her oddities. If something goes wrong and the boss is offended, you know what will happen."

Mother came out in white *kameez* and white *salwar*. Short and shrivelled, with lacklustre eyes and only half of her sparse hair covered with the *dupatta*—she looked only slightly improved.

Shamnath looked at her doubtfully. "That will do. If you have any bangles, put them on too."

"I have no bangles, son, you know that. I had to sell all my jewellery for your education."

"All right, all right! Why do you make a song about it, mother?" he said, "Why carry on about it? Just say you don't have any. Why bring in the fact of my education? The jewellery was sold to good purpose, wasn't it? I'm not a loafer, am I? I'll pay you back double what you spent on me."

"May my tongue be reduced to ashes, son! Does a mother ever ask a son to pay back? I did not mean it. Don't misunderstand me. Had I the bangles I would have worn them all the time. But I don't have them."

Now it was past five-thirty. Shamnath had to take his bath and get into his dinner suit. His wife was getting ready in her room.

Before leaving, Shamnath again instructed his mother. "Mother, don't sit silent as you always do. If the *Sahib* comes your way and asks you anything, reply to him properly. I'll tell you what to say."

"I'm illiterate, son. I can neither read nor write. You can tell them that your mother is ignorant, if that helps."

As time passed, mother's heart started pounding heavily. If the boss came to her and asked her some question, what would she say? She was scared of English *Sahib*s, even from a distance, and this one, they said, was an American. God only knew what sort of questions American *Sahib*s asked. She felt like going away to her widow friend, but she lacked the courage to defy her son's orders. She kept sitting there, dangling her legs from the chair.

Shamnath's dinner had reached a crescendo of success. The topics changed with every change of drinks. Everything was going superbly. The *Sahib* liked the Indian dishes and the

Memsahib the curtains, the sofa covers, the décor. What more could the hosts ask for? The *Sahib* had shed his reserve and was regaling the audience with anecdotes. He was as jovial now as he was strict in the office. His wife, in a black gown, a string of pearls around her neck, wearing a strong perfume, was the cynosure of the women guests. She laughed, she nodded; she was so free with Mrs. Shamnath and with the men: as if they were old friends.

Nobody realised how time flew by; it was now ten-thirty. They came out of the drawing room, Shamnath leading the way and the boss and the other guests following.

Reaching the verandah, Shamnath stopped short in his tracks. What he saw made him go weak in the legs. His smile vanished. Outside her room, mother was sitting exactly as he had left her, but both her feet were on the seat and her head swayed from side to side, as she slept. She snored, heavily. When her head fell to one side, her snores became louder, and when she awoke with a jolt, she was again swaying from side to side. The end of her *dupatta* had slipped from her head and her sparse hair lay in confusion, over the bald patch of her head.

Shamnath seethed with anger. He felt like giving her a wild shaking and then pushing her into her room. But the Boss and the other guests were standing by—what could he do?

The wives of the other guests tittered and the boss said, "Poor dear."

Mother woke up, flustered. Seeing so many people around her she got so confused that she could not utter a word. She covered her head and getting up awkwardly she stood before them with downcast eyes. Her legs shook; her fingers trembled.

"Mother, go to sleep. Why do you keep awake so late?" Ashamed, Shamnath looked at the boss.

The boss was in an expansive mood. He smiled and said, "*Namaste.*"

Mother almost shrank into herself. Hesitantly, she tried to fold her hands in greeting. But one hand was inside the *dupatta* with which she held her beads, and her effort looked clumsy. Shamnath was annoyed.

The boss extended his right hand. Mother looked at it, alarmed.

"Mother, shake hands with the *Sahib!*"

But how could she? She was holding the beads in her right hand. In confusion, she placed her left in the *Sahib's* right hand. Someone giggled.

"Not like that, mother! Don't you even know how to shake hands? Your right hand, please." Shamnath was furious.

But by now the boss was pumping her left hand, saying, "How are you? How are you?"

"Mother, say, I am well, thank you."

Mother mumbled something. Someone giggled again.

But the crisis had passed. The boss had saved the situation. Shamnath's anger started ebbing.

The *Sahib* was still holding mother's hand and she was standing still, utterly confused.

Shamnath said, "Sir, my mother's from a village. She has lived there all her life. That's why she's feeling so shy."

"Is that so?" the *Sahib* said cheerfully, "Well, I like village folk. I guess your mother must know folk songs and folk dances." The boss nodded his head and looked approvingly at mother.

"Mother, the *Sahib* wants you to sing. Any old song, you know so many."

"I can't sing," mother said in a weak voice. "Have you ever heard me singing?"

"Mother," he said, "Does one ever refuse a guest? If you don't sing, the *Sahib* may feel offended. Look he is waiting."

"But I don't know any song. I know nothing of singing."

"Come mother. Just sing a couplet or two. The 'pomegranate song,' for instance."

The Indian colleagues and their wives clapped their hands at the mention of this song. Mother looked with imploring eyes, first at her son, then at her daughter-in-law.

"Mother!" The son was getting impatient. She could detect a touch of asperity in his tone.

There was no way out. She sat down on the chair. In a feeble, cracked voice she started singing an old wedding song. The ladies burst into laughter. After singing two lines, mother pathetically trailed into silence.

The verandah resounded with applause. The *Sahib* would not stop clapping. Shamnath's anger suddenly changed into joy. Mother had introduced a new note into the party.

When the clapping stopped, the subject suddenly veered round to cottage industry products of Punjab; the boss wanted to be enlightened on the point.

Shamnath was bubbling with joy. The sound of clapping was still ringing in his ears. "We have so many of them," he said enthusiastically. "I will collect a complete set for you and bring it to the office, Sir. You will like it, I'm sure. Shamnath thought for a moment and continued, "The girls make dolls, Sir, and...and women make *phulkari*."

Shamnath inefficiently tried to explain that a *phulkari* was a sort of embroidered piece of cloth and then giving up the effort as hopeless turned to his mother. "Mother, do we have as old *phulkari* in the house?"

Mother went in to her room and returned with one.

The boss examined it with keen interest. It was an old *phulkari*, its threads had come undone in several places, and the cloth almost crumbled at the touch.

Shamnath said, "Sir, this one is almost threadbare, it's useless. I will have a new one made for you. Mother, you will make one for the *Sahib*, won't you? Make one for him."

Mother was quiet. Then she said, "My sight is not the same as it used to be. Old eyes feel the strain."

"Of course, mother will make one for you," Shamnath said, interrupting her. "You will really like it."

The *Sahib* nodded his head, thanked mother, and proceeded towards the dining table. The other guests followed.

When they settled down to dinner, mother quietly slipped into her room. No sooner had she sat down, than her eyes flooded with tears. She kept wiping her eyes with the *dupatta* but the tears wouldn't stop; as if the floodgates of years of old pent-up feelings had suddenly burst open. She tried to control herself; she folded her hands before the image of Krishna, she prayed for the long life of her son, but like monsoon showers, the tears kept flowing.

It was now midnight. The guests had departed, one by one. But mother kept sitting with her back set against the wall. All the excitement was over and the quietness of the locality had also descended on the house. One could hear only the rattling of plates in the kitchen.

There was a knock at mother's door. "Mother, open the door."

Her heart sank. Had she made another blunder? She was always making mistakes. Oh, why had she dozed off on the verandah? Had her son not forgiven her for it? She opened the door with trembling hands.

Shamnath hugged her wildly. "Amma, you have done wonders today. The Sahib was so pleased with you, Amma, my good Amma."

Mother's frail body looked even smaller against Shamnath's heavy frame. Tears came to her eyes. Wiping them, she said, "Son, send me to Haridwar. I've been asking for a long time."

Shamnath's face darkened. He let go of her. "What did you say, mother? Again the same thing?"

He was getting angrier. "So you want to discredit me before others, so that they will say that the son cannot even give shelter to his own mother!"

"No, son, don't misunderstand me. You live with your wife in joy and comfort. I've come to the end of my life. What will I do here? The few days that are left to me, I would like to spend in meditation. Please send me to Haridwar."

"If you go away, who will make the *phulkari* for the boss? I promised him one in your presence. You know that."

"Son my eyesight has become weak. It can't stand any strain. You have the *phulkari* made by someone else. Or buy a readymade one."

"Look, you can't let me down like this, mother. Do you want to spoil the whole thing? If the *Sahib* is pleased he'll give me a raise."

Mother was silent for a minute. Then suddenly she said anxiously, "Will he give you a lift in the office? Will he? Did he say so?"

"He did not say anything. But didn't you see how pleased he was with me? He said when you start making the *phulkari*, he will personally come and watch it being made. If the boss is pleased, I may get an even higher post. I may become a big officer."

Her expression started changing and gradually her wrinkled face was suffused with joy.

"So you are going to get a lift in the office, son."

"It's not so easy, mother. You don't understand. If only I could please the boss. There are others too, all wanting to get promoted. It's all a rat-race, mother. But I'll have a better chance."

"In that case, I will make one for him. I will...I will somehow manage it, son." Silently, she prayed for her son.

"Now go to sleep, mother," Shamnath said, as he turned towards the door.

Translated from the Hindi by
Jai Ratan and P Lal

11

GAUTHAMI TELLS A STORY

Masti Venkatesha Iyengar

[Kalidasa's play *Abhijnana Shakuntalam* ends with the reunion of Shakuntala and her emperor-husband, Dushyanta. In a story with the title *The Return of Shakuntala*, I pictured Shakuntala as visiting her foster father's *Ashram* some time after returning to Hastinavasti, the capital. She and her friends, Priyamvada and Anasuya, who in the meanwhile had been guided by their Granny, Gauthami, to marry Sharngarava and Sharadvata, respectively, had some happy times together during the visit. The present story describes something that took place on the first night of Shakuntala's visit to the *Ashram*]

1

The day that Shakuntala visited the *Ashram* of Kanva with her son, for the first time after she rejoined King Dushyanta, she and her friends spent half the night talking of many things.

In the joy of their old companion's return, as happy mother

and queen, Anasuya and Priyamvada forgot the affairs of their own little households, leaving even the task of swinging the children's cradles to their husbands, and sat down with Shakuntala.

Granny Gauthami, inconsistent with her years, sat with these young women for some time and then went out to attend to the affairs of the *Ashram*. When the work of the evening was over, and the residents of the *Ashram* had all retired for rest, she joined them finally to talk as long as they liked.

Priyamvada laughed at the grandmother and said to Shakuntala, "Thanks to your coming, Sister Shakuntala, Granny has walked about enough for a month on this one day. She was old before you came. She has now become a girl!"

"Who said that Granny was an old woman?" said Anasuya. "It is not only today that Granny moves about more actively than us. That is so even on other days. Only today she is more cheerful."

"You girls are clever, I must say," said the old woman. "You wish to feed me with praise and make me do all your work, while you spend time with your friend, the queen, idling and happy. If I did not become a girl, who would have attended to your work?"

"Anyhow," said Priyamvada, "Anasuya and I, together, have discovered a drug that makes old people young."

They soon came to the subject of how Gauthami did not rest until Anasuya and Priyamvada were married; when she returned from the capital, where she had left Shakuntala.

Why did the old woman insist so strongly that the two girls must marry? Did she fear that they might make the same mistake that Shakuntala had made with Dushyanta? Shakuntala was the daughter of a celestial Nymph. She had grown up with the expectation of someday marrying a royal person. Anasuya and Priyamvada, on the contrary, were girls of the *Ashram*. Their minds had not moved in the direction of marriage. There was no reason to fear that these girls would give way to love as Shakuntala had done.

The old woman said in her defence, "You are too young. You do not understand these things. Even children brought up to celibacy may suffer from desire sometimes. Listen while I tell you the experience of a young woman I knew when I was young. You will then agree that what I did in your case was necessary."

The three friends loved to hear a tale from Granny and huddled together, in front of her, and urged her to tell the story.

2

"The girl I am telling you about," said Gauthami, "was one of the children growing up in the *Ashram*. She came from one of these villages in the woodlands surrounding us. She grew up here as the rest of you. Children who do not have anybody to take care of them come to stay in the *Ashram;* sent either by their elders for spiritual pursuits or themselves desirous of the peace of the life here. This girl was one such. Her name was Malini, the same as the name of our river."

Malini was eight or nine years old when she joined the *Ashram*. As the days passed, she grew up to be a young, obedient girl. It so happened at the time that the other girls in the *Ashram* were either several years older or several years younger than her. The consequence was that almost from the day of her arrival, Malini was forced to find companions among the boys of the *Ashram*. She joined them in their tasks, like gathering flowers, bringing in grass, tending to the cattle and attending to visitors.

Among the boys who thus became Malini's companions, were two who were just a few years older than she was. One of them was of the Bharadwaja sect; the other was adopted into the Kashyapa sect.

"Of the time I am speaking about," said Gauthami, "Bharadwaja was nearly 16 years old; Datta Kashyapa a year or so younger and Malini was a year or so younger than Datta.

Growing up, from the age of nine, as a companion of these two boys, Malini seemed unaware even at 15 that she was not a boy herself. The young men too seemed not to know that she was different and interacted with her as if she were another boy, without any hesitation; in fact, with perfect ease.

This was nothing new in the *Ashram* of Kanva. The elders always wished that men and women should be able to interact with one another without each being overtly conscious of the other as a member of the opposite sex. All the residents grew up in this atmosphere, so this girl and these boys could, without any effort, live together as they did, untroubled by thoughts of attraction or intimacy.

Going about with the young men, Malini became adept in swimming. The finest swimmer in the *Ashram* in those days was Bharadwaja. Datta was nearly his equal, but could not be considered as inferior. As for Malini, there were not many women of the time, who could swim as well as she did.

As she went about with Bharadwaja and Datta, even after she had grown up, some people one day asked her in jest which of the two she was going to marry. She had not, till that day, thought of the matter. She gave no answer.

When, however, she went out with the young men again, the question came to her mind naturally; her mind said, Bharadwaja. Not that she did not like Datta! In truth, she liked the two equally. Yet, if it was a question of marriage, she preferred Bharadwaja.

One of those days, the head of the *Ashram*—the immediate predecessor of the present Chief—called Bharadwaja to his presence, and said, 'You and Datta have been Malini's friends for a long time. She is grown up now. It is now time for you to marry her and become a householder."

Bharadwaja did not refuse. He folded his hands and left. When the girl came to him a little later, he looked at her in the manner of a man who was troubled by a problem. It must have been because the person, who had only been a companion till then, appeared, for the first time, as a woman ready for marriage; that being so, he had to be wary of his conduct with her. He, however, said nothing.

The girl continued to go about with both the young men with the same ease as before. Yet it was clear that her mind turned more and more in the direction of Bharadwaja.

Bharadwaja's mind also must have slowly turned towards her. One day as they were swimming side by side in the river, he asked Malini whether she would like to marry him. She said, "Yes."

When they reached the bank, Bharadwaja told Datta of this. Just a shade of displeasure appeared on Datta's face. But only for a moment!

Returning to the *Ashram*, he communicated the news to others. When it reached the head of the *Ashram* he said, "That is good."

But for being affianced to each other, Bharadwaja and Malini treated each other exactly as before. The only small difference was that, now, the two would occasionally go out by themselves, without waiting for Datta to join them. They wandered together in the moonlit nights quite often as Malini loved the moonlight. The world, she would say, wears one kind of clothing during the day and quite another in the moonlight. To her, tree, wood and creeper seemed to each wear a mysterious charm, in the light of the moon.

On many a moonlit night she would call both the young men for a stroll in the woods. If Datta did not turn up, she would go out with Bharadwaja.

There is without doubt, some spell in the light of the moon. They who have been caught in it know it. Malini had lost her heart to it.

Datta went with her and Bharadwaja a few times, but then refused to go with them. Walking with Malini, Bharadwaja also was caught in the spell and he too learnt to desire Malini deeply; for her, the moonlight seemed to be a beautiful clothing for the world, to him it seemed to be a beautiful clothing just for her. He would sometimes stand still looking at her bathed in moonlight—he would feel that the very deity of physical charm stood before him, clothed in moonlight.

On many a moonlit night, when the river level was low, they would go and sit together on the swans' sand dune in the river. So seated, they would sink into a joy that transcended the limits of the body and was yet as real as the joy of physical union. They would no doubt have become husband and wife in a little while thereafter.

3

Gauthami continued her story. "The rains came. You know how

our river Malini fills with fresh water and gushes fiercely. It was a major sport for Bharadwaja to cross the river when it was in full flood, one day in the year. As Bharadwaja wished to do this, Datta would also join him. That year as in the previous years, when the floods came, Bharadwaja talked of the feat."

For some reason, Malini disliked the idea. She did not know why and she told Bharadwaja so.

He laughed and made a joke of it. "Why have you become so timid? I have not become old since I swam the river last year," he said.

On the night before the full moon, Bharadwaja and Malini went to the *Sahakara* tree on the bank of the river and sat on a boulder, where they spent a lot of time looking at the river and talking.

Bharadwaja had, so far, not touched Malini with any feeling of desire. That night, suddenly he held her face in his hands and gave her a kiss. Malini was surprised by this uncharacteristic behaviour.

As the flood in the river pulls trees on the banks and carries them away, love for Bharadwaja flooded her heart, removed all hesitations and pushed her into his arms.

They did not yield to desire. Yet, that night, spiritually, the pair became husband and wife.

The next morning had been fixed for the swimming bout. At the designated hour, practically all the young people of the *Ashram* gathered on the bank of the river.

Bharadwaja and Datta sprang into the water. The river was in full flood.

Gauthami now explained the way the river looked that day, "You have seen it; when the water touches the top steps, the river seems to have ceased to move—the middle of the river even more than the edges. You could see it running, because the grass and stick and branches floating in the water are floating away."

In this still-looking water, Bharadwaja and Datta swam shoulder to shoulder till almost the middle of the river. At the very centre, they could not keep together in this manner. Each had to cross that middle as quickly as he could without being carried too far down. Bharadwaja gained a lead in doing this and Datta fell behind. Even after crossing the middle of the stream, Bharadwaja maintained the lead and reached the further shore first. Datta joined him a little later. The two walked a few hundred steps, up and down, and then dropped into the water again.

"The way across lay to the left of our great boulder, Yogasaila. Our river has changed its course in the last few decades and the boulder now stands nearer to one side. In those days it was exactly in the middle of the river. The swimmer would have to make a special effort to leave the boulder on his right when he reached the middle of the stream. Without making this effort, he would be carried down by the force of the river and not be able to reach his destination," Gauthami explained.

That day it looked as if Bharadwaja was tired in his efforts to keep the boulder on his right. Besides, just as he and Datta reached that point in the river, a tree came floating down. Datta saw this tree. It looked as if it would bear down on Bharadwaja and he shouted to him. The people at the nearby shore, who were watching the swimmers, also shouted a warning to Bharadwaja. However, he did not realise what the warnings were for and looked in the wrong direction.

Alas! That very moment the tree bore down on him. The youth was caught under a branch of the tree and sank out of sight.

"Who just called?" Gauthami stopped suddenly to ask. She then got up abruptly and went out.

"Nobody called," said Priyamvada. "Why did Granny say that somebody called?"

Anasuya looked at Shakuntala. The old woman returned a few minutes later to continue the story.

4

It is difficult to say what happened. The tree was stuck between two boulders. The youth must have got caught in the branches and was trapped under water.

"Each moment was, to us, like an hour. Datta swam with tremendous speed towards Bharadwaja. The people on the bank would have to swim a thousand feet to reach the Yogasaila. Some offered to do this," Gauthami now shared the anxiety of the onlookers.

Some of them had wondered aloud, "How can Bharadwaja come to harm? There is no swimmer like him."

After a few minutes, two people dropped into the river and swam to the Yogasaila.

In the meanwhile, Datta was risking his life to reach Bharadwaja.

Finally, Datta and the two people who had earlier jumped into the flooded river brought the lifeless body of Bharadwaja to the bank.

The *Kulapati* heard of this and grieved terribly. He forbade swimming bouts when the river was flooded. In fact there were no more swimming bouts in the *Ashram* anymore. That, however, would not bring Bharadwaja back. The *Ashram* had suffered a calamity and the young man was gone.

Malini was among those who had seen the danger and called out to Bharadwaja.

She now remembered the previous night when they had sat together on the river bank.

Bharadwaja had said, "When I am in the water I shall be looking at you all the time. What strength will come to me from the desire to join you! How would a girl know this? I shall conquer the river tomorrow and then I shall win you; then life, then austerity." The youth had four wishes. He had failed in his attempt to acquire the first. Malini, the river, had played rival to Malini the girl, and taken him away

5

The story of the young man was over. What of the girl he had left behind?

The people at the *Ashram* could not fathom the depth of her sorrow. After all, Bharadwaja and she had not been married! Even if they had, it was not appropriate for the residents here to indulge in strong emotions. She would be expected to check her emotions even if she had been his wife. Only some came to Malini to offer her any kind of condolence.

For Malini, life had ended with Bharadwaja!

Gauthami explained, "Without becoming husband and wife, Malini and Bharadwaja had developed the pure love of ideal marriage. You girls hold a flower in your hand before wearing it, and find joy in just looking at it. Child Bharata, this evening, when we gave him a fruit, held it to his nose and caressed it before eating it. So, this youth and this girl, before tasting a life together, had heightened their expectations, by restraining their longing.

"But Alas! As a lizard drops on your plate of food, when you are about to begin eating, and you have to throw away the food, the life these people had planned for themselves had come to an end even before it had begun!

"What the young man might be feeling, where he was now, people here below could not know. But here, nobody noticed Malini's grief and helplessness. She did not cry fearing the taunts of the people and the sorrow seemed to choke her soul."

The unfortunate girl had lost Bharadwaja but her loss did not end there. It looked as if she had lost Datta too. The three of them had grown up together. When she and Bharadwaja had got engaged, Datta had distanced himself; not that he and Malini cared any less for each other, but they could not be to each other, what they had been before. Now, Bharadwaja had died and disappeared from Malini's life. Yet Datta maintained his distance. So, the unfortunate girl was now utterly alone. She would spend the minutes thinking of Bharadwaja; she remembered that broad chest, the bright eyes, that brave gait of his, the beauty of that waist. The figure of her love stood in front of her, moved in front of her, again and again. She remembered, again and again, the last occasion when they had sat together.

The voice that is expressing love gains a new tone; Malini remembered Bharadwaja's words of love to her on that night. As youth and maiden who were to be married, they had sat close together, touching each other. What joy did that touch bring! Even now, remembering that joy, Malini's heart swelled with happiness.

When her beloved said that he would get his strength to cross the river by just looking at her, she had believed him.

Standing on the bank that day and watching him swim, she had noticed the sparkle in his eyes as he looked at her.

It is believed that love does not die! Malini's love for Bharadwaja did not die with him. There was also no end to her grief. She could not accept that love such as theirs had now become a mere fable. She was overwhelmed with sorrow. But why did this abode of austerities not prevent her sorrow from overwhelming her? Not only this, the place seemed to bring back every memory of Bharadwaja and add to her distress.

She would go back to the sand dune of the Swans, where the birds came as couples and rested, and again and again remember her beloved Bharadwaja. Even now, she would imagine two shadows moving together. She soon began to ask herself why she should live.

6

Overwhelmed by the flood of her grief, she went to the river in despair one day and jumped into it to end her life. She knew how to swim and it was not easy for her to die in the water. The stream took her down some distance.

Datta happened to be on the shore, collecting flowers and sacred leaves. He noticed that the water was carrying someone down and jumped in to bring her out to the bank.

Malini revived and asked Datta, "Why did you rescue me? You ought to have let me die."

Datta replied, "Obviously, your destiny wished you to live."

Time went by; days and months passed by! Malini began to rediscover interest in life. The intensity of sorrow abated and she was at peace with her loss. She began to mingle with the other inmates of the *Ashram* as she had not been doing recently, and even began to conduct herself with Datta without any awkwardness.

In these years, Datta had grown in his austerities. The *Kulapati*'s regard for him had also grown. All the people of the *Ashram* had begun to show him special respect, as the prospective successor to the *Kulapati*.

It was the season of spring. The cuckoo called and the mango tree at the *Ashram* had flowered; the jasmine creeper by its side had grown around it and bloomed. That season brought Malini desires which she only half-understood; and she found herself yielding to them.

One day, she just wanted to be around Datta. 'Why am I feeling this desire?' she asked herself. She tried to engage herself in different tasks, but her mind continued to be restless. She soon realised the nature of this desire and it began to rule her thoughts. She fought with it for several days, refusing to yield, but did not succeed.

After much wrestling with her mind, she told herself, Bharadwaja was to be her husband. Destiny had come in the way. Why should Datta not be her husband now? She had tried to die, but he had saved her and brought her out of the water. Having saved this life, why could he not look after it, she convinced herself.

A few days later, she went to him when he was alone.

Datta greeted her. 'Sister, why are you here?" His voice reflected his surprise.

Malini without hesitation asked him to marry her.

Datta replied, "Sister, let us not think of this."

"Suppose the *Kulapati* had asked you, instead of Bharadwaja, to marry me, would you not have accepted me?"

"It is possible I would. My brother agreed. If he had not

been asked, I might have agreed. But what is the use of talking about that now? You became his wife and, to me, a sister-in-law, who I should honour. I have grown these years thinking of you as sister-in-law. I am unable to think of you as a wife."

"But this marriage did not happen," Malini protested.

But the idea that Bharadwaja and Malini were a couple had sunk into the depths of his being. How could he think differently now? He thought of Bharadwaja whenever he saw Malini.

The day it was decided that Bharadwaja should marry Malini, Datta had realised that it was his destiny to embrace celibacy. The Lord of my life is telling me that the householder's life is not for me, he had thought, and then decided to follow this destiny.

Now he told Malini, "This is my view and you, as my sister-in-law, have to help me realise my destiny."

Malini was distraught. "When fate took away one of two people who I could marry, did it not tell the other man that I was his?" said Malini.

Data replied, "It is possible that is so, but there is always the possibility of misunderstanding what destiny has planned for us; the possibility of interpreting it in accordance with our wishes. Destiny must be understood as saying that which our heart says is right."

"What do you think destiny is telling me?"

"As it told me that day that marriage was not for me; so now it is telling you that married life is not the life for you. The day that Bharadwaja died, destiny told you that renunciation was your way in life. I had thought, till this moment, that you had realised this and were acting in accordance with it."

"Then what about this desire? Is this not given by destiny?'

"Have you not heard the teacher say that desire is a serpent?

Our spirit has to be careful in this body, knowing that it is a hut in which a serpent is moving about.'

"Place a serpent and a mouse in one basket and tell the mouse to be careful? What is the use of this advice?' Malini asked him.

Datta did not reply. Malini also left things there at the time and turned her mind again towards renunciation.

7

The year passed somehow. Spring came and again the call of the cuckoo was heard in the woods and the Sahakara put out sprouts. The jasmine creeper blossomed and in Malini's heart, desire bloomed again.

The desire of the heart is a natural phenomenon and cannot be prevented, in much the same way as the blossoming of nature cannot be prevented. To a young heart, desire is just as natural. When the whole world woke up to a new cycle of life and seasons, love and desire woke up in the heart of young Malini.

Gauthami explains, "People do not seek desire. Desire seeks them. Does the jetsam and flotsam which the river carries in the hour of its flood choose to go to any particular point? Supposing it chose, can it go where it desires? In the flood of life, people too, for the large part, are helpless as the jetsam and flotsam of the river in flood. They know they are in danger but cannot save themselves.

"Could there be a stronger man than Bharadwaja when the stream swallowed him? Where is the strength of spirit that cannot be swallowed by desire in flood? And you know, desire does not rise in a flood after taking into consideration how much you can stand. It seeks hold of people and carries them on. A big tree floats for some time and sometimes stops beside a bank. The straw and sticks on the other hand are borne away by the flood. Our Malini too was caught like a straw by desire in full flood and it carried her away without mercy to its vortex."

Malini made up her mind that somehow she would get Datta. She went to him again and said, "I come to you again to ask for your benevolence."

Datta spoke to her, at length, explaining that it was against his way of life to marry her.

Malini did not say anything. She left

The next day was a full-moon day. The *Ashram* observed the festival of the full-moon spring. When the festivities ended, each person went to his place for rest. Datta sat down to meditate. Malini too went to her hut to rest. But, she could not sleep. She was very fond of the moonlight. She wished to wander in it and came out of the hut. For a while, she wandered, distraught, in the *Ashram* and then, without specifically thinking of it, came where she knew Datta would be sitting in meditation.

By this time, Datta had finished his meditation and was resting. He had covered himself with his shawl. But his shoulders and chest were open to the light of the moon. The face had on a peaceful and guileless smile, which it generally wore.

Malini, for the moment, seemed unaware that it was Datta who was lying in front of her. She seemed to think that it was Bharadwaja himself. She came close to him and sat at his head. She then caressed his cheek, touched his chin and touched her lips with the hand.

Datta woke up to the touch and sprang to a sitting position. "Sister, why did you come here at this hour? I suppose you could not sleep?"

He could have asked her why she was behaving foolishly. But, by nature, he was very considerate, very courteous. He was not a man to speak to people who had made mistakes in a tone which showed that he was offended. Even unintentionally he could not offend anyone.

"No," said Malini. "I did not get sleep. I felt a desire to come to you."

"That is right, sister. The moonlight is very beautiful, is it not? I too sat for some time watching how beautifully the light danced on the river. The night is really very calm.'

Malini said nothing in reply to this. After a minute of silence, she said, 'You must give me your answer."

"To what?" Datta asked incredulously.

"To my prayer to you."

"I gave you the reply then, sister."

"What reply?"

"That I do not wish to marry."

"Do not marry; have me as your companion."

Datta was not prepared for this proposal. It seemed to shake even his strong spirit. He took a moment to get hold of himself and then said, "We are together now."

"Do not pretend that you do not understand what I am saying. I feel no shame by your knowing what I mean. If I felt any, would I have come like this?"

"Sister, is this the path you show to a man who has chosen celibacy to achieve his goals?"

"I am asking for something and you are talking about something else. As for me, life has become impossible. Pay heed to my wishes just once. If you cannot do this, I shall go and jump into the river."

"Do you forget that destiny showed you that was not the way for you?" Datta reminded her.

"Was it destiny that showed me, or was it you? Why did you save me? Did you do it so that I may suffer as I am doing now? To have let me die that day would have been like saving my life. You saved me and are killing me now!"

"Sister, it is not in your power to die. It was not my power that saved you. There is another power that directs all life. Do not forget it. You are my elder brother's wife. You should guide me and show me the correct way in life. You are younger than I in years. But, spiritually, you are no less than I am. Show me the right way.

Malini sat still for some time, then, stretching out her hand, took hold of Datta's face and pulled it towards her breast.

Datta pulled himself away and fell to her feet. "Do not test me. I do not have the purity of spirit, which is vouchsafed to womanhood. If you do me this favour, I can have a good future. Do not insist that I lose my way. Have pity on me." The words were uttered in a tone of indescribable humility.

Something in the humble tone in which Datta uttered his petition touched a chord in her. Her desire had dragged her to that place. Now the veil seemed to have been lifted from her eyes. The youth who, till then, had seemed a strong-willed person, at that moment, became a helpless youngster who could save himself only with her help. The arms that had longed to hold him as a companion, now wanted to comfort him as a child.

Malini placed her hand on his head, patted his back, as if offering him a reassurance and got to her feet. Datta also stood up in front of her.

"What you say is right Datta. I agree with you." And then without waiting for a reply, she returned to her hut.

8

The blessings of elders and the power of Datta's spiritual practice saved Malini from being caught again in the whirl of desire. In the meanwhile, Datta made great spiritual progress. The head of the *Ashram* respected him for what he had become and announced that he would be his successor.

Malini began to look at Datta as though she was his mother or elder sister. She felt that all his achievements were her own and was very proud of him.

Datta achieved greatness and in the process Malini was saved!

Malini was saved because Datta was great. Supposing he had not been great, what would have been Malini's fate? Because Datta had remained strong, both had remained righteous and stepped across the hell that might have engulfed them.

Gauthami told the young women sitting in front of her, "Malini was fortunate. Even though she was caught in such a whirl of desire, she was saved by Datta's spiritual greatness. This is why I have always said to our young women, that they should marry early in youth. All are not Malini. All will not suffer as she suffered; condemned to live alone after losing her companion, the man she desired to marry.

"It is a different matter with those who decide to remain celibate. Those who think that they might get married when the possibility arose, should get a companion at the proper time in life. It was because you did not get such a companion that you, Shakuntala, my child—I beg you not to take offence—lost your heart to the King as soon as you saw him. And you, my children, that was why you too approved of her yielding to him when he wanted her.

"All three of you treated your Granny, who had brought you up, as a stranger, and the young man, who you had seen for a few hours, as a friend! This, my children, is the reason, why that year when Shakuntala went to the court, I would rest in peace only after getting the two of you married."

9

As Gauthami finished her story, the three friends sat in silence for some time.

Then, Priyamvada asked, "Granny, how do you know all the details of this story?

Anasuya smiled and looked at Shakuntala, "How does Granny know all the details? Do we know why, Shakuntala?

Shakuntala nodded her head in assent.

Priyamvada asked, "How is this? You two seem to know and I do not."

"If Granny permits me, I shall tell you," Anusuya responded.

"By all means, little mother, do not hesitate," Gauthami said, indulgently.

Anasuya finally said, "Malini is no one else, but our Granny Gauthami."

"That is true, my child."

"Oh! Granny, how you must have suffered! I shiver to think of it. If I may ask, where is Datta? What became of him?" Priyamvada asked curiously.

"I can tell you, if Granny permits," Anasuya answered for Gauthami.

"Yes child, you know. Tell her. Let her understand."

"*Kulapati* Kanva is Datta."

Shakuntala added, "If he were not Datta in youth, would

Kulapati be what he is today? He is the strong spirit that could swim across the most powerful flood of desire which might have caught him. Bharadwaja was a worthy youth. I concede that. But he would not equal Datta. One in ten million might equal the *Kulapati*."

"I realise now why he shows so much respect for Granny," Priyamvada responded.

Gauthami explained to the three young women, "He has often said, it is easy to cross a stream when it is low, but very difficult to cross it when it is in flood, and that his elder sister, Gauthami, crossed the stream of desire when it was in high flood. It is his idea that though not free from desire, he never experienced desire in the violence of the strength with which it assailed me. Yet, is there a way to measure the strength of desire?

"Our Chief is a man of infinite strength. That is how this *Ashram* has become such a great place. What do you think? The king of the country is our son-in-law and our grandson will be the Emperor."

Translated from the Kannada

12

A COCK-FIGHT

Amin Kamil

The moment Ghulam Khan entered the compound, Shah Maal got up with a start. She did not remember to wash and wring her *pheron* that had been soiled by her eight-month-old baby.

She seemed to have come by a treasure, the way she asked her husband, "Have you got it? I was afraid that you might come empty-handed even today."

She almost snatched the rooster off him and began to fondle its feathers and comb.

"It cost me four and a half *rupees*." Ghulam Khan put much emphasis on rupees perhaps to bring home the cost to her, lest she take it for some unworthy lame thing.

But Shah Maal was altogether unmindful of that; she simply was experiencing the boundless joy of feasting her eyes on it.

With her eyes raised, she cast her glance towards her neighbour's window. She said to her husband in a higher pitch this time. "This was really the sort of rooster I was after, for day in and day out numberless roosters are hawked in the market and the whole *mohalla* has gone to purchase that lot."

Ghulam Khan did not reply to that and directly went indoors.

A string was tied to the rooster's legs and it tried to walk around. By turns, it pecked at the string and seemed to take stock of its surroundings.

Janna Bitsh called out from her window.

Shah Maal was in fact wishing desperately for her to appear. However, she assumed nonchalance, to pretended to shake dust off her *pheron* and, shaking her silver ear-rings, said, "We have made a purchase, just now, for four and a half *rupees,*"putting much more stress on the word *rupees* than Ghulam Khan had done earlier. .

"It seems to have come from the village?" Janna Bitsh said, "It looks like that. It is a fine sort."

"Will you believe it is only seven months old?" Shah Maal fixed its age somewhat arbitrarily. "It is a different breed. They do not bring this sort to the city for sale. Then the thing remains that no one buys, even such a sort dear. Here, the stray roosters will do."

Shah Maal saw Janna Bitsh flushing crimson.

It had dawned on the water that it was she who was meant with the "no one".

Janna Bitsh abruptly said, "I have to dry the dishes. You better fill its crop." And with this she went indoors.

Shah Maal, with a smile playing on her countenance, pouted her lips and continued gazing at the rooster.

The matter, in truth, was that its purchase solely owed itself to a taunt from Janna Bitsh.

Shah Maal's neighbour, Janna Bitsh, owned five hens and a rooster, while Shah Maal owned only hens. Janna Bitsh's rooster would, once or twice a day, hop and jump down into Shah Maal's compound. Shah Maal, as she had no rooster of her own, would take it as godsend.

It was a different matter, however, when Shah Maal left some paddy, or some such thing, to dry up in the sun; its presence then was an eyesore to her as it stuck like a leech. It could not be prevented from scattering grains pell-mell, much as you tried to scare it off.

A fortnight back, she had been driven crazy because of this and had come close to killing it.

Janna Bitsh, showing herself at her window, had bandied back with a taunt. "If that be the case, why don't you buy a rooster of your own? If you are so fond of it, when it suits you, why should a few grains wrench away your pleasure?"

Shah Maal would rather die than bear this repartee. That very moment, she pestered her husband to buy a rooster.

Janna Bitsh, too, from then on, kept a vigil on her rooster, lest it should fly over to Shah Maal's.

Ghulam Khan, with one pretext or the other, dilly-dallied for a fortnight, but could not help buying one from a dealer at Maisuma for three rupees. He had added a rupee or so more to forestall her likely pert rejoinder, See what inferior stuff you have brought, as if you could not get anything else!

Janna Bitsh's rooster was henna-red. The one that Shah Maal now owned was white, snow-white—dazzling white to be precise. It cut a notch above, in its mien, to Janna Bitsh's rooster, which, it should be admitted, was much stouter in life and limb; or else both were of the same breed, a few *annas* more or less hardly mattered.

As the day wore on to a close and everyone went to sleep, Shah Maal, lying in bed suckling her babe with the entire weight of her head falling on her elbow, supported by a pillow, was, in the heart of hearts thinking of the rooster...How green with envy Janna Bitsh must have got, her jeering taunt still galls me. Let that rooster of hers move over to this side. I will not be worth my salt if I do not tear off a leg."

Ruminating thus, her eyes fell on her husband's face, sleeping aside in a separate bed. How handsome he looked to her now; indescribably handsome.

As she lifted her elbow off the pillow to finally get to sleep, she was startled by a sound.

Kuck-doo-koon, from the pen.

Shah Maal held her breath.

She pricked her ears to make sure she had not misheard. No, the rooster crowed the second time and her last breath seemed to slip out of her!

She sat up on the bed and called her husband.

'Hah, dear...get up. Here, listen to me..."

"Oogh! Why?" said Ghulam Khan half awake. "Did you say something?"

"Hark! The rooster just crowed and it is night yet." Shah Maal was getting impatient. "What an ominous devil of a rooster you have bought!"

"Crowing?" Ghulam Khan made a grimace. "How does it matter? We do not have to give a morning call to people to be awake for Ramadan fasting!"

"See! What rot he talks!" Shah Mal got angry. "Get up and slit its throat. Don't you know that a rooster which crows when it is night should be put to death? It turns out to be an evil portent."

"What nonsense! This prattle about portents! Please sleep and pay no heed to such rubbish." Saying so, he tucked himself under the quilt and fell into a sound sleep so that he could wake up at his wonted hour; seven in the morning.

Shah Maal, however, much as she tried, could not sleep.

She did not so much mind the off-time crowing as the likelihood of it having been heard by Janna Bitsh and then the probability of her jeering.

"Was this the much-vaunted rooster that you were after? All other roosters brought good tidings of morning light, whereas this ominous creature is possessed by the devil when it is night yet," Janna Bitsh would say.

This very fear, kept Shah Maal from even opening the door of the pen and letting its feathery beings in the open in the morning.

Otherwise, come what may, nothing would have stopped her because she would take it out on Janna Bitsh for days to come by hurling taunts at her through walls and the fences.

Now, she remained under the shade in the corridor and she saw the rooster along with the hens make its way to the compound. Seeing this, Shah Maal's heart sank. How loathsome it was to her eyes!

The rooster fanned out its wings and flexed them with relief. It spread a wing fanwise and amorously made four to five rounds around each hen. The hens, to save their skin, went helter-skelter, as if cautioning the cock, "Fie! What has befallen! Do not even look around, for shame."

The hens looked at the corridor as if to wonder why Shah Maal had not come out; not even to cast a handful of grains. They flocked straight to where she was. The rooster, too, got a hint and followed their tracks.

As she caught sight of its legs, her face distorted with contempt. Its legs, right up to its body, took on the hideous form of a donkey's skull in her mind.

But she did not scare it off, lest Jaan Bitsh know what had happened.

She just cast off two handfuls of rice towards the compound.

Across at Janna Bitsh's compound, when her rooster heard the unaccustomed *kroo*, it raised its neck up, put forward its breast, stiffened its body, as if all the sinews of its body had shrunk

Kut, kutok, kutock......,

It let out a shrill crow as if to throw a challenge at the bully that had entered the other compound.

Kutock, kut, kutock...

Shah Maal's rooster also lifted its neck, apparently in response.

"Beware, I am the white rooster. If only you cross over to this side will you know who you have to deal with. It would not do to show your fists from the other side," it seemed to say.

Shah Maal abhorred these shrieks of her rooster. If only it would behave normally, so that Janna Bitsh would not look out of her window.

She flung a sod of clay at its head, but missed it. It was only frightened and this made it hop up with a *Kutock*, which now made Janna Bitsh crane out her neck through her window.

"Why are you out of temper so early in the morning? What has the poor creature done to you?"

Shah Maal seemed to have been caught red-handed, sweating through and through, all her caution and care finally coming to nothing. She surmised from Janna Bitsh's tone that she was deliberately baiting her, knowing the cause of her anger

"Far be it from me, why should I be angry? Only the rooster does not let the hens approach the grains."

"Come, now, it is only because it is new to the place," Janna Bitsh said in a humorous vein, "By tomorrow it will offer the grains to them itself."

"That would be possible if we were to keep it, but we bought it to make a meal out of it," Shah Maal said, thinking that now her neighbour would not be able to find a pretext to mock her. "My husband might have got its throat slit right yesterday, but for his being tired out."

"What has happened to you? Why should you kill it?" Janna Bitsh remonstrated. "See, what a fine figure it cuts! And it has a good voice to boot!"

Shah Maal lost her colour. She took the phrase "good voice" to mean that she had heard the untimely crowing, but to throw her off the scent, she said again, "If I were to keep such stray roosters, then many were peddled up for sale. The sort of rooster I had set my heart on has not yet come by. Now somebody has given his word to procure one like that, at any rate."

When Janna did not respond to this, Shah Maal thought it would be better to go inside rather than listen to something unpalatable that she might eventually have to say.

Shah Maal put some embers into the *samaavaar*, but, all the while, was taken up in the rooster's quandary.

As Ghulam Khan returned home after ablutions in the mosque, she said to him while pouring him a cup of tea, "Get the rooster's throat slit; after all, we are to pass our days in this *mohalla*."

"Let me know what the locality has to do with it," Ghulam Khan asked her, chewing a loaf of bread. "This surely is not the month of fasting that one should be penalised for not knowing the right time."

"You do not care, you only talk," Shah Maal got incensed. "Well if you cannot bring yourself to do it, I will be the last to rear this ominous thing up."

"Do it then," Ghulam Khan said, cutting the matter short and adding, "But mind that you do not make a fresh demand."

"That I will not!" Shah Maal said angrily before pointing out, "Well, Janna Bitsh's rooster remains there in the compound the whole day."

As Ghulam Khan left for his job, Shah Maal got up and went to Samad Khaash's place. He was, so to say, a priest for slitting throats of all fowls of the *mohalla*. There were many others who did it, but the epithet *Khaash* (throat cutter) stuck to him only. That is why the curse "Shhhh... Let Samad Khaash take you," was hurled at the fowls.

Samad *Khaash* said over his window, "Get it here, I will slit its throat. But remember, I will also partake of it in the evening at your house. You man and wife alone will not take it. Yes?"

"Well, who the devil denies you that? You are welcome." Shah Maal replied with a smile as she made for her home.

She was pleased with the prospect that Jaan Bitsh would no longer be able to put her to ridicule or else day in and day out she would be the butt of her jibes.

As she entered her compound, Shah Maal witnessed a strange spectacle—the poor hens were terrified as Janna Bitsh's rooster was locked up in a high-pitched fight with her rooster.

God alone knew why they had raised quite a cloud of dust. As if that was not enough, Janna Bitsh was gloating over the spectacle occasioned by this fight.

Shah Maal imagined Jaan Bitsh was happy with the thought that her rooster would come out the victor, because it looked something of a bully dut to its stout frame. It had, besides, put to shame many a rooster in the *mohalla*. Shah Maal's heart began to pound and her face lost all colour.

Jaan Bitsh's rooster was red while that of Shah Maal was white. The small downy feathers of their necks bristled erect in rings. Their heads trembled with rage and their feathers seemed to let off electric currents. Their bodies stretched and their tail feathers spread out. They were face to face with outstretched necks, spitting around fire and swooping upon each other, unannounced, raising quite a tumult with their beaks.

When Janna Bitsh saw Shah Maal making an entry in the compound, she sat all the more at ease at her window. She then added, "Do you not see, how can this stray rooster of mine be a match for yours? But it is all the same for a rough street-tramp to give and take hiding. Let there be no mistake, however; it will make your rooster take to its heels, just as it has made all the roosters of the *mohalla* eat humble pie."

Fear choked Shah Maal. What could she say? She was repenting over the turn events had taken. She suspected that Janna Bitsh had, on purpose, let her rooster cross over to this side. She knew she had to say something in response to her neighbour's taunts.

"This rooster of mine is not meant for such brawls, a different breed as it is," she said finally.

The roosters, by this time, had raised a pandemonium; bleeding and stripping each other of its feathers.

Janna Bitsh, fastening herself close to the window, was expectedly bobbing her head, whereas Shah Maal turned crimson and then ghastly pallid. She gradually got desperate and bitter; even hurling curses on Janna Bitsh's rooster, although in a whisper.

"May your beak fall to pieces…may your legs be paralysed…"

One could not guess how far Jaan Bitsh's rooster had bled because of its red colour, but the white colour of Shah Maal's rooster showed that it was badly wounded.

Shah Maal could not restrain herself seeing its plight. "May it fall dead in your stead, may its beak fall to pieces," she said to at her neighbour's rooster.

"Why are you driven to extremes? It is too early yet. See, it will make yours turn its tail," Janna Bitsh bandied back.

Shah Maal grew desperate, over-wrought as she was by many a foreboding right from the previous night; she might have served so fitting a repartee that even Janna Bitsh could be silenced.

This inner battle might have mounted to vituperative recriminations and execrations, but alas! One of the roosters left the arena all of a sudden—it was Janna Bitsh's rooster.

The other rooster chased it all around the compound.

Shah Maal was by now sweating profusely because of all the excitement.

Janna Bitsh, however, in order to save face, had the cheek to pretend that she had nothing to do with the brawl.

"Oh, are you going to kill such a rooster?" she finally said, her chin resting on her palm, "If you do not mind my saying so, do bring it up. Do not kill it."

"Oh! Did you really take me for my word?" Shah Maal said haughtily, twirling her silver earrings to make them jingle.

"A rooster may be marred by one hundred flaws, it may crow untimely when it is night yet, I will be the last one to mind that. But it should give a stiff fight. Such indeed was the sort of rooster I was after."

Translated from the Kashmiri

13

A NARROW PLACE

Paul Zacharia

Along time ago, there lived a little boy who walked home from school every day well before sunset on a path which wound along a wall of boulders, guarding the plantations that bordered the high banks of a stream. During the unending rains of the monsoon, long viscous drops of a light medicinal flavour hung from the exposed roof-tips of the grass on the wall, bright and glittering in the occasional sunlight.

The stream wound its way through many bends and turns. In some places it had eaten deep into the bank. Here the boy either jumped down into the water, if it was shallow enough, and crossed over, or, placing his umbrella, tiffin-carrier and bundle of books on the wall, climbed into the plantation and walked through it till the bank reappeared.

He was a plump little boy who usually wore a blue half-sleeved shirt and shorts. He had a round face, soft cheeks and soft, fair legs.

The most important difference between his journey to

school and return lay in the weight and position of his copper tiffin-carrier; it went carefully hung from the boy's right wrist, which also held the bundle of books, and returned swinging on the fingers of his left hand.

His heart's greatest desire in those days was for a ballpoint pen which had refills of different colours.

He was prohibited from taking the path along the stream after a heavy downpour. Instead, he was expected to take a longer path that meandered through the plantations. He did so often, but only because he had discovered through experience that it was better, in his own interest, to accept the prohibition rather than be humiliated by the rain-swollen stream and be driven back into the thorny underbrush of the plantations in the pouring rain.

The boy carried an umbrella almost all the time.

His parents had given him a plain three-lettered name, which he did not consider fine enough. In fact, he harboured a great resentment towards whoever had thought up this name for him. Besides the one desire already mentioned, his other great longing was for a long, beautiful name, with many letters for himself. Often, he daydreamed of the good times, when he would be a grand person with another name.

He had a few small scars on his body from the time he had had a bout of ringworm. These scars were also the cause of considerable sadness to him.

One summer evening, when he was returning from school along the bank, the big toe of his right foot struck a stone. This was never considered an auspicious sign; for he knew that the axiom, *Hit your right foot on a stone and you'll be at the receiving end of a stick* was as much an absolute certainty as the one that said, *Hit your left foot on a stone and you'll receive a feast.*

For a more definite interpretation of this portent, he sat on his haunches and carefully picked a well-rounded leaf from the plant usually selected for this purpose, blew it into the air and watched it fall. Fluttering and turning several times, the leaf fell on its face. This only added to the confusion, since the meaning of the leaf falling on its face contradicted that of striking the right toe on a stone.

Pondering over this strange development, he continued on his way faster, picking up an occasional pebble and throwing it at the leaves floating in the stagnant water.

It being summer, the current was broken in many places. The sluggish water, dirty with soap, oil and moss, crept weakly through sandbanks overgrown with grass.

In the few pools of water that remained, women of all ages bathed, washed clothes, dried their hair or mercilessly scraped into cleanliness, children, who moved helplessly under their hands like clockwork figures. These half-clad women with their hair undone, rubbing themselves with the bark of the soap-tree, were mere parts of the landscape to his indifferent eyes. He knew that he too was a mere moving shape and nothing more in the attentive and knowing world of the bather's eyes, and he was not concerned or affected by this fact. Sometimes their breasts, shining with oil and extraordinarily large, surprised him. Among women on the whole, he considered only two as deserving of his attention and company: Susy, his youngest uncle's daughter, and Lakshmikutty, the girl with curly hair in his class. Neither had breasts.

His proficiency in whistling, an art he had only recently acquired, was noteworthy. He had undergone many hardships to master this art which, until then, had been the monopoly of his elder brother and his friends. Though he could now overlook the humiliation of having had to submit to the disdain of these tyrants in order to learn certain secret movements of the lips and the tongue, he could not forget the aching of his lips and the feeling of defeat, despair and hurt that marked the period of perfecting the technique. However, directing his entire mind and body to the effort with a vengeance, he had learnt to whistle some songs and certain secret questions and messages, loud enough to be heard at a good distance. He was very proud and satisfied with this, for it was only a month since he had produced the first clear, unmistakable note from his lips, standing under the dark umbrella of the trees at the spot where the path climbed steeply from the bank.

This path descended, narrowed into a footpath between high embankments of stone and earth, crossed a small stream and entered the plantation neighbouring his father's. His friend lived there.

It continued along the side of the small stream, till it reached the stone steps leading to his family's coconut grove. There was a bathing place at the foot of these steps. But he always preferred to go downstream to a deep pool of water between two forebodingly dark hillocks, surrounded by big rocks.

It adjoined his friend's property and was far enough from his house to conveniently indulge in the activities of fishing, diving and blocking the flow of the stream; all of which were part of the function of bathing. This pool was filled by a waterfall that poured through a crevice between two rock-faces, and it was very deep at this spot where little rainbows danced in the wind on sunny days.

A long time ago, a woman who had had an epileptic fit had drowned here. The boy and his friend sometimes gave themselves up to dread, thinking of the white figure, dead, drifting in the foam and froth of the waterfall; trapped in its undertow, with nowhere to go.

On one side of the pool was a broad, high slope of rock, which turned into a vast sheet of cascading water after the rains, its every inch slippery with moss.

The boy and his friend would regularly push a boulder up this slope and then let it go with unfailing extraordinary results!

Considering, therefore, the tremendous amount of time, energy and effort expended on their daily bath, the boy's parents had firmly prohibited him from bathing in this pool with his friend. The boy considered this prohibition very unfair and harmful to his general happiness, and had been forced to reach a secret understanding with his friend.

The last lap of the path he was now walking on, crossed a corner of his friend's plantation, went down some steps into the small stream again and climbed to a narrow bank, which ran at the foot of the stone-and-earth wall surrounding his friend's land. It passed the prohibited pool which could be seen from a narrow, dark ledge under the shadow of tall trees, partly hidden from view by overhanging vines.

The wall was built over a large rock at this spot.

The boy had made a pact with his friend that he would stand under the rock and whistle for him, as a signal to come over and plan the evening's activities.

During the rains, when the waterfall roared loudly, he would begin whistling even as he entered his friend's plantation, so that the sound of the waterfall would not drown his whistling, and his friend would reach the meeting place at the same time as he did.

When his toe struck a stone, the boy had been thinking of an important and compassionate mission; capturing the fish from the pool that was drying up under the summer sun, by draining the little water left in it, and transferring them, in a coconut shell, to a well in a corner of his plantation But, it was prohibited to keep fish in the well and therefore the matter had to be handled with utmost care and secrecy.

Since the experiment with the leaf had not given him a clear answer, he walked faster, whistling under his breath, throwing the tiffin-carrier high in the air and catching it as it fell. He was upset when he missed the carrier the third time, and it got a dent from the fall. All of which made it urgent that he see his friend.

According to him, his friend had several advantages over him. For example, in the boy's home there were only his father and mother, a servant who was his friend, a brother who came during the holidays with a trunk smelling of strange places, and a sister who often wore a red skirt with blue flowers on it. The boy had a grandmother, but she stayed with his youngest uncle and he visited her only occasionally. However, his friend not only had his uncle, aunt and their daughter Molly living with him, but his grandfather and grandmother as well, which was no small matter.

His friend's grandfather was a lanky old man, who had grey hair on his hands and prominent jawbones. He smelt of a wooden store room containing paddy and bananas. He always carried a tall walking-stick. When he hitched up his *mundu* as he always did, the hind-leg of his *langoti* hung out at the back.

Sometimes when the boy was bathing, Grandfather would defecate among the bushes on the bank and get down into the stream to wash himself. The boy thought that he made a rather shameful sight with the big hands, the lifted *langoti* and *mundu*, and his baldness and nakedness. But Grandfather never thought so himself, and even spoke to the boy while washing himself.

The boy always went to a hidden place behind his house with a brass jar of water to wash himself. One day, his sister had peeped at him while he was washing, and broken into peals of unreasonable laughter. He had rushed at her with great sorrow and indignation and attacked her with his wet hands.

Whenever Grandfather had too many drinks, the boy would know of it from the shouts and roars that rose from his friend's house at night. The boy didn't like these sounds, because it was always unpleasant to connect Grandfather with them the next day, at the bank, when he would seem like a stranger from the noisy night.

The boy also had a suspicion that Grandfather sometimes supplied his mother with information on his and his friend's activities. Still, he was on amicable terms with him.

He had agreed with his friend that he would never signal for him by calling out his name, since the friend's parents had keen ears. It was a safe signal to whistle, casually, the snatches of a song. The boy, therefore, now whistled the opening lines of the hymn *Praise be the Lord God.*

Actually, there was no need to whistle so early, as it was summer and the waterfall was silent. But he was in a hurry today. He could see the courtyard of his friend's house, partly hidden by the old coffee plants. His friend should have whistled in reply by now, picked up the bath towel from the clothes-line on the verandah and crossed the courtyard on his way to the rock.

But he was not to be seen. Surprised, the boy proceeded to the secret meeting place above the pool. He went down to the pool for a moment and prodded the greenish water with a stick. He returned and waited, leaning on the rocky outgrowth.

By now, a few dim clouds had gathered in the west, as a prelude to the monsoon expected to start in a few days, and the narrow place under the trees where the boy stood grew dark and lay in shadow, as if the sun had already set. The sense of an untimely sunset disturbed and saddened him; the feeling that time had advanced upon him from some place in the future made him uneasy. He didn't want to whistle again. He felt that his whistle might turn into a scream in that unnatural darkness.

With many misgivings, he climbed up on the rock on which he had been leaning and peeped over the wall to see if his friend was on his way. Not finding him, he stepped down and began to whistle again and again in the direction of his friend's house. He waited restlessly for a while, jangling the tiffin-carrier and biting on a leaf. Then he whistled again, looking up at the sky.

The boy didn't know that on the verandah of his friend's house, under the clothes line, people were gathered round the Grandfather's still warm body. He didn't know that his whistles had repeatedly fallen on the stillness of death and the hushed whispers that surrounded it. Nor did he know that his whistles had reached his friend's ears as a sound both familiar and unfamiliar.

The boy in shorts and a blue shirt, the plump nine-year-old fisherman and walker of the stream-bank, whistled once again, did not receive a reply, waited, and then continued on his way home slowly and at last climbed the steps, under the *champakam* tree in bloom, to his house.

As he sat down to eat the *dosa his* mother had made, the servant told him about his friend's grandfather. Suddenly, the coffee he was drinking turned into something else in his mouth. He could not bear its sweetness. He could not touch the *dosa* on which his mother had spread sugar and chutney. The taste of death seeped into his mouth and nostrils. He bent down and vomited on himself and the table. Everyone ran into the kitchen.

His shirt and shorts were removed and he was put to bed in a *mundu*.

A sound of unremitting whistling filled his ears. Thinking of the darkness under the trees, in the narrow place where he had stood, and of the death that had stirred so close to him, he crept to the middle of the bed. His head was filled with the resurrected clamour of the whistles that had issued from his lips over a dead man and fallen upon his dead ears.

In the growing darkness of the room now, he felt the ceiling had grown high as the sky and that he had become as small as an ant.

He silenced with a scream his sister, who came into the room to ask him something and with a great effort tried to drive out of his ears the endless sound of whistling.

For many days afterwards, he would not walk under the shadow of the trees, on the bank without the servant for company.

Translated from the Malayalam by
the author

14

MYSTERY OF THE MISSING CAP

Manoj Das

*I*t is certainly not my motive, in recounting this episode of two decades ago, to raise a laugh at the expense of Shri Moharana or Babu Vir Kishore, then the Hon'ble Minister of Fisheries and Fine Arts of my State. On the contrary, I wish my friends and readers to share the sympathy I have secretly nurtured in my heart for these two gentlemen over the years past.

Shri Moharana was a well-to-do man. His was the only *pukka* house, in an area of 20 villages. Whitewashed on the eve of India achieving independence, the house shone as a sort of tourist attraction for the folks of the nearby villages. They stopped to look at it, for none could overlook the symbolism in this operation that had been carried out after half a century.

Shri Moharana had a considerable reputation, as a conscientious and generous man. He was an exemplary host with two ponds full of the choicest fish and a number of pampered cows. He was a happy villager.

And then came India's independence. As is well known,

the ancient land of India has had four major castes from time immemorial. But, during the days immediately preceding independence, a new caste was emerging all over the country— that of the Patriots. The 15th of August 1947 gave a big boost to their growth. In almost every village, besides the Brahmins, Kshatriyas, Vaisyas and Sudras, a couple of Patriots came into being.

It was observed that the small fisheries of Shri Moharana were often exploited in honour of these new people. And observers began to notice that Shri Moharana himself was fast growing into a Patriot. As I found out later, he had even nurtured an ambition to be elected to the State Legislature.

The incident I relate occurred at the outset of his endeavour in that direction. A small boy then, I was on a visit to my maternal uncle's house, which was in the immediate neighbourhood of Shri Mohrana's.

In those early days of indigenous ministries, there were no deputy or sub-deputy ministers. All were full-fledged Hon'ble Ministers and, since Bapu Vir Kishore hailed from our district, the sponsors of Shri Moharana thought it proper that the latter's debut into politics should have the Hon'ble minister's blessings.

That was a time when a minister's daily life was largely made up of giving speeches at public meetings; there was no need for any specific occasion to accord a reception to a minister.

A reception was arranged for Bapu Vir Kishore, with Shri Moharana as the Chairman of the Preparatory Committee. Shri Moharana's huge ancestral cane-chair was laid with a linen cover on which the most gifted village seamstress had laced a pair of herons, holding two ornamented fishes in their beaks.

The children of the village lower primary school were made to practise a welcome song every afternoon, for a fortnight.

Among the many strange phenomena wrought by the great spirit of the time, was the composition of a song. The composer, the head-pundit of the school, has lived in my memory. Its literal translation would be:

O mighty minister, tell us, O tell us,
How do you nurture this long and broad universe!

The rest of the song catalogued the great changes nature and humanity experienced on the occasion of the minister's visit; how the morning sun frequently blushed in romantic happiness, how each and every bird chanted a particular salutation-oriented *raga*, and with what eagerness and throbbing of heart the womenfolk waited to blow their conch-shells in unison for when the minister would set foot on the village soil.

I know that nowadays ministers do not enjoy such glory. But it was very different then. We, the rustic children, wrangled over several issues—what does a minister eat? What does he think? Does he sleep? Does he ever suffer from colic or colds, as ordinary mortals do?

Shri Moharana himself was excitement personified. He used to be very fond of his hour-long afternoon nap. But, he gave up the luxury at least ten days prior to the day of destiny. He devoted all his time to examining and re-examining details of the arrangements; even then, he looked nervous and uncertain.

At last came the dawn of the big day.

The minister got down from the jeep as soon as it reached the very first welcome arch on the outskirts of the village. He was profusely garlanded by Shri Moharana, but was requested to step back into the jeep as the destination was still some distance.

But the minister smiled and made some statement, which meant that great though destiny had made him, he loved to keep his feet on the ground!

Moharana and his friends looked ecstatic.

While hundreds applauded and shouted "Babu Vir Kishore ki Jai" and "Bharatmata ki Jai", the minister, double the size of an average man of our village, plodded through the street, it seemed to us, to the embarrassment of the poor, naked earth.

And I still remember the look of Shri Moharana when the minister's long round arm rested on his shrunken neck, a look which I have seen only once or twice later in life, on the faces of dying people who had lived a content and complete life.

Shri Moharana's look suggested, *What more, what more, O mortal me, could you expect from life? My, my!*

At Shri Moharana's house, the minister and his entourage were treated to tender-coconut water, followed by the most luxurious lunch I had ever seen, with about 20 dishes around the sweetened, ghee-baked rice mixed with nuts, cloves, etc.

Soon the minister retired to the cabin that had been kept ready for him. Though it was summer, the main window being open to a big pond and a grove brought in enough air to lull even an elephant to a sound sleep.

Volunteers had been posted to see that no noise was made anywhere in the village to disturb the ministerial repose.

I had, by then, separated myself from my companions. Being rather ambitious, I was eager to see the great man as closely as possible; the minister sleeping was surely the most ideal condition for achieving my goal.

I mustered courage and slowly approached the window facing the pond. This was the rear side of the house. The minister's personal assistant and the entourage were on the opposite side.

While I stood near the window, suffering the first shock of disillusionment in life regarding great men, for the minister was snoring in the style that was ordinary and human, something most extraordinary happened.

Speechless, I was already; the incident rendered me witless...

Through the window, I had observed that the minister's egg-bald head rested on a gigantic pillow, while his white cap lay on a stool between his bed and the window.

Now I saw mischievous Jhandoo, the monkey, hop towards the window, like a bolt from the blue, and pick up the cap. Then, throwing a meaningful glance at me, he disappeared into the grove.

Even when my stupefaction passed, I was unable to shout, partly because of my deep affection for Jhandoo (knowing that the consequences of his crime could be fatal to him) and partly for fear that the minister's dream—must be on a patriotic theme—might be interrupted.

At that crucial moment I was in a dilemma as to which I should value more—the great man's cap or his snoring.

I retreated, pensive. But before long, I heard an excited but subdued noise. Crossing into Shri Moharana's compound again, I saw the minister's personal assistant flitting about like a locust and heard his repeated mumbling, "Mysterious, mysterious!"

The minister was obviously inside the cabin. But nobody dared to go in.

Shri Moharana stood thunderstruck, as did his compatriots.

The public relationships officer was heard saying, "The Hon'ble Minister does not mind the loss of the cap, so much as the way it was stolen. Evidently there is a deep-rooted conspiracy. The gravity of the situation can hardly be exaggerated. In fact, I fear, it may have devastating effects on the political situation of our land."

I could see Shri Moharana literally shaking with fear. He was sweating like an ice-cream stick, so much so that I was afraid, at that rate, he might completely melt away in a few hours.

The conflict within me, as to whether I should keep the knowledge regarding the mystery to myself or disclose it, was resolved. I signalled him to follow me, which he eagerly did. A drowning man will indeed clutch a straw!

I told him what had happened. He stood silent for a moment, eyes closed. Then wiping the sweat from his forehead, he smiled like a patient, whose disease had been accurately diagnosed but was known to be incurable.

He then patted me and said, "My son, good you told me. But keep it a secret. I will reward you later."

The incident had thrown a wet blanket on the occasion. The sepulchral silence in the minister's room was broken only by his intermittent coughing. Every time he coughed, a fresh wave of anxiety hit the people in the courtyard and on the verandah.

I went away to join my friends. They were wild with speculations. One said that the thief, when caught, was to be hanged on the big banyan tree beside the river. Perhaps all the villagers will be thrown into jail, said another. Among us, there were naïve people who even believed that the minister's cap was a sort of Aladdin's lamp, that anyone who put it on would find himself endowed with ministerial power the very next moment.

But the situation changed all of a sudden. I saw the minister and Shri Moharana emerging on the verandah, the former all smiles.

It was the most remarkable smile he had hitherto displayed. By then, at least half a dozen caps had been secured for him. But he appeared with his head bare. Even to a child like me, it was obvious that his bald pate wore an aura of martyrdom.

Not less than five thousand people had gathered in front of a specially constructed stage when the minister ascended it, that remarkable smile still clinging to his face. Shri Moharana's niece, the lone high-school-going girl of the region, garlanded the minister.

A thunderous applause greeted the event, for that was the first time our people saw what they had only heard in the tales of the ancient *Swayamvaras*, a young female garlanding a male in public.

Then the chorus of *O mighty minister* was sung in *kirtan* style, to the accompaniment of two harmoniums, a violin and a *pakhauj* drum.

Now it was Shri Moharana's turn to say a few words of welcome.

I saw him (I stood just in front of the stage) moving his legs and hands in a very awkward manner. That was certainly nervousness, I told myself. But, with a successful exercise of will-power, he grabbed the glittering mic and managed to speak for nearly an hour, giving a chronological account of Babu Vir Kishore's achievements and conveying gratitude on behalf of the nation to the departed souls of the great man's parents, but for whom the world would have been without the minister.

I was happy that Shri Moharana did well in his maiden speech. But the greatest surprise was yet to come—in the concluding observations of Shri Moharana.

Well, many would take Shri Moharana as a *pukka* politician. But I can swear that it was out of his goodness—a goodness befuddled by excitement—that he uttered the lie. He said, his voice rising in a crescendo, "My brothers and sisters, you and the world have heard about the mysterious disappearance of the

Hon'ble Minister's cap. You think that the property was stolen, don't you? Naturally. But that is not so, ladies and gentlemen, not so!" Shri Moharana smiled mysteriously. The minister nodded his big clean head, which glowed like a satellite.

Shri Moharana resumed, "You all are dying to know what happened to that object. Isn't that so? Well, it is like this. A certain nobleman of our locality took it away. Why? That's what you want to ask, don't you? Well, to preserve it as a sacred memento, of course! He was obliged to take it away secretly, because otherwise the Hon'ble Minister of Fisheries and Fine Arts, the brightly burning example of humility that he is, would never have permitted our friend, the nobleman, to view the cap as anything sacred!"

Shri Moharana stopped and brought out of his pocket, a bundle tied with his handkerchief. Dangling it before the audience, he said, "Well, ladies and gentlemen, the noble gentleman has requested me to place this humble amount, of ₹101, at his disposal, for some little use in his blessed life's mission, which is service of the people, through fish and fine arts." Shri Moharana then bowed and handed over the bundle to the minister who, with a most graceful gesture, accepted it.

Applause and cries of wonder and appreciation broke out like a hurricane!

Even the minister and Shri Moharana, both looking overwhelmed, clapped their hands.

The minister spoke for two and a half hours thereafter, drinking a glass of milk in between, at the end of which he declared that, as a mark of respect to the unknown admirer of his, he had decided to remain bareheaded for that whole night although the good earth did not lack caps and, in fact, a surge of caps had already tried to occupy his undaunted head.

Soon my shock gave way to a mixed feeling for Shri Moharana. At night, the respectable people of the area partook of the dinner that the preparatory committee had organised in honour of the guest. Glances of awe and esteem were frequently cast at the minister's head and homages paid to the honourable thief.

But when I saw Shri Moharana in the morning, I could immediately read in his eyes the guilt that haunted him, at least whenever his eyes fell on me. He, perhaps, had never spoken a lie; and now when he did speak one, he did so before a gathering of thousands! God apart, at least there was one creature—I—who knew that he was no longer a man of truth.

The minister, however, exuded sheer delight. He did not seem to notice how strained Shri Moharana looked, when conducting himself before him.

At last, came the moment for the minister's departure. He was served with a glass of sweetened *lassi*. While sipping it leisurely, he said, in a voice choked with curd and emotion and sporadic laughter, "Well Moharana, ha ha! The way things are moving, ha ha! I'm afraid people would start snatching away my clothes. And I may have to go about naked! Ha ha! But I don't mind! That is the price one must pay for winning admiration! Ha ha!"

The minister then came out to the rear verandah, facing the pond and the grove, to rinse his mouth. Shri Moharana followed him with a jug of water.

Except for me, there was nobody on the verandah. My presence was not accidental. I had spied upon the rascal Jhandoo, playing with the minister's cap, slowly emerging from the grove. Seldom had I wished for anything that ardently as I wished then for Jhandoo to go unnoticed by the guest.

When he was an infant, his mother had taken shelter under Shri Moharana's roof, in order to save her male child from the usual wrath of the male leader of her group. Shri Moharana had not been at home and his servants had killed the mother monkey.

Shri Moharana was extremely upset, did not eat for one and a half days and, to compensate for the wrong done, had nurtured the baby monkey and christened him Jhandoo with great affection.

Jhandoo, when he grew up a little, would often escape into the grove. He was half-domesticated and half-wild. He played with everybody, and they tolerated him. We children were extremely fond of him.

To my horror, I saw Jhandoo rushing towards us, from the other side of the pond. I made an effort to warn Shri Moharana of the impending crisis, but in vain.

Jhandoo got there in the twinkling of an eye. He sat down between the minister and Shri Moharana. He put the cap once on his own head; then taking it off offered it to the minister, in the most genial gesture.

My heartbeats trebled. Looking at Shri Moharana's face, I saw an extremely pitiable image—he was as pale as death.

The bewildered minister mumbled out, "Er...er...Isn't this the cap that was taken away by the nobleman?"

And something most preposterous came out of the dry lips of Shri Moharana who seemed to be on the verge of collapsing, 'Yes, yes, this is that nobleman...'

His eyes bulging out, the minister managed to ask, "What... What did you say? Well?"

But Shri Moharana was in no condition to say anything more. He broke down into tears. Next moment, I saw the

Hon'ble Minister of Fisheries and Fine Arts weeping too.

The Personal Assistant's voice was heard from the opposite verandah, "Sir, the jeep is ready, Sir."

The minister gulped down almost half of a jug of water and plodded towards the jeep. Shri Moharana followed suit. Their reddened eyes and drawn faces were interpreted as marks of the sorrow of separation.

Shri Moharana's political endeavour is not known to have gone any further. And it is strange that the Hon'ble Minister, Babu Vir Kishore, who was willing to be robbed of his clothes, was soon forgotten in politics.

I have a strong feeling that it was this episode of the cap vis-à-vis Jhandoo, that changed the course of their lives.

Translated from the Odia by
the author

15

THE BED OF ARROWS

Gopinath Mohanty

*B*ack from work, today he emitted a sweet fragrance. Turning on her side, her face contorted with pain, Kamala looked at his face from her bed.

She remembered her decision not to speak any more of her pain, nor to reveal the agony on her face; instead she would smile, or at least try hard to smile. Yet why does she feel dampness within?

Why does she find some happiness in the thought that her days are numbered? And that she should not prove herself a worthless burden on him?

Before she could sport a smile, Surababu, his face dry, had come near her. Pressing her head with his left hand and playing with her dishevelled hair, he asked, "Do you feel any increase in your pain today? Oh God, what should I do, how long to carry on this way?"

Kamala smiled. "What is new in my pain? It is the same old thing," she said.

His face seemed to dry up further before her sharp gaze.

"Why won't you say so! That is in your nature, I mean, the nature of the women folk. Never to say what is going on inside, even to yourself, let alone to another. You think that if you burn yourself out at the service of the others in a single-minded devotion the heavens will be yours first, isn't that so, Kama?"

Surababu extended his hand to caress her cheeks. But, as if in a desperate bid to escape his touch, she withdrew her face. She felt a stab of pain in the chest and a sudden dizziness as she closed her eyes and floated in emptiness.

Half a minute later, she was herself again and, biting her lower lip, said, "You have not even changed your clothes, you must be feeling wretched. Will you please go and eat something?" she said and then called out to their maid, Indira, in a nasal voice.

"I am going," said Surababu. "You won't have to shout. That will only aggravate your weakness and pain. How much do you think is left of your body?"

She sighed and closed her eyes. But Surababu was still there when, a minute later, she opened them.

How much is left of your body? These words echoed in her ears. The fragrance returned to her nose. Her vision was getting blurred. Things alternated between clear and hazy.

Now she could see a human body sparkling in the pale wintry light after the rains. That was her husband. His 46th birthday was approaching, yet the structure continued to be strong; rather, it had grown stronger. The wide forehead, the glow of knowledge on the face, the chin adamantine to fight and overcome obstacles remained unchanged. And that body was her property, only hers!

Kamala had gooseflesh, her face grew hot, there was burning around her eyes and she started at Surababu hungrily. She remembered his words of sympathy. His was a lovely body, but what once had consciousness suddenly became huge and there was intimation of rain. She pressed her teeth hard as she muttered. "What use for an empty wine-cup?"

Surababu, startled, asked, "What did you say?"

Kamala smiled with jealousy, but said, "Nothing much. But, see, it's a long time I have been telling you that I am bedridden, can do precious little for you and you need care. For my sake, you must..."

To her surprise, Surababu did not turn his face away, he did not blink repeatedly and there was no sign of sadness as before. Instead, there was anger in his voice, as he said, "What nonsense do you speak!"

Kamala felt herself sinking, not because of his anger but out of an unknown fear.

"Are you angry?" she said, "You have just returned after a hard day's work, why don't you go, change, have a wash and eat something? Why do you keep standing here?" And once again she squeaked, "Indira, can't you hear me? Babu is standing here!"

Surabau walked away. The breeze retained that fragrance only for a while. Kamala kept thinking, vacantly looking up, in her bed. Outside, the shadows lengthened. She could see the drumstick plant; its leaves had flashed a smile at the sun a little while ago and was now slowly becoming a column of darkness.

She went back in her memory, by twenty-two long years. Ghana was yet to be born. Manika and Suna were not there even in her realm of dream. It was the first year after their marriage.

"You exude such a fragrance, Kama!"

"Please move. Mother is in the other room and, look, someone, maybe one of your students, is knocking at the door. You came back after a hard day of teaching. Are you not hungry?"

All around there was fragrance. Covering his own face with her messy hair, he lay silent and still.

"Would you please go away?" she said again.

"Quiet! I can hear a song!"

"What nonsense!"

"There is music in the human breast, fragrance in the body and do you know what is there in the touch?'

"Fire? No you are wrong. The touch has the caress of the lotus and sleep!"

"Yes, everything is there in your language. You are, after all, a professor of literature."

"Let us not talk of literature. It is not greater than life nor is it a substitute for life. It is an act that leans on life. Wait, let me drink life."

"Are you not ashamed?"

"Shame is only a superficial mask. Why to have something in which you don't believe?"

Startled out of her reverie, Kamala tried to get up, but there was an explosion of all the familiar pain and weakness in her body. Piteously she kept lying and sulked and could recognise that the fragrance was nothing special, but that of an *attar*, available in the bazaar. From one who has applied it, the fragrance jumps on to another! It was a long time and she had forgotten all about toiletry. Forgetting all personal pleasures, all her tender habits, she had made herself into a tough housewife, rearing children. Now, they had emerged into the wide world.

Manika and Suna had set up their own homes. Ghana was a student of forestry at Coimbatore. Once he took up a job, he should get married, she thought, even though he was a child, so that there would be a daughter-in-law in the house.

She had sacrificed all her desires and pleasures, deriving satisfaction only in giving, in sacrificing and bringing up the children. The soft palms of her hand had grown rough in domestic chores; her complexion had become pallid and there was increasing loss of hair. Feeding herself was only a ritual after feeding all. For her clothes, she managed with whatever was available; a little coconut oil was enough for her body. Her only wealth was her right to work. And now, for a year and half, she had lost even that right and lay bedridden.

Doctor after doctor had examined her; so many medicines had her body absorbed, but to no avail. The same soreness in the waist and the legs, the weakness was on the increase. She knew that her body was slowly wasting away.

She and *attar*! But the fragrance had turned through his body perhaps only to tease her. He was unusual that way; never cared for perfumes; often even forgot to shave, comb his hair or dress properly. Great in knowledge, a professor, everything looked nice on him, but surely no *attar*.

Who then passed it on to him?

How good was her husband and indeed, how generous God had been to her!

Darkness was deepening. Kamala wept; only a few wet drops of tears in the hot eyes.

Indira brought in a lamp. Kamala enquired and was told that Surababu had gone out.

"Where did he go?" she asked. "He did not tell me."

She fell silent.

The *attar* was available in the market and there was nothing exclusive about it.

The world was full of human beings too and if you seek, you get. No one waits. And all the concerns, all shows of love, were only for a while—something of a lie.

Turning back in the bed Kamala lay quiet; there more tears.

Indira stood beside her. He was used to her tears, but he felt sad everytime he saw them.

"What should I make for dinner?" he asked.

"How long do you expect me to be here that you should keep asking me?"

Her voice sounded slurred.

The effeminate Indira asked as he kept chewing the tip of his *dhoti*, "You are crying, sister? Why, won't you get well soon?"

"Let this body go into the hearth-fire. What use is this kind of living if suffering is all? Who cares of whom?" Kamala responded, her voice reflecting her despair.

Indira left.

Kamala wiped her face. She had frankly declared her wish to die at least before one and now felt somewhat light.

She lay coolly thinking of death, which was surely better than doing nothing except blinking.

But when would it come?

As she lay still, she reflected back on her life. She could not recollect any instance of benevolence from anyone but there were numerous instances of murmur at not getting the service expected of her.

Ghana was deeply attached to her but his first love was his studies, his future. Four months ago, even when she was critically ill, could he manage to stay for more than four days? His father also insisted that he should not disrupt his studies for too long. In fact, that was the chorus. Manika and Suna had to take care of their respective households. How often could they come? Each one, after all, had a world of her own.

The one, who was her own, had gone away for a walk, without uttering even a word for her!

The lights were on. Kamala looked outside, her mouth half open as if she had stopped in the midst of saying something and her mind had flown away elsewhere.

She again sifted through her memories. In these years after her marriage, some acquaintances had suffered broken homes, some others had left for the other world. She thought of the day of Ghana's birth, twenty-one years ago; the hospital, the pain, a small operation, dressing, the unseasonal rain and the bitter cold wind that made one shiver to one's spine.

The peace-loving professor would wake up with the sound of her crying with pain and say, "Can't you sleep quietly? The child had now woken up too!" The baby also cried bitterly.

Life leans on happiness. It cannot continue with a sense of fear submerging it. Sometimes she had let herself go in self-defence; ignored the precepts of the scriptures. The body remained a body, suffered injury, recovered and only awaited other injuries.

After Ghana came Manika and then Suna. They were the fruits of happiness, if not ecstasy. Even then she persuaded herself; the body's desires must end.

Often she would tell her weakling friend Sovana "My friend, life seems to be only a stretch of suffering and agony. Where is happiness? It was so wonderful, those days in our father's home! Swimming plucking flowers, climbing trees, racing to nowhere. Can anyone get back those carefree days?"

Often she remembered the living shadow of the strong

and healthy limbs and heard the seductive whispers of the past.

Her friend had understood.

After the birth of her second child she had low haemoglobin. There were other problems, like indigestion and frequent loose motions. Soon her body was only a frame of bones. Her husband was a foreman in steel plant and he looked strong as a Bhima.

She always agreed with Kamala. "Alas, who knew the pain involved in building a home and raising the children? How flitting is one's shine, one's strength!"

Kamala would nod and keep mum. She could never think of Surababu as greedy or cruel. She had the keys to their chests and he always brought to her whatever he earned. He had no fancy for anything. He could never be compared to her friend's husband.

She would negate her own words and console her friend, "It is all a matter of destiny, dear friend!" Kamala could guess her friend's condition from her crumpled clothes, unoiled hair and weak body. And she knew that the paan-chewing bony figure was indeed a rebel, but it suppressed more than it spoke.

Her friend managed to live, containing within her a secret spirit of revolt, but once again she was in the family way. This time, however, she could not live to see the offspring's face. Her foreman husband had the baby boy in his arms as the mother lay on the bed like a dirty cast-out piece of linen.

Kamala had heard the tragic finale from Surababu. With tears in his eyes, the sympathetic professor, a lover of literature, had given a graphic picture of the event. In his elegant words the event had come alive.

Kamala had felt the loss inside as a woman. Her consciousness that was looking for deliverance had, as it were, met her friend somewhere in the sky. She had a sudden vision of that bony face, a curve of smile; ridiculing life. Kamala used to pity that but today she herself was an object of pity. She felt as if it was her friend who had won.

She felt like asking, All of us would depart, sooner or later. Why then suffer this life? Her pain was returning with a vengeance as she remembered things and pieced them together.

One evening Surababu introduced to her a Shrimati Chandra Midha alias Usharani Devi from Siam. She was a professor in the Ceylonese women's academy. She had come under an exchange programme for teachers and taught English but had acquired proficiency in Hindi, Bengali and Tamil. She spent two months in Puri earlier when she learnt to speak fluently in Oriya. She was guileless, almost child-like, Surababu had added, "I am now proving it to her that her ancestors were from Kalinga and hence her knowledge of Oriya lay dormant in her."

Chandra Midha kept smiling but there was a swaying motion in her body as she brought her arms together and then threw them apart, like a gymnast.

"Swagatam!" said Surababu.

"Welcome!' she reciprocated and uttered a few phrases explaining the genesis of the word.

"Did you see how much she knows?' Surababu commented with great appreciation.

Chandra Midha winked and tried to compare the words of love in English, Hindi, Bengali and Oriya. Kamala laughed. Surababu said nothing.

"Devi Chandra Midha! How many children do you have?" asked Kamala.

Surababu stared hard at Kamala. Chandra Midha laughed strangely, and its ripples spread all over her face and along the rows of her pearly teeth inside her coral lips.

She asked Surababu, "Wachat?" Meaning what was that...
Surababu played the host and Kamala did not struggle to get up.

Let him explain to her she decided. From the drawing room their laughter floated in. Kamala understood Chandra Midha was really wonderful and her laughter was not only music but also the voice of a life free and fearless. It was something to be envied. Kamala enjoyed neither that health nor that freedom. From her narrow tradition-bound bylane she started at Chandra Midha's unhampered highway. For the first time she had felt a trepidation, a secret shiver of fear. No one explained it to her, but her feminine instinct seems to have read the situation all right.

That evening, she prayed, "O God, deliver me from this life!"

Interpretation of an event depended on one's point of view and the point of view was moulded by one's mood which in turn depended on several other factors.

Sometimes, she recalled the events he narrated to her and his analysis of them. She was not illiterate even though she hailed from a village. She had studied at the local primary school, had read scriptures to please her mother, and had perused, for her own pleasure, novels that inspired one to look for a hero in life.

Looking anew at the past, she felt that Surababu had never loved her; he loved only himself and had used her as a mirror for his self love.

At the beginning, he had tried to educate her, but had failed and given up. He had taken her out only when obliged to do so; otherwise he sat lost behind his pile of books all the while.

The selfish meaning of his monologue came back anew to her, Only if someone was there to help me a bit, I could have gone much farther. Doing a D.Litt. would not have been that difficult!

She remembered her cooking, her pain, her household worries and taking care of the kids—surely these were of little use for his D.Litt!

Well, now that a Chandra Midha had appeared in his life, let him work for a D.Litt and have it. How could she, a dwarf in knowledge, have done anything for him!

Often he gave his observations on womenfolk in our society; they were good housewives, but no good *Sahadharmini*—a partner in a husband's pursuit of his duty.

"Do you understand, Kama," he would say, "Dharma is not idol worship, it is one's activity according to one's ideal. If the husband is a doctor and the wife's *dharma* is the kitchen, do you think that makes for a good partnership?'

She also recalled his comments on life and society, with literature as his yardstick to judge them,

"Look at the ethics. Clever ones have interpreted them to suit their own interests. They hide their lies, their false pretenses behind their ethics. They don't have any faith in their hearts, but the name of Rama is always on their lips. Our womenfolk are never tired of vaunting their ethics, but live in the dark, narrow cubicles of the mind. Trying to be careful, they end up being selfish; sometimes the fool passes off as the catholic. And those who revel in sordid rumours and whose imaginations run amok put on dazzling vermilion marks on their forehead and wear a brooch with 'husband is the greatest guru' inscribed on it. True ethics does not include merely reserving one's body for the husband and letting the mind be a heap of filth."

To all these she had nodded. He must, after all, be right. All this must be in the books he teaches. She never questioned the relevance of such doctrines in practice.

Bisibabu, a senior scholar, often used to come to consult his "Sir". Handsome, with his bushy eyebrows ranged above his eye-glasses, he was a lovable person, ever smiling bright and exuding a sort of familiarity. One always felt comfortable and happy in his presence. Sometimes when Bisi was closeted with Surababu she had brought in tea and snacks for them. But suddenly one day, Surababu poured venom against him. "Don't trust that guy, a veritable devil under a sweetmask. Don't forget."

Since then she had never appeared before Bisi.

He had such complaints against many other people. Kamala now recollected how he always had something bad to whisper against so many of the familiar faces.

Kamala now began to read his nature in a new light. He had mastered her mind and had put shackles on her feet, but perhaps he had never trusted her.

And these are known as ethics, affection and togetherness!

An empty co-existence gilded by illusions, life had taken a backward stride and she would never regain her adolescent days.

Sometimes she felt like blurting out, "Sure enough, your globe-trotting Chandra Midha has seen so much, known so much, that her mind cannot but be broad, unlike ours. And she has no husband, no children and she does not depend on someone else for a living. Why should she fear anyone?"

But, she held back the surging words. Always she recalled his anxiety-ridden face, his sleepless nights. Was it not only for her? The memory of the spring of yesteryears always put her with her husband on a swing where there was no envy, no meanness, but only bathing in the blessings of flower-petals.

Let him be happy, let everyone be happy, let my life's lamp burn out before him, but let him continue in happiness.

It was as if the body was dying away slowly from the feet upwards. Like an empty vessel, the mind resonated even with a slight touch. She felt that the body and the mind were not mutually dependent but both were prisoners in the grip of time.

She had danced uncontrollably, not the dance of youth but of a half-dead leaf trembling precariously on a branch in the cold northern wind; a dance bereft of hope or any priming of forgiveness.

How could she forgive another when she wanted to die, not prepared to forgive even herself?

How healthy he is even now! Like a rock shedding the last drop of the lashing rain with ease, he had stood unaffected by ordeals. Time had rolled by; they had grown older and poorer, but he had marched forward and enviably kept his head high. Their three children were now well-placed in life.

Even now he would get up in the morning, do his exercises.

The earth in the morning would lay open before him and the sky would be a page of poertry.

He continued to combine his studies with the practice of sitar late into the night.

And what of her world? It was one of suffering and pain; a scorched mind, a little bed and all the movement confined to crawling to the toilet and back.

There was a hedge of small and big trees, beyond the window and in some distance at the back of a house. Leaning on them was the curve of the sky. The lonely, empty sky. Would she go there? When? But inside the body, the last drop of vitality still insists on living, to see the changing seasons, the familiar crows, house-sparrows, the kites; their movements and changing moods. And when the sky looked deep blue and the drum-stick tree bent down with flowers, she would try to forget her illness.

She called out to Indira, "How beautiful are these drumstick leaves and flowers! Why don't you cook them for Babu? He loves them, you know!"

The sound of human voice outside brought her happiness.

She knew that it was foolish to expect the healthy ones to look after the invalid all the time. That would be a deception, an illusion.

That is why she would tell him now and then, "I have become a burden to you. Please marry again." And the reply always was, "Please keep quiet. Are you mad? Won't people laugh at this?"

She was, indeed, losing her sanity since the arrival of this Usharani. Surababu insisted on calling her by this name instead of her original name. Her name, in different contexts, came up every day. He sang her praise in various tunes.

And lying in her bed, Kamala would realise that a healthy man looked only at a rising sun.

Her attendant Indira alone listened to her. "This is the way of the world, Indira, never trust a man!" she would say. Indira hardly understood the significance of that statement, but he had an instinctive wrath against the male gender. How much he wished that he were born a woman!

He would say, "You will recover sister!"

The two decrepit boats touched each other through inadequate words and then floated apart. Kamala derived some peace from her loneliness.

But she noticed the changing mood of her husband and marked how he looked brighter day by day. His face and his eyes betrayed rejuvenation. Sometimes he kept quiet as if under a spell; sometimes he jumped out of his reveries. His sitar played a new music. He returned late from the college and then went for a walk after dark.

In the beginning he used to inform her, "I have to be with Chandra Midha for a while to discuss a paper in comparative linguistics." Then he began avoiding her name. But he spent more and more time outside the home.

Nobody had told her anything, but Kamala understood that life would triumph over death.

Her husband exuded that fragrance once again; he was out on stroll once again!

What was that streak of fire on the horizon? The round large moon rose, beaming. Even the drumstick tree looked like a beauty in its haze.

She too had once hoped and desired to be like that.

Suddenly, she felt gigantic waves of a tide roll over her entire consciousness.

She had found something. She had something to say. But she was unable to articulate it in words. In any case there is no use for it. Yet her mouth remained half open.

Surababu returned at half past nine. He too was thinking of life all the way. He felt certain that life and happiness were inseparable.

So too were death, misery and narrowness.

Kamala, lay there, face upward as if looking at the moon. The mouth was slightly open; she had not been able to say what she wanted to say.

Translated from the Odia by
the author

16

ALI BABA'S DEATH

Ajeet Cour

*E*ventually, that man who belonged to the breed of lesser mortals, who was part and parcel of that faceless crowd which runs the network of offices, that creature called a clerk, jumped from the topmost floor of his Town Hall office.

Next day, down below the columns of the third pages of newspapers, where local news of robberies and rapes, suicides and accidents are printed, there was a two-and-half-line story: *Ram Lall, a clerk in the Municipal Corporation, jumped to his death from the top floor of the Town Hall.*

The same afternoon, a kitty party was in full swing at Mrs. Midha's house. Mrs. Mathur always felt a little uneasy at such parties because her husband had been stuck for the last five years in a very "unprofitable" department of the Defence Ministry. She could neither afford to buy the latest *sarees* nor the solitaires that other women exhibited with pride on such occasions. But she couldn't just sit back and let the world go by. She had to do something, to be a part of the crowd;

otherwise how could she go through every single boring day week after week?

So, she equipped herself with the latest news and took special care to read the newspaper more thoroughly on the mornings of the parties.

Yes, newspapers were the only source of news, if any. News on the idiot box was only about the powers that ruled, not only the box but the whole country, and that was no News.

It seems that the box believed in the happy dictum that *No news is good news*.

Mrs. Mathur had read the papers carefully in the morning, so she poised a piece of chicken *tikka* on the tip of her fork with great delicacy, and sighed, "Who knows who that poor Ram Lall was, who jumped to his death yesterday, from the top floor of the Town Hall office!"

Nobody else had read the paper that morning. A few clusters of diamonds glittered on a couple of perfumed earlobes, a few eyelashes fluttered, showing bewilderment and Mrs. Midha fulfilled the duty of an accomplished hostess by whispering, "Poor devil!"

Next afternoon, at lunch time, a group of journalists were busy draining beer bottles at the Press Club, with rickety tables and not-too-clean surroundings. They were talking loudly about the Tarapore Plant and the Peace-keeping Force in Sri Lanka, about Indo-Chinese relations and the Punjab problem.

Gupta, who brought out a four-page evening tabloid and had been nominated as a member of the Rajya Sabha a couple of years back, asked his neighbours on the table, "Any news about that Ram Lall?"

"Ram Lall is making use of the usual routine gimmicks. Every Chief Minister does the same when he is removed from power and is replaced by someone else. He starts looking for the dissidents, starts a whispering campaign against the current incumbent and unearths all his shady deals, to be then presented to the High Command. It is a vicious circle that never ends; one Humpty Dumpty being replaced by another! Ram Lall is also going through the same routine exercise these days," said Raj of *The Hindustan Times.*

"No, it is not the former Chief Minister I am talking about. I am referring to Ram Lall, who committed suicide yesterday."

"It is being investigated by our crime reporter. If there is any meat in the story, it would be filed tonight."

But actually everybody connected with this case had already got the "story" in his or her pocket. It was Pawan Manchanda who helped them get to the bottom of every truth related to the story, when he met them last evening, though we know that at the bottom of every truth there is a residue of that little something, called "Untruth".

Pawan Manchanda? Don't you know Pawan Manchanda? Strange! He is always around at all the social functions in the capital, where the glitterati of the city appear with the sole object of being seen by others; one of those all-powerful jugglers whose job is to make others see what is not ordinarily visible to the naked eye.

No, you are mistaken. There is nothing fraudulent about it. It is simply a part of the poor chap's job! He has been employed in the Corporation for this purpose only. Every large company, every public sector undertaking, every government organisation, every respectable business house, even the Prime Minister's Office, has such people on their payroll.

Yes, your guess is correct. Pawan Manchanda is a public relations officer. It is another thing that he, like all other cousins of his clan, hardly finds time for the "public" because he is too busy manipulating the all-powerful "fourth estate"; the media.

Such deaths and suicides, strikes or lockouts, labour unrest or any other ugly incident like that can be a matter of great embarrassment for any "respectable" organisation. So any news connected to such things is to be suppressed; if it can't be made to disappear, it has to be made palatable. That's what is known as "watering down" in the newspaper language; toning down the harshness of the mishaps by twisting the facts.

In fact, the previous day, around midday, the Municipal Commissioner had called Pawan Manchanda to his room. "What is happening? Who the hell was this Ram Lall? How did the news leak out to those vultures in the newspaper offices? I've already had six calls since morning! Why couldn't you do anything about it?"

Pawan Manchanda pasted a greasy smile on his pleasant face with its prematurely receding hairline and said in a meek, humble voice, "Sir, when Ram Lall came tumbling down with a bang and lay sprawled in the open space below, dead, how could I just make the dead body disappear?"

"I don't want excuses. If you couldn't make the dead body disappear, you could have at least seen to it that its news did not appear on the papers." The Commissioner Sahib's fury couldn't be extinguished today with placating smiles from Pawan Manchanda.

Anyway, both of them agreed on one point; that these journalists are very ungrateful. When they smell a meaty story, they forget about all the goodies that they have gulped down at the expense of their benefactors.

Pawan Manchanda was now a man on a mission! .

Firstly, he tried to trace down the trail of the suicide to the victim's own house. So many people commit suicide because of their domestic unhappiness, don't they?

There could be a million causes: Ram Lall's wife might be having an affair with someone else; Ram Lall's unmarried daughter might have become pregnant; his son might have got himself involved in a robbery. It could be anything!

But all investigative efforts in that direction came to a dead end!

Ram Lall's wife looked haggard in her early 30s, and was clad in a faded rag of a *saree*. Ram Lall's daughter was only seven, so there was no chance of her eloping or getting pregnant. His two sons were studying in the sixth and seventh standards in a government school, where children are not given lessons on conducting robberies. As you know, it is only the privileged sons of all-powerful politicians or heavyweight industrialists who go to the best public schools of the country and learn how to commit million-dollar frauds and yet evade the law.

But something must be done, brooded Pawan Manchanda. After all he was paid month after month, to manage these kinds of things. And that too with all the perks!

So he prepared a file. The file moved in rather an unprecedented hurry from table to table. This fast-moving file contained an initial complaint from some Mr. Bhardwaj—Pawan Manchanda was in a terrible hurry, so he couldn't think of a better name—for it was with one Bharadwaj's daughter that a matchmaker was trying to work out Pawan Manchanda's marriage and Ram Lall had demanded four hundred rupees from him as bribe to bring down the slab of his property tax.

The complaint was followed by a detailed enquiry which revealed Ram Lall was allegedly caught "red-handed" accepting the bribe.

All of us know quite well that occasionally some small-time clerks and *babus* are caught "red-handed" accepting bribes, running into three or four digit figures: Lighter bribes cannot help floating on the surface and are therefore readily visible. The heavier ones sink because of their weight and are not visible. You can look back on four decades of independent India; you will always find a small fry getting nabbed in these dirty acts.

The "file" also contained a chargesheet and suspension orders, which were allegedly awaiting the final signatures of the top boss.

It is evident that when chargesheet and suspension orders are making a stroll in the corridors of any office, the concerned person cannot be unaware of the approaching guillotine, Pawan Manchanda explained to the journalists over the phone and invited them over for a drink and snacks in a five-star hotel in the evening. For such important press conferences he was allowed to book a suite in a five-star hotel and serve scotch with the choicest of snacks.

Scotch, as you know, is very helpful in "watering down" any scandalous story!

The most exciting thing about the whole operation is that both parties think that they are befooling the other.

This bastard PRO is smiling like prostitute. As if we don't know...contemplate the reporters, downing glasses of Scotch and munching the choicest of *tikkas* and *kababs*.

In the meanwhile the PRO's mind is also at work... Enjoy your free drinks! You mean bastards! From your lousy salaries you can't even afford to have country liquor. Who doesn't know you are prostituting your pens?

But, the PRO and the reporters keep smiling at each other, because that's how all the dirty jobs are done honourably.

Don't you know we are cultured and civilised people? Cultured people shun naked truths. They keep themselves and the truth decently wrapped up.

Every PRO knows that after downing free Scotch, the reporters would be in no position to go to their offices and file their stories. They would just go home and collapse on their beds. And well after midnight, when they will be swinging between sleep and intoxication, they would sleep with their wives, taking them to be the Hema Malinis and the Madhuri Dixits.

In that case, what happens to the story? Where does it end?

But then, every problem has an inborn solution. Pawan Manchanda's scheme works and the "story" is successfully kept away from the press for the time being. Everybody slips it in his pocket and goes home. Each one of them would now present it to their news editors the next day.

Every profession has its own ethics after all!

So, Ram Lall's dead body was deprived of the knowledge of his own misappropriations. In all probability the story would be published when his body had already been reduced to a handful of ashes.

What about his soul? It is just a whiff of air. Moreover, who bothers about souls these days? One shouldn't get unnecessarily worried about something which you can't see and which can't harm anyone.

The next day, which was third day after Ram Lall's suicide, there was a news story in every newspaper that Ram Lall had been chargesheeted because of a complaint of corruption and bribery against him. Fearing that he would be suspended, he had ended his life by jumping from the top floor of his Town Hall office.

During these two days, Ram Lall's widow and children felt as if they had got buried under a heap of rubble. His death had shaken their world like an earthquake.

Since Ram Lall's death, the neighbours had been bringing them food.

Now this is something that does not happen in the upper-class homes. There, a deathly silence prevails in the house where someone dies, but life goes on. In any case, the servants have to eat. So food is cooked and everybody eats. Then, the people who call for condolence have to be served tea all the time, and as a result the kitchen never stops functioning.

As compared to the lower middle-class people, sorrow in the upper classes is expressed in a much more cultured and civilised manner.

The lowest strata of people also don't face any of these problems, because most of the time their hovels wear the look of deathly gloom. Their hearths remain cold most of the time. Death in the family means just loads of extra worry about the burial or cremation. Worrying about these extra expenses and running around to borrow from friends and neighbours doesn't leave any room for mourning their dead in a relaxed and leisurely manner.

On the third day, when newspapers published the story of Ram Lall's corruption, chargesheet and suspension, his wife didn't come to know of it. A newspaper is a luxury which people like her can't afford. These people hear only the news which comes flying like crows and perch on their roof-tops; "Flying News", which are popularly known as rumours.

Usually such news is connected with the happenings in their neighbour's houses. Most important ones are connected with the affairs of the sons and daughters in the neighbourhood.

Gradually, the important news of the city also filters in, which is usually of robberies or killings or suicides. On the national level, the news generally whispered around is connected with the affairs of important persons; news, that Indira Gandhi didn't cry when her son died in an air crash, that Rajiv Gandhi used to fly airplanes and now he is flying a kite named India, etc.

If you think objectively, the other news would hardly matter for these common people. The Gorbachev-Reagan Treaty and the Non-Aligned conference are as immaterial as the presence of a red or black government in Spain. What is happening in Kampuchea or Yugoslavia doesn't concern people who are worried about things like having to fold their legs, and lie like a crumpled ball on their beds, because their bedsheets are too short to cover them completely.

Ram Lall's wife hardly found any time to gossip, and was certainly not aware of what was happening in the world. She was a deeply religious woman, but didn't find time even to sit down and meditate in front of the small clay idol in the house. She bowed her head before it every morning and said a brief prayer for the welfare for her family. Flowers and incense sticks are costly, so their *Bhagwan* evidently couldn't enjoy this luxury in Ram Lall's house. But on some particular days, like *Janamashtami*, Ram Lall plucked some flowers from the park, on his way back from the milk-booth, and offered them to the deity. An incense stick and these flowers were enough to say "happy birthday" to *Bhagwan*.

Though Ram Lall's wife had no information about the newspaper story concerning her husband, it had already begun to spread around as it was the same type of juicy news which grows wings and reaches people who find it spicy enough to go running and whisper it into the neighbour's ears!

Eventually the news came flying and landed right in the lap of Ram Lall's widow, Prema.

She beat her breasts and cried, "It is wrong. A gross lie. Only I know how I went through the 30 days of the month. His salary never lasted beyond the 20th, and for the rest of the month we were always in debt. Anybody can check up from the grocer; we always owed him money. If my husband took any bribes, I wouldn't be sitting here today, worrying about how I am going to feed my children tomorrow."

The neighbours listened to her, expressed their sympathy, and went about their work.

These people, who belong to the lowest depths of the covered cauldron called "middle-class," are very selfish. They are worried about their own hearths and simply don't have time times for others.

Ram Lall's widow couldn't sleep at night. She felt she was lying on live coals.

And suddenly a thought flashed through her benumbed mind: he was a very quiet man. Always engrossed in his thoughts. Hardly talked. There might be another woman in his life, who he was spending all the "extra income" on. You never know these men!

And thus that man, who was less of a human being and more of a bullock, yoked to an oil press with blinkers on because he was a mere clerk, lost all his credentials within two and a half nights of his death.

He was naïve like many others of his clan—though his clan is getting extinct gradually. He thought that his children would at least be able to keep their heads high and feel proud of him because he was thoroughly honest: It was immaterial that his salary couldn't see his family through the month; that he hadn't bought himself a new suit for the last 20 years; that the soles of his shoes were so worn out that he could feel the heat of the tar road searing his skin. His consolation was bringing up his children in an atmosphere untarnished by the all-pervading, suffocating smoke of corruption. He was proud and untiring and had high moral values, though he knew that these values sold cheaper than even onions in the market!

He was guilty of the twin sins of poverty and honesty!

A poor man should be able to claim his rights or grab them by force. If he is unable to do either, he would himself be robbed of them.

Ram Lall was thus destined to be robbed, though it was to happen to him after his death.

In fact, he came to know about the "robbery" a little before his death. When his knowledge dawned on him, he decided to call it a day.

This is how it happened.

It all started with this transfer, which brought him to the chair of the private secretary to the commissioner who was in charge of the Public Works Department in the Town Hall of the city.

His fellow clerks congratulated him.

"What for?" he said in a little bewilderment. "This is not even a promotion. A clerk is just a like bullock under a yoke; it is immaterial whether he ploughs the field or pulls a cart. What difference does it make?"

"Unbelievable! You talk about the difference when you occupy that magical chair. Tons of money exchanges hands in the room of your new boss. And when devotees come with their offerings to the God, the priest also gets his share," one of them said with meaningful glee.

Everybody laughed, and Ram Lall was very uncomfortable. The light-hearted chatter seemed to hit him like pebbles. He merely sighed and thought, Oh God, please save my honour and integrity in this infernal place.

When he started working, his boss dictated to him a list of important visitors with a standing order, "If they call, connect them to me immediately. If they drop in, let them into my room at once."

All the rest he had to understand himself, gradually, with experience. He also had to learn to read the subtle changes in the boss' moods, manifested by little gestures like the look in his eyes or his raised eyebrows. Correct response to these different moods became an essential part of his job.

He had to make instant decisions on who he should allow to enter the all-powerful boss' room, who he should offer tea to if the boss was busy. He had to learn to identify people who were nothing but mere nuisance and also those it was not "profitable" for the boss to meet. Who wants to waste his time for nothing!

Sitting in his private secretary's chair, Ram Lall entered a mysterious world where money was God; The Almighty one! If someone higher in the political hierarchy rang up the boss and wanted him to "help" somebody, it only meant that money had changed hands elsewhere.

Ram Lall realised that he was surrounded by thieves. He felt that he was Ali Baba. Yes, that's what he was. Surrounded by not forty, but forty thousand thieves!

He thought of lot of councillors, members of parliament and of state assemblies, big politicians and their cronies, who helped them during elections and who needed to be carefully nurtured all the time. He now thought that they were all thieves!

There were a lot of smaller thieves behind every big thief, like the wooden Russian dolls. You open the bigger one, and hidden inside is a smaller one. You open that one, and there is still a smaller one inside. Dolls within dolls, thieves within thieves.

The Ali Baba of *Arabian Nights* was able to make those forty thieves lick dust, but Ram Lall was unable to do anything. He just cursed the day he was transferred to this post. He felt all these thieves were only out to rob him because he was a minuscule version of India, a symbolic heir to the whole country which was being robbed.

Sitting in that chair he felt that his third eye had opened. It was, what they call, "Shiva's eye." But unlike Shiva, he was incapable of destroying the universe with an angry look of his third eye. Now he could see through things. Like Shiva he was drinking the poison of his new awareness.

With the third eye, he realised how millions of people did without medicines, why children did not have access to education, why the bones of young people *are* eaten away by termites and only they rotted away because there were no jobs for them even when they wanted to work, how freshly-built tar and coal roads developed bumps and potholes after the first monsoon shower and why every politician spent millions to fight for elections, though after being elected his total salary was less that of Ram Lall's.

But Ram Lall could not do anything about it. Like a dutiful assistant he was supposed to just say, "Yes Sir" or "All right Sir", and nothing else. He was supposed to take dictations from his boss, type out letters, take notes and attend telephone calls.

In fact, his job was his only identity.

"Ram Lall? Which Ram Lall?" "Ram Lall, son of Bhairon Prasad."

"Who the hell is Bhairon Prasad? In this country, millions of Ram Lalls and Bhairon Prasads are sold cheaper than turnips, and millions rot in the warehouses."

"The Ram Lall who is private secretary to the Commissioner of Public Works, and works in the Town Hall."

"Ah well, *that* Ram Lall!"

This was what distinguished him from the others.

He had three children who needed food, clothes, medicines, fee for their schools, money for books and notebooks. They were the future of the country. It was immaterial if they never had enough to eat, and never had new books when they went to new classes. Their trousers were always coming off at their seams and their shirts always had worn-out collars.

Ram Lall's wife, Prema, was like a juggler, who always managed to make their shirts by cutting off the frayed portions of Ram Lall's worn-out ones; she could shorten the length, alter the size of the cuffs, with her magic touch after trimming the sleeves but she could never learn to stitch new collars. That is why the same collars travelled from Ram Lall's neck down to the necks of the children.

Like the country's hunger and poverty, these collars descended from one generation to another and adorned the necks of those who were the country's future.

They were always accused and reprimanded by their teachers: for coming late, for not doing their homework properly and for not depositing the fee in time etc.

Because Ram Lall was carrying the burden of this "future of the country" on his tired shoulders, he couldn't even shrug them off like the mythological Atlas. But Atlas is a god after all. Gods are free to do anything.

But Ram Lall couldn't even think of shrugging his shoulders, because if he did that, he and his family would get buried in the rubble of the ensuing earthquake.

So Ram Lall kept doing his job silently, gulping down all the poison of his newly acquired knowledge.

The monsoons set in. It rained incessantly for two days, and on the third morning, the roof of a newly-constructed school collapsed like a pack of cards and four children died on the spot. Twenty-three of the seriously injured were taken to the hospital.

Ram Lall knew the contractor who had been commissioned to build that school. It was through Ram Lall that his boss had hinted to the contractor that he needed a good architect for his thousand-yard plot of land The contractor had given an all-knowing smile and said, "Why only an architect? I shall get the house built. Ask Sahib to leave it to me and stop worrying about it."

Ram Lall knew it was a dirty deal, but dutifully conveyed the message to his boss.

But afterwards, he felt he was one of the accomplices to this act of corruption.

The contractor kept his word and the house was constructed within six or seven months—one-and-a-half storeyed bungalow. Marble was brought from Makrana, and tiles from Bombay. Sanitary fittings, lights and chandeliers, fans and air-conditioners, everything was purchased under the personal supervision of the Commissioner Sahib's wife.

Ram Lall was sometimes ordered to take Mem Sahib to the market where she selected the fittings and accessories, and the contractor made the payments.

After completion, the house looked not only beautiful but was also sturdy enough to be used by the next three generations of the boss.

Who bothers about school buildings, even if they collapse a few days after their construction! The children who die under the rubble don't count. Thousands are born every day!

And if you ask me honestly, who asks these children to go to schools? Why should they? They can also shine shoes on the pavements, clean plates at the wayside *dhabas*, work as domestic servants or in the backyards of factories, carry luggage, hawk newspapers at road-crossings. Well, they can do anything. Why the hell should they pick up their satchels and walk to the schools? Don't they know that school buildings are make-believe structures and come crashing down in the first monsoon shower?

Ram Lall was angry.

He was angry with the children who were dead, with the boss, with the contractor and with himself.

In the afternoon the boss called him in and with honeyed politeness asked him to collect all the files concerning the construction jobs given to the contractor who had built that school, and come to the *kothi*, his new bungalow, in the evening.

In the evening, when Ram Lall reached Sahib's house, carrying a huge load of relevant files, he found the contractor and his son in the drawing room, having drinks with the boss.

The boss told him, "Well, Ram Lall, keep the files on that table, and mark the concerned documents of the contract for the school building."

Ram Lall started doing what he was told quietly and mechanically.

The contractor realised Ram Lall's importance, filled up a glass and offered it to him but he, in a meek voice, said that he had never touched liquor.

But the contractor persisted, "Ram Lall. You must have a sip. If you don't we will feel really hurt."

The boss was smiling silently, and was looking on with a kind of patience he was not generally known to possess.

Ram Lall looked at him, and feeling grateful and vengeful at the same time, took the glass and gulped it down in one go. He then held out his empty glass. The contractor refilled it.

After gulping down the second peg, he sat back and relaxed. He opened his eyes and looked around. He had come to this room many a times, but always with downcast eyes. Today he looked up for the first time in his life, and saw TV, the video player, the Persian carpets, the flowers in the cut-glass vases, the dinner sets, the music system.

And he got up and walked out.

On his way home he kept abusing himself, Ram Lall, you worthless man, what did you achieve in life? What the hell did you accomplish? You couldn't give two square meals to your family, nor give them any happiness. You couldn't even save those unfortunate children who died under the rubble of the school building. You are worse than a dead dog, Ram Lall.

He was drunk and therefore keenly aware of life.

The whole night he kept arguing with himself…the whole long night he kept talking to himself. He was angry with the whole world.

In the morning he got up.

He was sober and very serious

He took out a new blade, shaved, took his bath, changed, and went to office.

He kept climbing the stairs till he reached the top floor. From there, he jumped down.

Translated from the Punjabi by
the author

17

COME RAIN COME SUNSHINE

Sant Singh Sekhon

Since the day Mangal Singh got himself recruited in the Army, Basant Kaur had to perform the ordeal of fetching green fodder, for the buffalo from their field.

Of the last six months, two were of rainy the season, when there was abundance of grass in the village meadows and there was no need to feed the buffalo at home. Since Basant Kaur's buffalo was not yielding any milk those days, it had to suffice on what it grazed in the meadow.

The cowherd took the buffalo out every morning to graze and for this he was paid two rupees every month. But for the last two months, especially since it had calved, it needed to be fed green corn-fodder. That had to be fetched from their field, which had been let out to share-croppers. Basant Kaur's mother-in-law, the old Mohan Kaur, had poor eyesight and was constantly worried about her going to the fields alone. Had her sight been good, she would have watched Basant Kaur's every step, to and from the fields. Unfortunately for her, even the household food lying scattered was no longer discernable to her.

"My child, the time is bad. One has to be on guard to save honour and self-respect." She would warn Basant Kaur.

"Don't you worry, mother. Nobody can dare cast an evil eye on me," Basant always answered confidently.

"Yes, dear, if one is good, no one can dare make a pass."

Though Basant was a picture of stoic aloofness, Gurdev Singh, son of the landlord, Hardayal Singh, did have designs on her.

For the last 15 days, assuring himself of Basant's timings of going to the fields, he invariably crossed her path and coughed meaningfully while near her. Basant Kaur kept her feelings in control and neither liked nor disdained his counterfeit cough.

In fact, she prided herself for not being excited at all by his attentions.

She laughed inwardly at Gurdev's futile attempts to pursue her. She had the pride and self-assurance of a skilled swimmer who rejoices at the rapids and the currents in a river. She returned home daily with the load of fodder on her head, proud of her unfaltering steps.

Mangal Singh had enlisted himself in the Army, against the wishes of his mother and wife. In fact, there had been no other alternative. Though the price of the produce was quite good, his landholding was too small to sustain his family.

He laboured hard, sweated and heaved, yet, in spite of his best efforts, he had incurred a debt of a thousand rupees. If he had continued tilling his meagre holdings for a few more years, even these would have slipped out of his hands. Tired and helpless, he decided to join the Army.

He had paid off some of his debts and with the sale of the pair of oxens and then some unnecessary farm implements the debts were further reduced to some five hundred.

The land was precious to them, but more than that was the family honour.

Mohan Kaur was worried that Basant would surely attract unwanted attention. She would have endured another five years of poverty and privation if Mangal Singh had stayed home to keep an eye on Basant. But he had chosen to go.

After Mangal left, Basant was inconsolable for a few days. Then, after two months he sent a money order of 50 rupees. Mohan Kaur spent 20 rupees to buy a woollen suit for Basant and warm clothing for her one-year-old daughter. She purchased a light suit for herself too. Another 20 rupees were spent on buying mustard cakes, cotton seeds etc. to mix in the fodder for the buffalo. The special care of the animal resulted in an increase of the milk yield. The level of the *ghee* (clarified butter) in the tin can also began to rise.

Gurdev found some pretext to come in front of Basant for about 15 days.

In the meanwhile, Basant had a feeling that though her dress had undergone just three or four washings it had begun to show signs of fading. Next day she changed her suit. That day she took her bath rather leisurely.

On her way to the fields, in her musings she laughed, saying to herself, today Gurdev will not to be able to laugh. He will be impressed.

That was what happened exactly. When Gurdev Singh and Basant Kaur came face to face, he did not cough as usual to attract her attention.

Instead, he blurted, "Basant Kaur has Mangal Singh come on leave?"

"No, Gurdev."

"Well, is he expected tomorrow?" Gurdev fired another question.

"We have no information about his arrival." Basant maintained her shy manner and continued on her way.

Three days after this meeting, Gurdev Singh appeared in front of Basant Kaur, right at the moment when, after cutting fodder with a sickle and binding it into a big sheaf, she was looking for somebody to help lift it to her head.

Gurdev Singh extended a helping hand, unsolicited. She was startled at his sudden appearance and, without uttering a word of thanks, continued towards her home with the fodder.

Reaching home, the first thing she heard were the usual words of warning of Mohan Kaur, "Be careful, my child, you must not be mesmerised by anybody's oily words and bring shame to the family. The village folk do not behave decently and the landlord's son is utterly unrestrained."

Basant Kaur heeded her advice, but all the same she felt as if caught in a vice. She prayed, God better instill some sense in Gurdev Singh.

She promised to buy sugar-bubbles, worth five paise, as offering, if somehow Gurdev desisted from confronting her from the next day onwards. She once again assured Mohan Kaur, with great confidence, of her moral strength. But her urge to dress well did not abate.

She changed her suit, if not every day, then at least every third day.

One day, a neighbourhood scallywag had the audacity to say, "Hey dame, where do you think you are going, to bring fodder home or to some festival?"

Basant Kaur brushed his remark away with a contemptuous laugh.

She now changed her timing of leaving for fodder by a few minutes, this way or that, every day. Gurdev sometimes missed helping her lift the fodder sheaf. Anyway, he still found opportunities to meet her on the way.

After a fortnight, a letter came from Mangal Singh, stating that he would be coming home on leave for a month, in some 15 days time.

Mohan Kaur felt relieved.

Basant Kaur too was elated. Her days and nights passed, anticipating the pleasures and joys of being with her husband. She felt irritated at Gurdev for coming forward to help her lift the fodder to her head.

One day, while helping her, Gurdev intentionally touched her hand.

She was infuriated and soundly swore at him.

But Gurdev smiled, waving away her remarks sportingly.

Even after that incident, neither Basant Kaur changed her style of dressing up nor did Gurdev cease to bother her.

In fact, when he learnt from the village gossip that Mangal Singh was expected to arrive very soon, he decided to make some sure move before it was too late.

Basant Kaur, in her efforts to avoid encountering Gurdev, started leaving for the fields earlier or later than her wont time, but still in his insistent manner he was found invariably loitering around while she cut and bundled the fodder. He would pass some remark appreciating her beauty or expressing his ardent love for her. She remained unresponsive as ever.

There were times when he said something so brazen that she had to tell him curtly, "Leave it, I will manage it myself." Cut with such disdain, he continued to shamefacedly help her lift her burden.

One day, before helping her lift the bundle, he took her hands in his, firmly, and looked at her face cajolingly.

"Leave my hands, Gurdev Singh," said Basant Kaur, a picture of self control, "My husband is due on leave tomorrow."

Gurdev immediately released her hands.

"How long is his leave? He asked

"One month."

Without uttering another word, Gurdev Singh helped her lift the fodder to her head and she continued on her way.

That day, again, Basant Kaur felt victorious. She could not however fathom what made her feel that way; her victory over herself or Gurdev Singh.

Next morning, Mangal Singh arrived home and Basant Kaur's duty to fetch fodder temporarily came to an end.

Next evening, when Gurdev Singh arrived at his usual time looking for Basant Kaur, he found Mangal Singh bundling the fodder instead. He contemplated moving away but then thought it more prudent to meet the latter.

"When did you arrive, Mangal Singh?" he asked

"I came this very day, Sardar Gurdev Singh. But how do you happen to be here?"

"I was just loitering aimlessly." Gurdev Singh was tactful and asked. "Who fetched fodder earlier?"

"Basant Kaur used to come for it."

"I have seen her heaving her load a few times, but you should have hired some helping hand for this job." Gurdev said, showing one farmer's empathy to the other.

"If we had the capability to hire a fieldworker, there would be no need for me to enlist in the Army. Anyway Basant Kaur lost no grace fetching fodder home."

Gurdev Singh laughed unabashed. "What did she have to lose in your absence?"

Mangal smiled as he shared the joke, but then concentrated on his work as Gurdev moved away.

"How long are you going to remain in the Army, Mangal Singh?" One day his mother asked him.

"They are not going to send me on pension so soon, mother. I have been in the Army for six months only," Mangal Singh replied.

"Pension, my son is a long time away. What will become of the house when I am gone? I am like a tree at the edge of the bank. Why don't you take Basant Kaur along with you?"

"What is there to worry about, mother, as long as you are here?"

"There is nothing to worry, of course. Basant Kaur, I do not want to praise her in her presence, is pure gold. But time is bad, indeed."

"Who cares about time?" said Mangal Singh sure of the moral strength of his wife.

"My son, we suffer no shortages. You have returned another ₹150 to the money lender. Only 400 are left of the loan and if we sell the buffalo, even that can be paid off."

"What do you want me to do?"

"Come back home and till your land, what else?"

"We will need ₹500 to buy a pair of bullocks."

Mother had not looked at the problem from this angle.

"We are certainly going to sell the buffalo," Basant Kaur joined the discussion, "Within six months our heifer is going to calf."

This two-and-a-half year old young buffalo was a gift from her parents and was still in their care.

"But, what about the oxen?"

"Oxen" Basant Kaur thought for a while and said, "I have a few items of jewellery that we can sell. We can buy new ornaments when, God willing, we have good harvest."

"No daughter, under no circumstances shall we take away your ornaments," said Mohan Kaur, "If we have a good harvest, we will be able to return any loan incurred against the purchase of the oxen."

"Look mother," Mangal Singh said, "Good harvest is never certain. It will require at least two good harvests to pay off our debts. If the harvest fails, the debts will increase, leaving us adrift. I get 50 rupees on the fifth of every month—come rain come sunshine. You better be helpful and not discourage me."

The women were left silent by these words of Mangal Singh.

On their insistence, Mangal Singh sold the buffalo for ₹300 and got rid of the debt he had incurred.

There was a tin of *ghee* in the house. The day before Mangal Singh was to leave to join his regiment, Basant Kaur put the tin over the kitchen fire, to melt the butter oil.

Mangal Singh asked about its need. To which she shot a question in reply, "Will you not take some with you?"

"What am I to carry it for? We get all our requirements from the Government," Mangal Singh said.

"That useless oil," she remarked, proud of the quality of her *ghee*, "How do we know what that contains."

"That must be the vegetable oil, my son," Mohan Kaur added.

"I have not returned any weaker for that," Mangal Singh said sarcastically, "Now you do not have a milch animal anymore. Use this for your bread, till Basant Kaur's young buffalo calves."

In spite of protests from the two women Mangal Singh removed the tin can from the fireplace.

"Let us warm it," Basant Kaur said.

"You warm it after I leave."

Even then, dry pudding was prepared for him, to take along.

That night, when Basant Kaur was alone with Mangal Singh, she snuggled closer to him and softly said,

"Please send for me wherever you are and soon."

"Who will take care of mother?" Mangal Singh said.

Basant Kaur had no answer for this.

Still she insisted, "I cannot be happy here anymore."

She embraced Mangal Singh, sobbing inconsolably. She was like a bird, wet and tired, seeking safety and comfort of her nest.

Translated from the Punjabi by
Ranjit Singh

18

NEITHER SONG NOR FICTION

Popati Hiranandani

$\mathscr{I}$ was a school girl, barely on the threshold of my youth, when I saw him.

Sheela had just joined our MJ Higher Secondary School for Girls, in Ahmedabad. Her father had been transferred here from Jaipur. Our class teacher made Sheela sit beside me on the same bench. Soon, we became friends. Whenever we had to study together, we visited each other's house.

On one such visit, I saw Sheela's brother Pratap. They called him Partu at home. From that moment, he became the centre of my world. My thoughts and emotions revolved around him. I would think of nothing else except him.

In his absence, I would call his name with my eyes closed. In his presence, my face would turn crimson and my heart used to beat fast, I was afraid the others would hear the sound of my heartbeats. Whenever I saw a movie, Partu became the hero on the screen and I, his heroine, pining for him.

Everyone knows that when two people become emotionally

involved, there is an unspoken bond of communication between them. And so it happened that whenever we met, Partu would stare at me and smile. What did he want to say, I often wondered.

I had heard from friends that boys are generally shy in these matters. Hence, if a girl is interested in a boy, it is she who has to make the first move. So, I wrote a letter in the form of a verse, expressing my feelings. The words were:

A bewitching smile adorns your lips when I look at you
Is this jewel for me or somebody else?
A shadow seems to accompany you when I see you
Is it me or somebody else
I don't know your feelings
But, I kiss the feet of my idol
who adorns the throne of my heart.

I waited for one day, and then the next.

On the third day, I started crying from sheer disappointment.

But on the fourth day Partu approached me, hurriedly handed me a piece of paper and walked away in the opposite direction.

I opened the letter with trembling fingers. Ah! My heart soared with joy and my feet danced as I read his reply. He had written:

In my mind a name produces the music of Veena
And my heart cries aloud like a flamingo
Separated from his sweetheart
Like a creeper, her image clings to me always
The name is Manorama
And for me she is Tilottama
The celestial beauty.

I was so happy. It seemed the sky, with its millions of shining stars, has come down to bless me! I don't know for how long I continued to live in this dream world which belonged to me alone.

And one day, I heard that Sheela's father had got his transfer orders. He had to go back to Jaipur and so all of them left Ahmedabad.

For me, the world came to an end. My dreams were shattered. I withdrew to my room, where I spent hours thinking of Partu and shedding tears.

Time passed and I grew up. Partu became a hazy memory. I passed my matriculation and joined college. I had just finished my first year when I was married to a staid, serious-looking young man.

Yes, I fell in love with my husband the very first night! There was a great difference between my love for Partu and my love for my husband. The emotions of my first love were like the foam on the mouth of laughing waves, and the love for my husband was like a swan studded with gems and diamonds.

But even then, I was romantic and was always busy with my dreamy thoughts of sailing in white silvery boats or flying along with crimson clouds in the sky!

But alas! My husband was not a romantic man. He was neither a Dushyanta nor a Devdas. He was not a sentimental lover like Shah Jahan or King Tamachi. He never told me that I was beautiful or paid me any compliments.

I have read in books that when a man is in love, he says to his beloved, *Oh! you are just like a creeper of sweet-smelling saffron!* or *Oh! my sweetheart your face is just like a fully bloomed rose flower!* My husband never expressed his love for me.

One day, I said to him, "You do not love me."

He smiled and then turned his face away as if he wanted to conceal his feelings. After a while he said: "Do you want me to compose a poem of love for you?"

His reply unnerved me, particularly the words "love" and "poem". I did not want him to know anything about my school days' romance. From that day onwards, I never spoke of love.

I had become a mother of two children and enjoyed looking after my loved ones, yet, there were moments when I felt unfulfilled because I longed to hear endearing words from my husband. I knew he loved me. But he was always a little distant and undemonstrative.

One day I saw a reddish mark on his shirt collar.

This aroused my suspicion and jealousy became an obsession with me. It pursued me everywhere like a ghost. I became a foolish, irrational woman. I forgot all about the tender care with which my husband looked after me—his politeness, his kindness and his unfailing generosity.

I tried to keep him home, as much as possible. Though we had servants to do the household chores, I made him go to the grocery shop to buy tea, salt and soap.

Under one pretext or the other, I pretended to be busy, making him sit with the children to help them with their homework. I knew that when he returned from the office, he was exhausted, as he was the chief accountant in a private company, and his duties were demanding.

Even so, I would make him accompany me to a play or a musical programme for which I used to buy tickets in advance, without even asking him if he would like to go.

He was quite baffled by my strange behaviour. He would look at me with a question in his eyes. But he said nothing and tolerated everything quietly.

That made me more suspicious and angrier. I said to myself, "He must be guilty, otherwise how can he be so quiet."

I went to the extent of opening his letters, searching his trouser pockets and shirts, looking into his files and papers. Almost daily I called up his office, under some pretext or the other, to find out if he was there or had gone to some restaurant or hotel.

One day, my cousin invited us for *Satyanarayan Puja*. The Brahmin, who had been called to perform the ceremony, made the married couples go round the *havan* fire. Tying the knot of the husband's *kurta* with the *pallav* of the wife's *saree*, he told the couples that they would always remain happy and united.

Seeing this, I told my husband, "Let us go round the fire."

He replied, "If two persons could be brought closer by tying their clothes together, then all the people in this world would have solved their problems in this way."

I was hurt by this reply. It confirmed my worst suspicions. I was sure there was another woman in his life. Who is she? I must find out who she is…All sorts of questions kept whirling in my mind.

After a few days, his colleagues decided to go on a picnic to Matheran the weekend. They hired a bungalow there. When my husband told me about this picnic, I readily agreed. At least he will be away from that woman, even if it is for a short period, I said to myself.

It was wonderful in Matheran. We loved its scenic beauty, the peaceful surroundings and the pure, cool breeze of the mountains. Everybody was in a good mood. Mrs. Patel would rest her head on her husband's shoulder every now and then. Mr. Kamat and his wife liked to sit on the swing in the garden.

Mrs. Iyengar whispered something in her husband's ear and both of them disappeared for hours.

It was only my husband who would not relax in this manner. He said he did not believe in such a display of emotions. "It is shallow to display your private feelings in public," he would say.

Among us there was one Mrs. Deshmukh who had come alone. She would go for long walks every morning and evening.

The next morning, my husband got up early and said, "Why don't you get up? We can go for a long walk."

That's it! She is the one in my husband's life, I thought. Tears welled up in my eyes. "If you like, you can go," I replied.

Without a word, he got dressed and went for a walk with her.

When he returned, I bombarded him with questions. "Why did you go? And where did you go? How dare you go with her?" and I started crying.

"After thunder, the rains must come," he said smiling.

Then he sat down beside me, took my hand in his and said gently, "Manorama! Our friends are waiting for us outside. What are you saying? At least lower your voice."

But I raised my voice even more and cried, "Let them be there, when you don't care for the people, why should I? Why don't you bring her home?"

He was taken aback. "Bring who home?"

"Your lady love, who else," I said.

He was angry now. "Are you mad?" he asked.

"Yes, I am mad. You are trying to make me lose my mind, so that you can bring her home. But rest assured, I'll never let that happen."

He smiled again and said, "I really don't know what you are talking about.

His smile added further fuel to the fire, and I became furious and shouted, "Don't pretend to be innocent. Bring that Mrs. Deshmukh woman here. I have to settle accounts with her."

"Mrs. Deshmukh?" he asked and added, "Don't you know she left Matheran yesterday, by the early morning train?"

I was confused. My head started spinning. I stuttered "Oh! I thought you and she...I mean she and you..." And my voice trailed off.

"Oh! So you are still that school girl Manorama, who thinks life is fiction, a romantic story that has no end. My dear, I am not a hero of your love story or a poem. Listen, do you remember Partu? He was my classmate, and it was I who wrote that verse in reply to your letter. But I thought you had grown up. You are a married woman now, with two children. How can you be so foolish?"

Tenderly he took my hands in his and said, "Get ready and wipe your tears, we must go and join our friends."

Translated from the Sindhi by
the author

19

HAPPY NEW GEAR

Ashokamitran

"Not going for practice today?" Mallayya's sister-in-law asked.

"Hmmm...I will go." he gave a rub to his left cheek. The master had said that the driving lesson would be on the main roads today. Mallayya felt too limp to leave the hut today. He could dilly-dally for a little while more. But it would have to be a yes or no within 15 minutes.

The time to tarry was cut short.

Mallayya's brother, a tuner in the workshop nearby, came back early too. "Not yet at the driving school?" he asked Mallayya.

The workshop was near a school. The noise emanating from the workshop could be very distracting. And so it remained closed from 10 in the morning to four in the afternoon. It was very unusual for the workshop to close before 10 in the morning. This was one of those days.

Mallayya got up and put on his shirt. It was his brother who had paid an advance fee of a hundred rupees so that

Mallayya, who had grazed cattle in Warangal till then, could learn to drive.

His sister-in-law brought a tumbler of something they all called coffee for her husband. It was the colour of ash.

Actually, she had Tamilised the whole family. Within months of marriage, Mallayya's brother was three-fourths de-Andhraised. Their two children spoke nothing but Tamil. But Mallayya's sister-in-law refused to learn even a few words of Telugu.

Mallayya dislodged a piece of looking glass from the thatched roof and came out into the open to have a look at his face.

His left cheek was slightly swollen, with the result his eye had narrowed a little. Mallayya passed his fingers through his hair in a manner of combing. What good was groomed hair when everything else was in an awful shape? He fixed the mirror back into the slit in the roof.

"You'd better have the gruel," his sister-in-law said as he was about to leave.

Mallayya almost threw up. That blessed Tamil gruel was awful. Maybe not! It tasted well. Only he was in no mood to relish it.

Mallayya walked along the rail track till he came to the level-crossing. On his right was T. Nagar and the driving school. Straight along was the Mambalam suburban station. On the left was old Mambalam. He wondered if he should go there and sit idly by the dirty pond. Buffaloes were washed in that pond. Some Brahmins performed funeral rites there. Only beliefs connected with death could prod anyone to get into the pond; that and the brave boys splashing water as they washed the buffaloes.

Nagarajan came over the railway crossing just then.

"Master not there yet?" he asked Mallayya.

"I have just got here," Mallayya replied.

Nagarajan too had a slightly swollen left cheek. "On the main roads today, isn't it?" he asked. His left eye too had narrowed a little. His face also wore an expression of doom.

The shoe shop had not opened yet. Nagarajan stood at the steps, while Mallayya opened the adjoining gate and walked up to the old car standing in a corner of the garden. It was a tiny car, to seat two tiny people in the front and two tiny people at the back.

The bungalow people charged 20 rupees a month for letting them park the car in their premises. Mallayya wiped the car clean. He walked around the bungalow to get some water from the well for the radiator. When he got back, he saw that the master had arrived. Nagarajan stood still beside him.

The master shouted at Mallayya in his own brand of Telugu which was like this: "Why sir you late so are? Why not did you come like in time that day?"

"I had to help my sister-in-law," Mallayya lied. He wished the master wouldn't make it a point to talk to him in Telugu.

"Hurry up! No more delay," the master said.

Nagarajan stood as though in a daze.

There was a difference between students like Nagarajan and students like Mallayya. The latter had to clean the car and see to the oil and water. Not Nagarajan. Otherwise, all students were treated alike. All had their left cheeks bashed by the master during practice.

The master slapped Mallayya for having flooded the radiator.

Nagarajan took out a bottle from the dashboard. The master switched on the ignition, opened the bonnet of the car, anointed the carburetor with drops of petrol from the bottle.

He dived into the engine after that, and pulled the accelerator wire. The car kicked...four to five times again... and then came to a standstill.

The master straightened his back and, placing his hand on his hips, shouted, "Push!"

Mallayya and Nagarajan pushed the car. The master steered from outside, helping the car slip into the street. Then he got into the car.

Just then a fruit seller placed her basket right in the way; the master shouted at her and she moved aside.

Mallayya and Nagarajan continued to push. They were now panting.

The street was congested and they had to stop every now and then. After about 15 minutes of pushing and cajoling, the engine purred.

Nagarajan and Mallayya got into the car.

"You!" the master shouted at Mallayya. "Sit here!"

Mallayya sat next to the master.

Master drove towards Saidapet. The car slowed every time a temple was sighted. The master left the steering to fold his hands in obeisance before every deity.

He brought the car to a halt at the Saidapet crossing.

"You first," he said to Mallayya.

Mallayya changed the gear to neutral.

"Start!" the master yelled.

Mallayya obeyed. The car sputtered—once, twice, thrice. And then, everything went dead.

Mallayya sat in a daze.

"Start the damn thing," the master suggested.

Mallayya tried again. The car did lurch forward. But, it also jumped backwards.

The master simply stared. "Start again," he said tonelessly.

Mallayya went through all the motions. The car inched forward and went ahead, with jerks.

The urchins, who had collected on the road to watch the fun, gave a loud, gleeful howl.

A hen, inevitably, just then, decided to cross the road. Mallayya dodged the hen and pressed the brake. The hen stood in the middle of the road and gave a contemptuous look. The engine died under its stare, kicking a little.

There was no stopping the master this time.

Mallayya could dodge only a few of the master's blows.

"How should I often you tell? Gently the clutch release?" the master said frighteningly. Even in anger, he spoke to Mallayya in his own version of Telugu.

The set of urchins surrounded the car again.

"Get out now! Get you Sir just out!" the master ordered Mallayya.

"You, now!" the master beckoned Nagarajan.

Nagarajan slipped into the driver's seat. He banged the door shut in two attempts; partially the first time and properly the second time.

"Start," the master ordered.

The gear coughed horribly. The master slapped the pupil. "Gas!"

The car hissed forward. Nagarajan changed to third.

Mallayya was tortured.

Nagarajan had always managed the gears smoothly from the very first day. But that alone was not enough.

"Slow, slow…" the master said. The car moved in a relentless zigzag. Cyclists attracted the machine like pieces of magnet.

"Honk!"

Nagarajan squeezed the horn in despair.

A cyclist looked back and screamed, "Oh, God!"

The master turned the steering the other way round with all his strength.

A huge lorry, carrying sand, overtook the car dizzily. Those at the back of the lorry gave a loud mocking howl at the novice.

In a daze, Nagarajan pressed the accelerator and the car shot out at top speed.

"Stop!"

Nagarajan stopped.

The car now stood right in the middle of the road. There was no end to the blows now on Nagarajan.

Cars overtook the lifeless car from both sides. The drivers flung the choicest of abuses at the master and his pupils.

"You!" the master shouted now at Mallayya. "Come over."

Nagarajan tried to reset his ruffled hair.

A military truck at the back honked its guts out.

The master tried to start the car. No use. The smell of petrol inside was overpowering.

"Push," the master ordered.

The two pupils pushed. Two cyclists seemed to greet Nagarajan. He was too much in a daze to respond.

The engine remained dead.

The car had been pushed beyond the soft drinks factory. Even the Guindy slope failed to revive the dead engine.

The master signalled with his hand and Mallayya and Nagarajan stopped pushing. The car now stood still near the pavement.

Folding his *dhoti* to his knees, the master stepped down, walked along the factory wall, and disappeared behind the bend.

Mallayya wanted to go too. Nagarajan seemed to be catching his breath, at last.

When he returned, the master gave Mallayya a packet that had been tucked into the *dhoti*.

Mallayya took a small bag from the dashboard of the car. He then walked over to a shady spot on the pavement and started grinding the betel nut with the mortar and pestle from the bag.

"Stop!" the master shouted.

Mallayya stopped.

The master gave him a betel leaf smeared with lime to grind.

After he had finished, the master stuffed the pounded contents into his mouth, topping it with tobacco. His eyes now fell on the onlookers who had gathered round Mallayya, Nagarajan and himself.

"What are you all staring at?" he snarled at them. "Get along now, get going, will you?"

He then spat mightily and slipped into the driver's seat.

The car this time was obedient.

The master then looked at Mallayya, sitting near him. "Back get you!" he spat.

Mallayya, along with Nagarajan, now sat at the back. The car whined and then sped on, grumbling.

Till they reached Alandur, the traffic was terrifying. The master kept a steady pace through all this chaos. Outside the Military Hospital, he honked impudently.

Mallayya was horrified as that was a 'no horn' zone.

The Meenabakkam airfield was visible now. "Five litres of petrol—that is what the two useless fellows have consumed and broken the car on top of it! Chchchi!" the master spat out.

He then stopped along the pavement near the aerodrome and stepped out of the car. "Practice! Only I seem to be getting practice!" he said and then turning to Nagarajan asked, "How about a cup of coffee?"

Nagarajan nodded in assent and meekly followed the master. No invitation was extended to Mallayya. He stayed in the car.

The master and Nagarajan went to a roadside canteen.

In the meanwhile, Mallayya looked inside the car. Clutch, accelerator, brake, clutch, brake accelerator...gear, one, two, three and four...one, two, three and four. He had not tried the reverse gear ever.

He could only drive in the first gear properly, provided there was no traffic on the road; not on the main road ever. As if anyone would learn to drive only on deserted playgrounds and airfields!

However, behind the wheel, Mallayya tended to agree with the master. The master's strength was concentrated in his right arm, something like Duryodhana and his thigh. It was with that sledgehammer of a hand that the master socked his pupils on their left side.

The master and Nagarajan came out of the canteen. The master was actually chatting with Nagarajan!

"Have you checked the radiator?" he now asked Mallayya.

"I'll go now," Mallayya said and entered the canteen with the tin for some water. The master was at the steering wheel.

The car faced the city.

Mallayya finished pouring water into the radiator. He then went for the bag in the dashboard. "No", said the master.

The master sat behind the steering wheel for a while. He switched the engine on. It started without protest and the master drove slowly.

"Get in!" he barked, moving aside.

Nagarajan opened the door.

"Not you!" he hissed. "You!" he pointed at Mallayya.

Mallayya slipped with alacrity into the driver's seat and Nagarajan sat at the back.

Clutch, brake, accelerator...Mallayya repeated the magic formula.

The car slid forward, without protest, without kicks.

"Hmmm! Second!" the master growled.

Mallayya obeyed. Not the car. There was a jerk.

The master rapped the pupil on the head. "Easy. The time next you clutch release like that I'll you murder," he said in his Telugu.

"You better do that!" Mallayya said. "I've no mother, no father. Nobody will protest". He choked.

"What gain will I by you killing?" the master asked with genuine surprise. "I want you learn to drive, I want to you get married. I want you settle down as a driver at least with the Transport Department. What gain will I by you killing?"

At the Military Hospital, Mallayya accelerated. The Mount Road Crossing was a few yards away.

The Guindy climb was a death trap. Mallayya slowed down instinctively.

"Go on, now!" the master yelled. Mallayya felt the steering wheel rebel right under his hands.

The policeman at the crossing gave the signal. Mallayya steered round the policeman.

"Second," the master ordered. The car coughed slightly.

At Alandur, traffic was heavy.

"Honk, now!" the master said. He was surprisingly gentle.

Mallayya continued to honk and move forward. The street was all his. He felt the sweat from the back of his neck pour in a steady stream and collect round his trousers. He slowed down, expecting the master to take over. He could surely not manage the crowd there, without mowing it down.

"Go on, go on, now," the master pressed on.

Mallayya dodged all the passengers, getting off and on the three buses parked there.

Just near the third bus, a van from the opposite direction left Mallayya exactly six inches to manoeuvre the car.

They crossed the bus stop, the Guindy railway station, the doctor's house and finally came the long climb on the overbridge.

The policeman was looking somewhere else.

The slow climb was almost over.

At the triangular junction, no vehicle was in sight, by God's grace. Now the bridge.

Oh, God! A giant of a truck! Right there!

The policeman signalled halt.

Mallayya braked and he rattled even more than the car.

In a trice there were cars all over; so many behind him.

The policeman gave the signal.

God! God! The car should start all right, not roll behind, should not hit anyone in the front or at the back. I shouldn't mow down the policeman, Mallayya chanted to himself.

"Go," shouted the master.

God, the car should slip into the first gear without jumping ...
It did.

Thank you, God. But...the engine died.

Mallayya felt his blood freeze.

"Start again," the master said.

Mallayya's fingers froze on contact with the ignition key. He remembered to change to neutral.

The policeman looked angry.

Mallayya waited for the spade-like hand of the master to descend on him.

It didn't.

The car started. It went round the policeman, in a smooth curve, in the first gear. Mallayya felt weightless. Now every limb of his was functioning in magical harmony. The car was no longer a mystery and an enemy.

"Slow! Slow!" the master yelled. The car nosed right into a herd of buffaloes, finding its way through. Once away from the herd, Mallayya accelerated. Without permission. The third gear coughed, but the car did not stop, making Mallayya smile.

The master gently boxed him. "What are you grinning at?" he asked.

Mallayya knew the master was pleased.

Mallayya gently veered the car to the left and stopped it along the pavement. Now there was nothing the car wouldn't do for him; except, of course, the reverse gear.

"Don't here you, live?" the master asked.

"Yes."

"You here Sir get down!" the master said.

"I'll get off at Mambalam…" That was Nagarajan in a subdued voice.

"Your class tomorrow," the master said. "Coming tomorrow or no?" he then asked Mallayya.

"Yes, of course! I'll come early!"

Mallayya relieved himself against the wall. He then went home.

There was no need to die now. He would certainly get a driver's job with the Transport Department. He was terribly hungry.

Now any woman, speaking any language, could serve him anything, and it would taste good.

Translated from the Tamil by
the author

20

VALUES REALISED

Yaddanapudi Sulochana Rani

"Oho! Such a small injury on your leg and you are behaving as if your whole life is over. Manju, what is this madness? The doctor said you'll be alright in a week's time," said Sekhar to his wife who was looking at her leg all the time, as if she had lost it for good.

She was reclining on a circular pillow on a cot drawn nearer to the window. She was looking like a queen who had lost her kingdom.

"It is okay. There was pus on the wound because it was the iron blade of the vegetable cutter. It is taken care of now and you are okay. No need to get scared." Sekhar was standing in front of the dressing table mirror, trying to put the tie-knot.

"Of course, you would say that! How can you understand my pain? I have been sitting on this bed for the past 10 days without putting my foot on the ground. If you could understand the hell I am going through, you wouldn't talk like that. Anyway, why should you be worried? It is not going to affect your life, your club or your meeting." Manju did not look at him but her face was red and her lips pouted.

"Don't start that again! I am getting ready to go after taking your permission. Okay, I won't go if you are feeling so bad. You know, the club's annual day is fast approaching and I am an important member of the executive committee. Otherwise I would not have bothered at all. Okay, it doesn't matter." He removed his tie, and throwing it aside, sat by her side.

"No need for all this. You go. It is, after all, not a one or two-day affair. You go now. If I am alone at home I feel very lonely. When you are by my side I just don't think of anything else. If you go out for a while, this injury magnifies itself into a huge devil and scares me. It mocks me and threatens me that I may be a cripple and may never be able to walk normally. I don't get scared if you are with me. I feel very bold. Whatever may be the circumstances I may have to face, whether I am beautiful or not, healthy or not, even if I am physically handicapped, I feel assured that there is someone with me, always, to take care of me. You are always there; that's my strength. That's all. Did I ever behave like this before? You know it, don't you? Can you not now understand the reason for my insecurity?" She covered her face with both hands to hide her sense of shame and pain.

Sekhar looked at his wife intently for a while, and moving closer to her, kept a hand on her head and said, "You know, Manju, you take every small thing to heart and get very sensitive and sentimental. I can understand the reason why you don't want me to go out. But what can I do? I'll be away only for half an hour. I'll just give them instructions and come back. You keep my watch. If I don't come back by seven o'clock, you can give me any punishment you like. Okay, look at me now!" He removed his watch and tied it to her hand.

"No, it is okay. You go now." She did not allow him to tie the watch on her wrist.

Sekhar put it on her hand by force. He came to the mirror again to knot his tie.

"Take your medicine. The doctor said if you don't get fever today you would not get it again. I'll try to come earlier than seven. Okay." He left, talking to her.

Manju could hear the gradual moving away of the car. She sat straight and touched the watch—*I'll be back by the time the needle touches seven*—She could feel his touch on the chain. Anyway, this injury on the leg had given her a new experience. In one way, she was very happy.

Ten days ago Sekhar had gone to a camp on office duty. He had been gone for eight days as a higher officer from Bengal was visiting the site. He could not take Manju along with him as it was an inspection tour. Eight days had dragged on like centuries.

At last, the day of Sekhar's return, had come.

It was very late in the evening. Manju took a bath and wore the white *sari* he liked. Her mind was set only on the call that she would hear any time—his voice calling out to her, "Manju!"

She wandered about the house for want of any work. The cook was busy in the kitchen preparing the night's dinner. Manju was getting coffee ready, to give him as soon as he arrived. She was just about to put the coffee in the flask when she heard his voice.

"Manju."

How had he come so silently? Half an hour earlier than the scheduled time! She could not believe her ears and ran into the hall. While running, her foot hit the vegetable cutter that was lying on the floor—once given a chance the blade did not want to lose the opportunity and cut into her foot deeply. Manju paused for a second, pushed the cutter aside, with the same foot, and ran into the hall like a whirlwind. By that time Sekhar had removed his shoes and was pushing them towards the wall with his leg.

"You came quite early. Oh God! This evening was so particularly dragging. At last you are here. How nice! This whole week, I was so bored every single minute," she said as she went straight into his arms. She was not aware of the wound on her foot, and the bleeding caused by it.

"Wait, wait a minute! Let me remove my socks," he tried to remove her hands from around his neck.

The truth was the cook had come into the hall following Manju and was peeping at them with wide-open eyes.

"What is this? What are these marks on the floor?" Sekhar, who was embarrassed at the cook looking at them, had looked down at the floor.

He realised that the imprints were of blood. It was then that Manju thought of her injury.

"Arrere! Let me look at your leg. It is bleeding so badly! What happened?" He sat on his knees in front of her and took her foot into his hand.

Her pink and rosy foot displayed a two-inch deep cut. It was still bleeding. He was stunned at the sight of so much blood.

"Oh yes! While coming I stepped on a vegetable cutter. It did not hurt then."

"You stupid girl, you are always like this. What was the hurry? Once I was home, would I not come into the house? Could you not come out normally? Why would you run like that? Actually, what were you doing in the kitchen? And who kept the vegetable cutter on the floor?" He kept his arms around her and carefully led her to a chair near the wall. Every step she took left its mark on the floor, red and bloody!

"Oh my God, look at the blood," he took out his handkerchief from his trouser pocket and pressed it to her wound.

The servants and the cook ran into the hall on hearing his angry voice—so unlike him to shout as soon as he entered the house.

"Shh, it is hurting," said Manju, leaning back in the chair and closing her eyes. It was not pain that caused her to close her eyes. It was the feeling she had at the concern and anxiety in his voice. He was holding her foot in both his hands now.

Without changing his clothes, he took her straight to the doctor.

The doctor assured them that there was no need to worry, though it was a deep cut. It would heal quickly. He put a bandage on her foot. Manju did not feel anything. She walked up to the car with her bandaged foot and was quite cheerful.

"You should be more careful! You are not aware of what is happening to your body at all. It is not always good, you know. See now, you got hurt unnecessarily. You have lost a lot of blood too," Sekhar admonished her in the night, before going to bed.

"It's okay! I'm not worried. I like this. I have not seen you worrying about me so much earlier. In the evening when you were holding my foot in your hand while it was bleeding, I was just looking at the expression in your eyes, and it was so soothing. I would like to see that kind of expression every minute of my life." Manju looked tired but her eyes reflected a bright inner light.

Sekhar did not understand. But he was overcome with some peculiar feeling that she had got hurt while running out to meet him.

The next day also, it did not pain much. Manju moved around quite normally, though Sekhar shouted at her for not taking rest. But on the third day, her foot had swollen enormously and she could not put it down. She was in pain too. The doctor came home that day. By the evening, she had developed fever. The wound had become septic. The doctor advised an operation to remove the pus.

"No, no! He may amputate part of my foot or he may even cut one or two toes. No, no! I don't want any operation. I'll be all right quite soon. Don't let them make me lame, please," Manju pleaded.

"What is this, Manju? You are not a small kid. Why would he cut your toes? You magnify everything," Sekhar chided her.

"If you act now, it will suffice with a small operation. If you now refuse this operation, we may have to remove your entire leg later on. I have no objection if you like that idea." The doctor picked up his bag and got up to go.

"To remove the entire leg! I am worried now about losing two toes and he is talking of removing the whole leg." Manju's whole body trembled with fear.

At last, after a long time, she hid her face in Sekhar's shoulder and told him, "If it needs to be done, let them do the operation. But see that they do not cut my toes. My aunt once had to lose three toes when her wound developed pus. I can't tolerate that ugliness."

"There is no need to be afraid at all! Why don't you believe me? Why would they cut your toes? Even if they say that your toes should be removed I would give mine in replacement. Okay? Maybe they would look rough, unlike yours. Can you tolerate them at least?" Sekhar laughed at her.

That was Manju's nature. By mistake, on the road or at the crossing, if she saw a lame or blind person, she would turn her face away. Once, Sekhar remembered very well, they were coming home after dinner at a friend's house. They stopped at a petrol pump, where they saw a beggar woman in a destitute condition. Manju could not sleep for two days. The poor woman had an infant in her hands, which looked like a lump of flesh. Manju looked at the baby.

"Sir, please have mercy on my baby and give something!" Manju turned her face away in fear and Sekhar was not affected by any of these things. He simply took out a coin from his shirt pocket and threw the piece at her.

They filled up the petrol and were soon on their way.

Manju, who had been talking and laughing till that time, fell strangely silent. Sekhar noticed this and asked her why

"People say that God is the creator. How can there be such ugliness in a creation when God is involved! We are so happy and healthy, why are they like that?" She continued, "Whether God created this ugliness or not, my only appeal to him is that if, at all, he is kind and merciful, as people say he is, he should show it in abundance to the poor and do justice to them."

Sekhar did not make any comment, neither did he argue. He wondered how certain things he wouldn't even notice caused such deep impressions on Manju's mind and ate away her peace of mind. He wondered why they moved her so deeply while not touching him at all.

Sekhar recalled all these things as she was preparing for her operation. After the operation was over he went to her and told her, stroking her hair, "Nothing to worry, you will be alright within a week."

Doctor said she should not strain her leg at all and advised complete bed rest. It was hell for her, but there was no other option. Sekhar bought one calendar and kept it front of her. With his nursing and the cook for help, Manju somehow managed.

Sekhar cancelled all his appointments to be with her. It was six days since the car had been taken out of the garage. It was the first time after their marriage that he was spending so much time with his wife. Now she stopped getting fever in the evenings. The wound also healed, almost, by 75 per cent.

While it was still slightly raw, the doctor had advised her to start walking a little without straining her leg. Sekhar used to make her put her hand around his neck and then, holding her carefully, would help her walk from the cot to the wall and back again. His soft nature, his patience, surprised Manju no end. She began to see new depths in his character. He always remembered to give medicines exactly on time, to check her fever every evening, to read to her in the afternoons.

Manju started feeling it would be very nice indeed if she continued to be bedridden throughout her life. If she got well he would disappear and get busy again with work, friends, meetings, parties and celebrations. Of course, she would always be by his side. Manju did not mind this earlier. But now, this leg injury had given her the taste of a new experience. She learned to see him in a different light. With this mishap, the two of them were always together. There was no one to drag him away from her to play cards or cricket.

One day, while watching him keenly mixing medicine for her she said, "If you were a doctor and I were your patient, if both of us could go to some corner of the world in beautiful surroundings—if we could live on top of a small hill, in small house—how nice it would be. If I sit every evening like this, reclining on the cushions and you would get medicine for me. How nice it would be."

Sekhar stopped mixing medicine and looked at his wife over his shoulder. Manju appeared to be living in a world she had created for herself.

"Why do you look like that? Don't you think it would be nice?" Manju asked.

"Well, it would be nice. Only we may get tigers and lions as our visitors. I will have to start shooting lessons to be on safe side. I should get the gun out from tomorrow. Here, take the medicine. Really Manju, I cannot understand one thing. I break my head everyday over this. Why didn't you ever become a story writer! People like you, who live in an imaginary world, should become fiction writers. It is quite dangerous for us who have to live with you, or people like you."

"What do you mean?" asked Manju without taking the medicine glass from his hand.

"What else? Lot of people imagine beautiful things and forget. But you insist that you should get all these things in real life. You want to experience your dreams in reality."

Both of them laughed. It was a glorious moment for both of them.

Manju's eyes had a faraway look. But now, they dropped to the watch. The needle was moving lazily and indifferently. It was ten minutes to seven. Somehow she could not believe that Sekhar would be back by seven as promised. He only wanted her permission to go out. That's why he was so obliging.

Her suspicions proved true. It was seven, and then seven-fifteen. But there was no sign of her husband.

"I can't blame him. It is my mistake. I told him to go. Had I been silent for a few more minutes and sat with a sulky face, he would not have gone at all. Once he has gone he would not be able to come back as per plan or as he wished. What can I do?" she lamented

But, how long could she hold him this way? How long could she go on impressing upon him that she craved for his attention? Could anyone enforce feelings of affection by such tactics?

I wish I wasn't hurt. Then I would not have come to know what depths of affection he was capable of. Manju sighed and closed her eyes. She did not take her medicine; just kept looking at her medicine glass on the table.

The clock in the hall chimed eight and nine too. There was no sign of Sekhar. She was deeply hurt though she tried to console herself. How nice it would be if I get fever again. He would then come home, feel my forehead and get concerned for me again. It would be nice to experience that concern. But that cannot happen. All these thoughts made her feel weak and she got a severe headache. But there were no physical symptoms of illness.

Manju heard the horn at 9:10 p.m. She quickly removed the watch, kept it on the table, turned to the wall and closed her eyes. Her ears strained to hear his call "Manju."

But he did not call her.

"Is Manju sleeping? Has she taken her medicine?" She heard him ask and Shambhu simply said a yes to both the questions. He knew his mistress would not neglect her medicine and since she had switched off the light long time ago, he assumed that she must be asleep . She wouldn't be so silent if she was awake.

Sekhar did not want to wake her up and remind her that he was late. So he got busy reading the scripts for the annual day programme.

Next morning, by the time Sekhar got up, Manju was moving around normally.

"You are moving around as if you are totally normal. Why don't you take rest for two more days? The wound is still raw." He knew she was angry about his delay the previous evening, so he talked to her first in an attempt to pacify her.

"It is okay! I should be the one worrying about my leg. It is okay with me even if it doesn't get cured. You don't have to skip your meetings for me."

Sekhar was angry at her sarcastic manner of speaking. "Yes, of course! That's all. All women are like this, so typical. You forgot all that was done for you in just one evening."

He did not talk to her further.

She asked herself, why he could not just tell her why he had got delayed. After, all she had waited for him anxiously. He would probably be happy if she didn't get well completely.

She gave a holiday to all the servants in a fit of anger; the cook had been asking for a leave for a long time. She wanted to go to Vijayawada to see her sister. Manju now gave her leave and train fare too. "You stay for four days if you want. My leg is alright." Shambhu too was very old now and had been coughing severely at night-time. Manju told him to take rest for four days and take proper medicine. Raju was next— nobody needs to give him a holiday. He takes leave anyway at every small pretext.

"Why did you let them all go on leave at the same time? Who is going to do the household work? Your leg is not totally cured. Why didn't you tell me before sending them all away? Am I so insignificant in this house?" Sekhar was hurt and angry at his wife's behaviour. Now, she would have to do everything, even though she was limping around. He knew her nature. Whenever she got angry with him, she would show it on herself.

"After we got married, this is the first time I have done something independently, without consulting you. Whenever I ask something, you always say, 'Do as you like'. I have never taken a decision independently. I always consulted you. I thought this is a small matter and I need not ask you permission for this. How do I know that your 'Do as you like' is just lip service. This is the first mistake I have committed since our wedding. You can surely forgive me," she said softly but emphatically as she came very close to him.

Sekhar forgot to blink.

Till yesterday she was like a baby, like an angel. What happened to her today? Why does she think I am saying this? Is it not for her good? She just refuses to understand. Sekhar thought seethingly.

"Okay, your wish. Do as you like. Move around as you please. Don't complain of pain hereafter."

"I won't, I won't! I promise you, okay! Not even if it hurts. Even if my legs, hands or eyes are taken out I won't complain of any pain or ask for your help," said Manju as her eyes filled with tears.

"Manju."

Sekhar tried to hold her but she ran away, crying bitterly.

Sekhar went to his office without eating anything that day. Manju knew that he was not in the habit of eating outside in restaurants and was disturbed. He had not even taken coffee that day.

At 12 o'clock she packed his lunch in a multi-tiered tiffin carrier and sent Raju to the office. She sent a note to him along with the lunch carrier—*Don't skip lunch in protest or anger. Raju*

will be there keeping a watch till you finish. He will report to me if
you do not eat. Come home quickly.

"Yes, I must adjust. He is a man working outside throughout
the day. He must be having lots of work outside. I can't expect
him to be with me all the time, holding my *palloo*. I am only
one among his many interests. For me he is everything. Not
so with him. I should understand this," she told herself.

She finished her lunch and sat in the hall waiting for Raju's
return; her eyes were on the wall clock and her ears were
keenly waiting for the sound of Raju's feet. Her hands were
embroidering a pillow cover but her mind was busy elsewhere.
Raju must be in the office now. He must have kept the carrier
on the table and given him the note. Sekhar must be reading
it now. Once he finishes reading he will come and sit before
the carrier in an angry mood. Then he will remember my note
and look up to see if Raju is watching. His mood will then
change and he will start eating his food, smiling to himself. He
may otherwise have finished his food in an indifferent manner.

Manju looked up when she heard the cycle bell. Raju came
in with the carrier.

"What did your master say?" She asked anxiously.

Raju did not reply nor did he take any note out for her. He
came to her slowly and said, "*Amma*, he is not in the office. He
was in the office for 10 minutes only in the morning. I believe.
I brought the food back."

Manju threw aside the pillow cover she was embroidering.
Her eyes which were on the wall clock till a moment ago now
turned red with anger. But she controlled herself.

"Okay, go inside and do your work," she told Raju.

Manju now got up and came to bed. Where could he
have gone? Where else? He must have gone to the club. The

annual day is only a few days away. He could have taken his lunch at least. He must be enjoying himself over there after taking his lunch with Raja at the club; chatting away with a cigarette in hand. She looked at her foot. It is good I got this injury. Otherwise I would have never known his true nature. He could have told me before that he was going to the club. And I never object to his going there.

All the anger that had deserted her earlier returned in full force. Now, not for a day or two or six days or even six months—in fact she would not talk to him with any affection for six months. If any other man treated his wife this way, she would also do the same. She would just give him the courtesy and respect a husband expects from a wife; not a grain of affection would she show him, she promised herself firmly.

When the hall clock chimed three in the afternoon, she heard the car horn outside. She did not get up, as she knew it was Sekhar's car. Raju ran to the gate and opened it. She heard the car coming inside. She sat down on the bed, just hearing the sounds outside.

Raju came into the room, running. "*Amma*, Sekhar babu has a bandage over his eyes. Dr. Yoganandam is with him too."

Sekhar, by this time, had come into the house. Both his eyes were covered with a white bandage. Dr. Yoganandam, holding his hand, was slowly leading him to a chair near the wall. Raja, Sekhar's friend, was also with them.

"What is this? What has happened?" Manju asked, coming into the hall.

Sekhar was occupying the same chair she had when her leg was wounded.

Raju looked at her.

Dr. Yoganandam said "Today is a lucky day. He escaped a major accident, just by a split second. He could have lost his eye totally. You are very lucky."

"What happened?" she asked again, rooted to the spot.

"You know, tomorrow is the annual function. We were all making arrangements on the stage. We are actually putting up special curtains for our drama. The curtains were draped on an iron wire and we were trying to fix the wire at each end. We were on stage to check if it was all okay when this accident happened. The person who was standing in the upper storey did not see Sekhar. He pulled the wire hard, in the process hitting Sekhar on his face, just missing the eye."

Raja explained, coming forward. "There is no need to worry. But he should not strain his eyes. That is why we bandaged the other eye too. You should see that he doesn't move out of the house. It is your responsibility. Tomorrow is the annual day in the club. Sekhar should not move out of the house. Do you hear me, Sekhar?"

Tomorrow is the annual day. Manju knew that he had been making plans for this occasion for days. Tomorrow he would not even be able to open his eyes. He had been looking forward to this day, and the great event was going to bypass him totally.

There was no change in Sekhar's expression. He was sitting there as if he had just accepted this situation.

"Don't worry, I will take care of everything," Raja said before leaving.

Sekhar did not appear to be upset about his injury. He did not call Manju near him. He was simply sitting and talking to the others, explaining to them all the things he had done so far and the things that had to be taken care of.

Manju stood listening. For a moment she thought, maybe

he is not hurt; he may be just acting so as to tease her. The next moment, she wondered at his supreme confidence and his ability to take care of everything and at the same time stay above it all. She was totally impressed by his personality.

After some time, Dr. Yoganandam and Raja left. Before leaving, Sekhar made them promise that he would be allowed to give his speech the next day and his bandage would be taken off briefly during that time. Manju went to the door to see them off and came back into the hall.

"Manju, come here," he called her as he heard her approaching feet.

"Now, at least, you recall my existence." She stood slightly away from him.

"First come here. Have they all gone? Raja and all?" He extended his hand in the direction of her voice. She quickly came forward and hid her face in his outstretched hand.

"What is this? Chhi, chhi! Are you crying for this? There is no danger at all to my eyes. Haven't you heard Dr. Yoganandam? It is all your luck. How is your leg? I did not see it at all today."

"My foot is okay. First tell me. Even when you hurt and your eyes have barely escaped damage, how can you be calm?" She sounded astonished as she took his hand in both her hands.

"Why not? In fact, I am now happy. I can close my eyes and sit with you all the time. That's what you always say you want. Isn't it? I will now sit in front of you all the time. Let me see how soon you get tired of me" He held her hand.

"If I say that you should be with me, always, does it mean that I want you to go blind or lame? Is this why you got hurt deliberately?" She pulled her hand away angrily.

"Look, you are getting angry again. If you move away from

me in anger, I cannot come after you. You have to come to me on your own when your anger subsides."

Manju came to him again and gave him her hand. He pulled her closer and said, "Manju, look here, you should learn to take things in your stride. If there are situations in life where you feel pain, you cannot avoid them. But, if you keep anticipating that something is going to happen, it is a sign of weakness and foolishness too. A wise man feels sorry for the things that have already taken place and a coward gets scared at some imaginary pain that might befall him in the future. Do you understand? I got hurt in the eye. I surely feel some pain. But if I lose my peace of mind by magnifying it, what do I achieve? What is the use? Tell me"

"But the injury I had on my leg also was not much. But why was I feeling so bad? I felt the whole world had come to an end and everything around me was in total darkness. Was it a sign of weakness? Does it mean I am a coward?"

"No, it is not cowardice. It is a beautiful feeling. You were actually not worried about your leg. But you were afraid that I would neglect you if anything happens to you. No, let me finish. I am not afraid that way. Even if I were badly hurt, even if I had lost my eye I would not worry. I know I have you with me always. If I lose my eyesight you will be my eyesight. Am I not right?

"You seem to have forgotten that I have not eaten anything since morning. I am feeling hungry. You feed me now with your hands. First, take me to our room. You must take me to the club tomorrow. The driving you have learnt for fun is now going to help us. What are you thinking about? You are very quiet."

"No, no, it is nothing. Let's go to our room." She supported him as he got up from the chair.

"What is it? Tell me?"

"Just what you told me now. Get involved in everything, but be above it all."

"Is that all? Are you not going to tell me that you are not afraid of losing me, that you have confidence in me? I thought that's what you have realised." Sekhar stopped in his tracks, questioning her.

"No, no. I have complete confidence in you always. I just talk like that sometimes. I have no fear complex at all. You must have known it too. Let's go."

She wiped her eyes and walked along with him. But some inner voice in her shouted, *Not now, even after hundreds of years, would there be any change in the nature of the relationship between a man and a woman and the delicate difference that lies between their attitudes towards each other.*

Translated from the Telugu by
Syamala Kallury

21

HOUSEWIFE

Ismat Chughtai

The day Mirza's new maid ambled into his house, there was a sensation in the neighourhood. The sweeper, who normally avoided work, stayed on and scrubbed the floor with great vigour. The milkman, notorious for adulterating his ware, brought milk clogged with cream.

Who could have named her Lajo, the coy one? Bashfulness was unknown to Lajo. No one knew who begot her and abandoned her on the streets to a lonely, weeping childhood.

Begging and starving, she reached an age when she could snatch a living for herself. Youth etched her body into bewitching curves and this became her only asset. The street initiated her into the mysteries of life.

She never haggled; if it was not a cash-down proposition, it would be sex on credit. If the lover had no means, she would even give of herself, free.

"Aren't you ashamed of yourself?" people asked.

"I am!" Lajo would blush brazenly.

"You will regret it someday."

"I couldn't care less!"

How could she? With a face that was innocence itself, dark eyes, evenly set teeth, a mellow complexion and a gait so swinging, so provocative!

Mirza was a bachelor. Flattening and baking *chapatis* daily had flattened out his existence. He owned a small grocery shop which he pompously called, General Store. The shop did not give Mirza any leisure time to go to his hometown and get married.

Mirza's friend, Bakhshi, had picked up Lajo at a bus stop. Bakhshi's wife was nine months pregnant and they needed a maid. Later, when Lajo was not required, Bakhshi deposited her at Mirza's. Instead of squandering away at brothels, he thought, why not let Mirza enjoy a free dish?

"God forbid, I won't have a tart in the house!" said Mirza, warily. "Take her back!"

But Lajo had already made herself at home. With her skirt hiked up like a diaper, broom in hand, she was sweeping Mirza's house in dead earnest. When Bakhshi informed her of Mirza's refusal, it fell on deaf ears. She ordered Mirza to arrange the pans on the kitchen shelf and went out to fetch water.

"If you wish, I will take you back home," said Bakhshi.

"Out with you! Are you my husband to take me back to my mother's? Go! I will tackle the *Mian* myself!"

Bakhshi's departure left Mirza helpless. He ran out and took refuge in the mosque. He was not prepared to incur this extra expenditure. Moreover, she was bound to pilfer and cheat. What a mess Bakhshi had got him into!

But on returning home, his breath got caught in his throat. As though his late mother, *Bi Amma*, was back!

The house was sparkling.

"Shall I serve dinner, *Mian*?" Lajo asked and disappeared into the kitchen.

Spinach and potato curry, *moong ki dal* fried with onion and garlic just the way *Ammaji* used to cook!

"How did you manage all this?" Mirza asked, baffled.

"Borrowed from the *bania*."

"Look, I will pay your return fare. I just cannot afford a servant."

"Who wants to be paid?"

"But..."

"Is the food hot?" Lajo asked, slipping a fresh *chapati* into his plate.

Not the food but I am certainly hot from top to toe! Mirza wanted to shout, as he went into his room to sleep.

"No, *Mian*, I am here for good!" Lajo threatened, when he brought up the question again the next morning.

"But..."

"Didn't you like the food?"

"It's not that..."

"Don't I scrub and clean well?"

"It's not that..."

"Then what is it?" Lajo flared up.

She had fallen in love; not with Mirza, but with the house.

Bakhshi, the bastard, had once rented a room for her. Its previous occupant had been Nandi a buffalo. The buffalo was dead and gone, to hell, but had left behind his stench. And Bakhshi did not treat her well either.

Now here she was, the unrivalled mistress of Mirza's house. Mirza was uncomplicated. He would sneak in, softly and quietly, and eat whatever was served.

Mirza, for his part, checked the accounts a few times and was satisfied that Lajo did not cheat.

At times, she went across to Ramu's grandmother for a tête-à tête.

Ramu was Mirza's dissipated teenaged help in the store. He fell for Lajo the minute he saw her. It was he who told her of Mirza's frequent visits to the nautch girls.

This hurt Lajo. After all, what was she for?

Wherever employed, she served well in every capacity. And here a full chaste week had passed! She had never felt so unwanted before. Several offers came her way but she was Mirza's maid. She rejected one and all, lest Mirza become a laughing stock. And here was Mirza, an iceberg, or so he appeared!

Lajo could not see the volcanoes erupting within him. He kept away from home deliberately.

Lajo's name was on every lip—today she had slapped the milkman, yesterday she had aimed a dung-cake full in the face of the *bania*, and so on. The schoolmaster insisted on educating her. The *Mullaji* of the mosque burst into prayers in Arabic, beseeching God to ward off impending danger!

Mirza came home annoyed. Lajo had just had her bath. Strands of wet hair clung to her shoulders. Blowing into the kitchen fire had flushed her cheeks and filled her eyes with water. She ground her teeth at *Mian's* untimely entry.

Mirza almost toppled over!

After a silent, uneasy, meal, he picked up his walking-stick, went out and sat in the mosque. But he could not relax. Ceaseless thoughts of home made him restless. Unable to hold out any longer, he got back and found Lajo on the threshold, quarrelling with a man. The man disappeared the moment he saw Mirza.

"Who was that?" Mirza's tone was that of a suspicious husband!

"Raghav."

"Raghav?" Mirza had been buying milk from him for years and yet did not know his name.

"Shall I prepare the hookah, *Mian*?" Lajo changed the subject.

"No! What was that man up to?"

"Was asking me how much milk he should bring from now on."

"What did you say?"

"I said, 'May God hasten your funeral! Bring the usual measure.'"

"Then?" Mirza was furious.

"Then I said, 'Bastard, go, feed the extra milk to your mother and sister'!"

"The scoundrel! Don't let him set foot here again! I will myself fetch milk on the way home from the store."

That night, after dinner, Mirza put on a starched, freshly laundered *kurta*, stuck a scented piece of cottonwool in his ear, picked up his walking- stick and walked out.

Jealousy wrung Lajo's heart. She cursed the nautch girl and sat dumbfounded. Was Mirza really indifferent to her? How could that be? she wondered.

The nautch girl was hanging with a customer. This upset Mirza. He turned away and made for Lala's shop.

There he cursed inflation, rising prices, national politics and returned home at midnight, spent and irritated. He drank a lot of cold water but the fire in him continued to blaze.

A part of Lajo's smooth golden leg was visible from the open door. A careless turn in sleep tinkled her anklets. Mirza drained another glass of water and bundled in his cot, cursing everything under the moon.

Ceaseless tossing in bed reduced his body to a blister. Litres of cold water bloated in his stomach. The suppleness of the leg behind the door was irresistible. Unknown fears strangled him. But the devil egged him on. From his bed to the kitchen he had to walk so many miles but now he couldn't move a step.

Then an innocent idea crossed his mind. Were Lajo's leg not so exposed he would not be so uncomfortable. Gradually, this idea took strength and so did Mirza. What if she woke up? Yet he had to take the risk—for the sake of his own safety.

He left his slippers under the cot and tiptoed across, gingerly lifted the hem of her skirt and pulled it down slowly. He stood a while, indecisively, and turned away.

With one quick move, Lajo grabbed him.

Mirza was speechless. He was never so wrong in life before. He struggled, pleaded but she wouldn't let him go!

When he encountered Lajo next morning, she blushed like a bride!

Lajo, the victor, went about her chores boldly, humming a *kajri*. Not a shadow of the night's happening flickered in her eyes. When Mirza sat down to breakfast, she sat at the doorstep, as usual, fanning the flies away.

That afternoon, when she brought his lunch to the shop, he noticed a new lilt in her gait.

Whenever Lajo came to the shop, people would stop by and enquire about the price of groceries. She sold in a short while—what Mirza couldn't during the entire day!

Mirza began to improve in his looks. People knew the reason and sizzled with envy. Mirza, in turn, grew nervous and ill at ease. The more Lajo looked after him, the more enamoured he became and the more afraid he was of neighbours.

She, on the other hand, was utterly brazen. When she fetched his lunch, the entire bazaar throbbed with her presence.

"Don't bring lunch any more!" he told her one day.

"Why not?" Lajo's face fell. Staying home all by herself bored her.

The bazaar was an interesting break.

Having stopped her from coming, many doubts assailed Mirza. He dropped in at odd hours to spy on her. She would insist on rewarding him full for his attentions!

The day he caught her at a game of kabaddi with street urchins, his anger knew no bounds. Her skirt was billowing in the wind. The boys were engrossed in the skirt. Mirza passed by, holding his head high with affected indifference. His discomfiture amused the onlookers.

Mirza had grown fond of Lajo. The very idea of separation drove him crazy. He was unable to concentrate on his shop. He feared that some day she might desert him.

"*Mian* why not marry her?" Miran *Mian* suggested.

"God forbid!" he shouted. How could he form so sacred a relationship with a slut?

But that very evening, when he didn't find her at home, Mirza felt lost. He thought, the confounded Lala had been long on the wait. He had offered her a bungalow! Miran *Mian*, a friend from all accounts, had himself made a proposition to Lajo on the sly.

Mirza was losing hope, when suddenly Lajo appeared. She had just gone across to Ramu's grandmother!

That day Mirza made up his mind to take Lajo for a wife, even at the cost of his family's pride and prestige.

"But why, *Mian*?" Lajo asked, surprised at his proposal.

"Why not? Want to have a fling elsewhere?" he asked crossly.

"Why should I have a fling?"

"That Rao*ji* is offering you a bungalow."

"I wouldn't spit on his bungalow!"

The need for marriage completely escaped her. She was and would be his, for life. A master like him was not easy to come by. Lajo knew what a gem Mirza was. All her previous masters inevitably ended up as lovers. They would first have their fill, then beat her up and kick her out. Mirza had always been tender and loving. He had brought her a few clothes and a pair of gold bangles. No one in seven generations of Lajo's family had worn ornaments of pure gold.

When Mirza spoke of his plan to Ramu's grandmother, she too was surprised.

"*Mian*, why tie a bell around your neck?" she asked. "Is the slut making a fuss? A sound thrashing will set her right. Where beating up can do, why think of marriage?"

But Mirza was obsessed with the idea.

"You there, are you hesitating on account of the difference in religion?" Ramu's grandmother asked Lajo.

"No, I've always regarded him as my husband."

Lajo looked upon even a passing lover as a husband and served him well. Riches were never showered upon her, yet she gave of herself fully—body and soul.

Mirza was an exception, of course. Only Lajo knew the pleasure of the give-and-take game with him. Compared to him, others were pigs.

Also, marriage was for virgins. How did she qualify to be a bride? She begged and pleaded, but Mirza was bent upon entering into a legal contract of a *nikah*.

That day, after the evening prayer, *nikah* was solemnised. Young girls of the neighbourhood sang wedding songs. Mirza entertained his friends. Lajo, renamed *Kaneez* Fatima, became wife of Mirza Irfan Ali Beg.

Mirza imposed a ban on *lehangas,* prescribed *churidar pyjamas.* Lajo, however, was used to open space between her legs. This new imposition was a big irritant. She could never get used to it.

One day, at the first opportunity, she took off the *pyjama* and was about to get into the *lehanga*, when Mirza turned up. In her confusion, she forgot to hold the *lehanga* skirt around her waist and dropped it to the floor.

"The devil may take you!" Mirza thundered a *Quranic* curse. He hurriedly threw a bed sheet over her.

Lajo could not understand his annoyance and the granilloquent oration that followed. Where had she erred? This very act had taken Mirza's breath away so many times in the past. Now he was so upset. He picked up the *lehanga* and actually fed it to the fire.

Mirza left, leaving Lajo shocked and in confusion. Discarding the sheet, she examined her body. Maybe some repulsive skin disease had erupted overnight.

When bathing under the tap in the open, she kept wiping her tears.

Mithwa, son of the mason, would climb the terrace daily on the pretext of flying kites and watch her. She was so sad today, she neither stuck out her thumb nor hurled a slipper at him. She wrapped the sheet around and went indoors.

With a heavy heart she got into the long trousers—as long as the devil's intestines. To add to her misery, the cummerbund got lost inside the waist band. She shouted for help. Jullu, the neighbour's daughter, appeared and the tape was located.

Which sadist could have adopted this rifle case for a feminine dress? Lajo wondered.

Later, when Mirza returned home, the tape played truant once again. Lajo tried desperately to catch it with her fingers. Mirza found her nervousness endearing. After a combined concentrated chase, the tape was found.

But a greater problem popped up for Mirza. What used to be intoxicating coquetry in Lajo, now turned to brazenness in his wife! The indecent ways of a flirt are unbecoming of respectable women! Lajo failed to be a bride of his dream—one who would blush at his amorous advances, be annoyed at his persistence and feign indifference to his attention. Checking her every step, Mirza curbed her excess and tamed the wild in her—or so he thought. Also, he was no longer in a hurry to get back home in the evenings. Like all husbands, he spent more time with friends, to avoid being labelled as henpecked.

To make up for his frequent absences, he suggested engaging a maid. Lajo was furious. She knew of *Mian's* renewed visits to the nautch girls. She also knew that every man in the neighbourhood went there.

But in her own home, she would not tolerate another woman! Let anybody step into her kitchen and tinker with her glistening vessels, Lajo would tear her to bits! She would share Mirza with another woman but certainly would not share her home.

Mirza seemed to have installed Lajo in his house and forgotten all about her. For weeks he only spoke only in monosyllables.

When she was Mirza's mistress, all men had their eyes on her. Now that she had gained respectability, she became *mother, sister and daughter*.

No one cast even a stray glance at the jute curtain—except the faithful Mithwa. He still flew kites on the roof, although only when Mirza was away and Lajo was bathing in the courtyard.

One night Mirza stayed away, celebrating Dussehra with friends. He came home the next morning, had a quick wash and went off to the shop.

Lajo was annoyed. It was then while bathing, that she looked up at the terrace. Or maybe that day Mithwa's stare pierced her wet body like so many spears.

Suddenly, his kite snapped. The broken cord brushed sharply against Lajo's body. Lajo was startled. She got up quick and got into a room, absent-minded or deliberately forgetting to wrap the towel around her.

From then on, Mithwa was always found hanging around Mirza's house.

Whenever Lajo wanted something from the market, she would draw the jute curtain aside and shout: "Mithwa, don't stay put like a dunghill! Get us a few *kachoris*."

If Mithwa did not appear on the terrace during her bath, she rattled the bucket loud enough to wake a corpse in its grave. The love, which she had given so lavishly all her life, was now Mithwa's for the asking. If Mirza did not turn up for a meal, she would never waste the food, but feed someone poor and needy. Who was needier than Mithwa?

Mirza was convinced that, chained to wedlock, Lajo had become a genuine housewife. Had he not seen for himself, he would never have believed it. Seeing him on the doorstep so unexpectedly, she laughed uproariously. She could not, even in her wildest dreams imagine that Mirza would be so offended!

But Mithwa knew. Clutching his *dhoti* firmly with one hand, he bolted and stopped for breadth only after he had crossed three villages!

Mirza flogged Lajo so much that, had she been made of softer stuff, she would have breathed her last.

The news, that Mirza had caught his wife with Mithwa, spread throughout the village. People came in large numbers to watch the fun and were solely disappointed to know that Mithwa, the hero, had fled and that the wife lay dismantled.

Ramu's grandmother arrived and took her away. One would think a flogging like that would turn Lajo against the very idea of Mirza.

Far from it! Beating helped achieve what marriage could not. The bond was stronger. The minute she came to, Lajo enquired after Mirza.

All her previous masters had ended up as lovers. After giving her a sound thrashing, the question of pay was set aside. She slogged free and was beaten from time to time.

But Mirza had always been good. Other masters had even "loaned" her to friends, but Mirza regarded her as his own. Everyone advised her to run away and save her skin, but she did not budge.

How was Mirza to face the world? He saw no way but to kill her in order to save his honour.

Miran *Mian* held him back. "Why must you stick your head in the noose for the bitch? Divorce the whore and forget her!"

Mirza divorced her immediately and sent 32 rupees of dower—*mehr*—her clothes and other belongings over to Ramu's grandmother.

When Lajo heard of the divorce, she heaved a sigh of relief. *Nikah* had proved unlucky. All mishaps had been due to that.

"Is *Mian* still angry?" she asked Ramu's grandmother.

"Shall not set eyes on you. Wants you to get lost! Drop dead!"

The news of Mirza's divorce rocked the village.

Lala sent out a feeler, The bungalow is ready!

"Dump your mother in it!" Lajo retorted.

After a fortnight in bed, Lajo was up on her feet again. The beating seemed to have spring-cleaned her and left her more glowing than ever. When buying *paan* or *kachori*, she took the whole bazaar by storm.

Mirza died a thousand deaths. Once he spotted her at the *bania's* shop, arguing over something. The bania drooled. Mirza left, avoiding getting noticed.

"You are crazy, *Mian*! Why care for what she does? You have divorced her, haven't you?" Miran *Mian* asked.

"She has been my wife."

"If you want to know the truth, she was never your wife!"

"What about the *nikah*?"

"It was thoroughly illegal."

"How?"

"It was never valid. No one knows who begot her. And I suppose *nikah* with a bastard is not valid." Miran *Mian* passed the verdict.

"So the *nikah* never came into effect?" Mirza asked.

"Never!" confirmed Miran *Mian*.

"And I never lost face either? My family's reputation is safe." Mirza felt immensely relieved. "But what about the divorce?" He asked, worried.

"My dear, no *nikah* no divorce!"

"So the 32 rupees were wasted!" Mirza said sorrowfully.

In no time, news travelled all over the neighbourhood that Mirza was married to his 'wife,' that the *nikah* and divorce had both been unlawful.

When Lajo heard the news she danced with joy. The nightmare that was her marriage, and divorce, was over.

What made her happy was the fact that *Mian* had not lost face, after all. She had genuinely grieved that he had lost honour because of her. What a boon it is to be a bastard, she thought. God forbid, were she a legitimate child...even the idea of such a possibility made her a shudder.

Lajo was feeling suffocated at Ramu's grandmother's. Thoughts of the house kept her worried.

Mian could not have had it cleaned or dusted it for fear of theft. The place must be in a mess.

One day, Mirza was on his way to the shop when Lajo waylaid him.

"*Mian*, shall I resume the duty from tomorrow?"

"Damn," said Mirza and walked away briskly. "But I will have a maid sooner or later." He thought. "Maybe this wretch, if none other."

Lajo did not wait for Mirza to make up his mind. She jumped into the house from the roof, tied up her *lehanga* and set to work.

That evening, on his return, Mirza's breath caught in his throat. It was as if late *Bi Amma* had come back!

The house was sparkling clean. A smell of incense filled the air. The pitcher was filled with water and over that was placed a well-scrubbed bowl.

Mirza's heart went heavy with nostalgia. He ate the roast mutton and *paranthas* in hushed silence.

As usual, Lajo sat on the doorstep fanning the flies away.

At night, she spread a jute mat on the kitchen floor and went to sleep.

Mirza once again had a severe bout of thirst. He tossed and turned, listening to the provocative tinkle of her anklets. It clutched at his heart, as also a feeling of guilt. He felt he had been very unfair to her and had grossly underestimated the poor creature. A deep sense of regret overtook him. He lay cursing himself.

Then with a sudden, "Damn it all," he got up, ran across, and collected the housewife from the mat.

Translated from the Urdu by
Fatima Ali

22

LOWER DEPTHS

Sagar Sarhadi

Crying is a tough job. Not really up my street. Could have performed this miracle during childhood: weep a bucketful when hungry. Considered it a couple of times when young. Let loose into a rhythm after drinking; that would have embarrassed any classical singer

Crying is now an expensive proposition. Think of a way to laugh whenever things turned sour and reached a crying point. New formulas; I am an expert at this.

But my wife must get a *Padma Bhushan* for her expertise at crying. Dropping tears if there is no ration; let out a downpour if a child has fallen sick, tears again if the neighbour's wife demanded repayment of loan—as if she has an ice factory inside her; a little sunlight of gloom and out comes a cup of tears.

But then, there should be a place for the factory! She is like a dry bamboo—as if bones had been pasted together with gumpaste. Touch her anywhere, and you will have burns. Like a thin stem. I told her so.

She thought I was devising a new technique to make her laugh.

But I told her lovingly, very seriously. Called her sister! Isn't it wise to make my wife a sister? She would be happy, I would be free, I even suggested that she fall sick and take a ticket to heaven. I will organise a feast for the locality. Alternatively, she could go the village. Just stand there in the middle of the fields with hands spread wide like a scarecrow. Leave aside the fields, the thieves wouldn't even step into the village on seeing your ugly face!

But then, women are foolish. They have brains in their ankles. Neither my wife nor my mother understood my sentiments the wife was ready with tears, and mother picked up the broom and started hitting me, showering the choicest of abuses simultaneously. I was happy performing *Kathakali*.

I said, "Enough mother! I am a father of three ugly, starving children. I too have some respect. People of the locality talk to me and strangers pay respect to me."

This infuriated mother. She threatened to bugger my status. My mother looked like my wife who had been living with me like a sister for a long time now! But the old bones were tough for she kept up the beating. To make matters worse, I could not stop laughing.

Then the *qawali* programme started!

First a son started blowing a trumpet; then the daughter started playing the *tanpura*. Some neighbouring women descended.

One of them was solid stuff! Something or the other would come to hand wherever one touched her. Really sumptuous! I had my eyes on her for long. But she would not let me touch her. I often thought of sneaking into her house, but mother put me off. She frightened me. The woman also never encouraged

me. Why would she? A bankrupt man, looking like a sick
pony—I was also stick thin like my wife.

Mother continued beating me. Finally, I apologised in front
of all of them. Said I was just joking. And even though mother
understood the situation, she kicked my ass a couple of times.
In front of all of them!

Now, how much time can anyone waste in such a house?
I had been stripped of my dignity in front of everyone in the
locality.

And that fat woman. Chewing betel leaves beneath her
small teeth she let out a breath through her luscious lips: The
lips that turned me on; lips that have excited me through years.
But why would she sleep with me? A man should be able to
tackle his woman in the house. But I had been unsuccessful.
It was only me who converted the whole thing into a joke and
came out into the street saving up a semblance of respectability
in the process.

But once in the street, my position was no better than that
of a broom-beaten puppy; making strange sounds, looking for
a place to hide finally to find refuge under the parapet of some
shop or a ditch.

On top of it all, it was dusk seductively smiling at me like
that fat woman, chewing *paan,* leaving her lips half open and
swinging her hips. I was smouldering. A wound had been stirred.
The mind turned crazy. What should one do if everything
turned sour? No trick worked. The body itched wherever it
has been beaten by broom or the *chappals.* I couldn't hide like
a puppy to save my skin. I touched my back. Even the tail had
disappeared! Had there been one I would have held onto it to
find some other support. Who will fall into the trap? I was
born broke. Who would hear my tale of woes?

I wondered if I could fleece my daughter's silver locket. But the girl had become clever. She had slipped out of the father's hand and landed into the mother's lap. Besides, mother was still angry. Now even my daughter had the same opinion about me. Not finding any other corner, I decided to walk over to Dubey's house, thinking, God is great and merciful. He will find a way out.

Sitting cross-legged on the mattress, wearing his 32-year-old vest, Dubey was scratching himself. A heap of newspapers lay in front of him. A newspaper addict, he dabbled in politics and commented on international affairs. His thinking was warped and distinctly his own.

Whenever someone wanted tea, he would present himself and pretend to listen intently. I found the situation uncomfortable and detested it. Listen to Dubey's crap for two hours without laughing! Just for a cup of tea! Laughter would burst like crackers inside the stomach, desperate to come to the lips. The cup of tea would break in front of our eyes. We would pinch one another to suppress laughter, deliberately, to induce pain.

But in those moments, the cup of tea would be dearer than life; therefore the necessity to talk about Vietnam or Kampuchea or discuss the political situation in Poland or any other name that came to the lips. And seek his expert opinion. He would stop scratching himself for a while, look at us as if we were a bunch of fools. Then he would close his eyes, as if lost in deep thoughs; as if the TV cameras of the whole world were focused on him and his comments were to appear in the next edition of *The Times*.

Dubey had the same attitude towards leaders. He would drop names of Che Guevara, Khrushchev, Zhou Enlai, Henry

Kissinger, as if they were his chums and had just left that ugly, narrow, stinking room after a cup of tea.

This was the crucial moment. One of us would suggest tea before he started speaking. He would adjust the lines on his forehead, give a stylish turn to his 'asshead,' because it was important to have a cup of tea before deliberating on international affairs. One of us would call out to the vendor outside and order tea. And then Dubey would let out his fiery speech.

He would close his eyes, lick his lips and go on endlessly. The moment tea got over, we would disperse, bursting out with uncontrolled laughter. Then one of us would give it to him, "Fuck off, you bastard. Don't you know we heard that crap because we wanted tea? Go shove up that crap where it does not stink."

And we would run, and Dubey would chase us in his 32-year-old vest, flicking his dirty *lungi* which would often open. The urchins and stray dogs in the lane would join us in this game. Ruin Dubey's evening and have our fun!

Apart from politics, Dubey suffered from another fallacy; the misconception that every beautiful woman in the lane was in love with him. Whenever he returned from a tour, he would have umpteen tales up his sleeves How, where and which woman took the initiative and praised his manliness.

Dubey looked no better than the million sons of the soil who crowded the streets and fields in the country, wandering aimlessly. Sunken cheeks, as if someone had pasted them there with a shoe! He was short and always wore dirty clothes. Perhaps never even changed them! Or maybe he did on some festive occasion. When he spoke, half the sentences remained glued to his lips, some turned into murmurs, and the rest came out of his throat like dry spit. And the joke was that in these things, he fathomed, lay hidden his manliness that could turn any woman on.

But today Dubey wasn't sitting on the mattress in his usual cross-legged position. Instead, his head was on the pillow and his arms were covering his eyes. As in deep meditation! The pillow did not have a cover, but had the map of every Indian state imprinted on it, for the years of 'unwashed' usage.

"Are you sleeping, Sir?" I asked.

"Do you think I am the Indian public?"

I felt uncomfortable asking another question. He seemed to be in a difficult mood.

"Sir, that woman on the second floor was asking about you."

"Don't take me for a fool. Con someone else, I've no money."

Too bad, I thought. I was losing hope. But I wouldn't let him off so easily. I continued...

"What do you think of the Assam situation?"

"Ask the Mullah who teaches the Koran to the kids."

The evening was getting on and all my efforts seemed to lead nowhere. Dubey was one man in the neighbourhood who was never frustrated over anything. An incorrigible optimist! All of us would break down and get worried on the smallest pretext—food, clothes, sickness in the family, the school fees of the children. They would all make us miserable. But this man sat on the mattress, in his 32-year-old dirty vest, as Gautama Buddha sat under the Bodhi tree. I seemed to be losing my bearings. I felt like crying. I literally started begging. "I am in agony, Dubeyji. I will be nowhere if don't help. Think of something. It is a tough night ahead."

There was nothing else I could say.

One-eyed Siddiq had a joint in Kamathipura's 13th lane.

It had the cheapest liquor in town; three rupees a bottle. All the whores of the area, pimps, pickpockets, loafers and the eunuchs from *Safed Gali* landed up there; a filthy place with leakage all over. I had some position there, though Dubey enjoyed more clout.

We used to undertake the four kilometre walk in the hope that under the impact of liquor I would recite a Mir or a Ghalib couplet and Siddiq would close his good eye too and give us a quarter free or a credit of a rupee or two. Beyond this, neither we nor he could afford.

No one was allowed to sit there. He was tough with everyone, especially the whores. So everyone had to gulp their drink and get lost. But we were allowed the privilege, to sit for an hour or two; lick salt, and take a bite.

The reason for the cheap liquor was that Siddiq mixed acid and oxide water from rusted batteries so that it brewed faster and gave a quick kick. The residents of Kamathipura had just one need; a fast kick.

Dubey put his right hand into his dirty *pyjama* pocket and made strange movements there. I wondered if he was going to masturbate! But I checked myself from saying anything and sat with bated breath. This was the last hope. Besides, when Dubey's hand was in action, it was bound to do something! Finally, he showed me a fifty-paisa coin like a magician would show a trick.

I shouted, "Keep up the magical game, brother. It is a tough night. After the beating it wasn't possible to face the three women in the house."

Dubey lifted the mattress and together with a heap of dust picked up some loose change. Then he searched into the pockets of his solitary terelene trousers.

The trouser carried interesting tales about it. He frequently said that when he was three inches above ground, after three quarters of liquor, the trouser did wonders!

One day, when we left Siddiq's joint past midnight, we were happy. Each one of us had consumed more than half a bottle. The dust and battery-cells had done their trick. Our skins had stiffened like that of cattle. Each part of the body felt like a separate detached piece, miraculously stuck together. That night we were six inches above the ground. We had had our share of fun with our favourite whores. Dawn was round the corner. Only the tail end of the night remained.

We assembled at the Madanpura crossing. With his Liliputian height, Dubey resembled Napolean Bonaparte. He removed his "historic" trousers and unfurled it in front of us like a flag, each of us wondering if we could tell its colour. Battery cells danced in front of our eyes. Yet, each one of us stared, smelt, touched and tasted it but none could pinpoint the exact colour of that "historic" pair of trousers. I wasn't the one to give up easily. I counted all the colours one by one. Dubey lifted the trousers, imitating Spanish matadors with the red cloth. The stitching had come undone and the zipper had lost its original place. It looked as though it was laughing at us.

Finally, the moment arrived when priests and *maulvis* say their prayers, go to the temple or the mosque to remember their gods. Dubey said whenever he was in trouble, and hope abandoned him, the sky slipped down three inches; then when night turned into day or day turned into the evening, if he searched his trouser pockets, he always found a fiver or a tenner. At times even more! But then it had to be at that precise moment.

All of us bowed our heads to the pair of trousers in reverence; that colourless pair of trousers which had been with

Dubey ever since terelene was first manufactured! We prayed and hoped it would be our benefactor once again. So today, when Dubey dug out a fiver from that classic trouser of his, our happiness knew no bounds and we briskly marched towards one-eyed Siddiq's joint.

We did a sensible thing that night. Saving two rupees, we put all the money in front of Siddiq, pleading, "You alone can help us tonight, Siddiq Bhai. These days God has forsaken us and befriended the rich. But you don't be so cruel on us tonight. The dreaded dawn will come with a lot of demands. We are in trouble. The fear of morning will make the night difficult. You are an old friend. So have mercy on us."

The praise made Siddiq close even his other eye. But this appeal had such an impact on a eunuch that it started crying. A couple of prostitutes also started sobbing. And putting these citizens of India to work, we started gulping down the yellow liquid. In no time we were ready to face the night. We were literally staggering.

I told Dubey, "Brother, you go to that corner and piddle. Meanwhile, I will go and fix Radhabai. If I manage credit, we will get rid of our depression and then go home and sleep in peace."

Almost swaying in the air, stretching his legs wide, his eyes glued down, Dubey was searching for the lost four-anna coin. He suddenly remembered a 32-year-old song. But he couldn't recite the whole couplet even once...

Saajan ki galiyan chod chale
Dil roya aansoo beh na sake!
(I am leaving behind the lanes of the beloved.
The heart cries but yes shed no tears.)

He would either forget the beloved or lose his way in the lanes. At times, forgetting everything else, he would collect the tears in his lap.

My skin has stiffened like that of dead cattle. Everything we stood for, we had left it back at Siddiq's stinking joint. The nagging thought now was the need for a woman, man or even an animal! Otherwise, there would be frustration. Dubey had given me the remaining two bucks. Now what could one do with that little money? Credit was the only hope.

I had been to Radhabai before. She was a whore in her 30s. Seeing me, she could screw up her nose and call me a drunkard. But she was the only one I knew in that area. Dubey was loitering around in the streets.

When I shouted back a third time seeking mercy, she simply said, "Alright. But come back soon."

It seemed even Radhabai had overheard Dubey. She shouted even from a distance, "Hey, you drunken bastard. What're you coming here for?"

And then when she saw my face, indicating a 130 degree angle after eight drinks, she gave me a sumptuous pat on the back with her fat hands. She pushed me down the stairs when I said I was broke, saying, "Get lost, what have you come here for without money?"

Stumbling, I returned to Dubey like an unstamped envelope. By that time Dubey had reached a stage which only poets, sufis and saints could achieve. He was simply swaying his head, as if someone else had been singing for him. His own voice was lost. His face was calm and there was a thin smile on his lips.

This was the difference between Dubey and me. I would get restless and loiter around after drinking; as if ants were crawling over my body.

Somehow, I pushed Dubey till the next crossing. His body continued to sway, complete with a smile.

I ran towards the toilet round the corner. Once in a while, Chameli *jaan*, the eunuch, waited there for a customer.

The toilet and Chameli *jaan* were like bedfellows. After midnight, this toilet was a unique place; lost and troubled souls came here for shelter. Sticking to the walls, many appeared to be hanging on nails, silently watching. Breaths stumbled, and wandered in the atmosphere, and died at some lonely spot. Foul smell merged into the body like warmth. The moisture on the walls was like colour on one's face. And the yellowness of the urine was spread on the spirits. Having tried her luck, a tired Chameli *jaan* would often stand there by the wall, well past midnight; sometimes in search of a customer, sometimes looking for a companion and sometimes to kill the unbearable time. Silently, almost holding her breath!

And whenever I found myself near the toilet, I knew I was lonely and sad. There were times when I stood near a leaking roof, like an old battered tree, and the wind blew over. This upheaval took place within it also, as if wandering in the ruins. The leaking water would travel down from head to toe.

But Chameli *jaan* always stood there, unmoved, holding her breath silently; almost becoming a part of the wall, she was standing against. I have met Chameli *jaan* in that position three or four times. But we have always met like two units meet, or two zeroes meet!

Hoping against hope, I rushed towards the toilet. Seeing some activity there, I also stopped by. Policemen were abusing, arresting and blowing *lathis* on people. Several of them were being hustled into the parked van. Fortunately, Chameli *jaan* was not one of them.

I once again returned to Dubey like an unstamped envelope. He wanted to know what was next on the agenda. It was obvious he had returned from the beloved's lane. He behaved as if he had not had a drink too many. I suggested we could loiter around a little.

"Let's go to *Safed Gali*," I suggested.

Dubey was silent. Heaving a long breath, he enquired if I too was sad. He said whenever someone tries to laugh all the time it means he is troubled within.

"Do what you want to do," he finally said, "I am with you. But do get me a *paan* with the remaining money." Now who would not be subservient to Dubey's memory? Even in those desperate moments, he remembered the saved money.

Adjacent to Safed Gali was the road that led to the graveyard. A tall, good-looking eunuch stood there waiting for a customer. She measured me up and instantly understood that we were freaks just loitering around. I went close and pulled her towards me. Both of us had nothing to do and were just trying to have some fun! She had the upper hand because my need was writ large on my face. Then there was not enough money. Besides, she was good-looking.

The eunuch was clever. The way she moved her hands over my body alerted me to her intentions. But she was quick and in a split second, I realised that the remaining money was gone.

Had it been any other time I would have searched the eunuch's body for the money. But now I was hit by a sense of despair; where to bury the night, where to go, what to do? But then I decided that I had to recover it. So, I moved onto the only course open into me.

"Give me back my money," I said.

"I don't have it," she answered.

"Very clever, huh!" I argued.

"You are a hoodlum?" she countered.

"What do you mean?" I enquired. "All this, after the way you fleeced me! Bloody pick-pocket," I said, angrily.

"What money are you talking about, anyway? she asked.

I moved forward.

By this time, another eunuch had arrived. The money would probably now be transferred.

"Listen, I am asking you in all decency, please return my money."

She let out a tirade, and shouted, "You bloody...how dare you touch me. Come to have fun and then trying to be tough, huh?"

Dubey just hung around chewing *paan*. He was waiting for some untoward incident; something that he could store in his dirty head and later narrate to others.

I had forgotten that the lane belonged to eunuchs. Ugly scenes were not an uncommon phenomenon. New customers came, got looted and were beaten and then chased away. There were times when even murder did not seem improbable here! .

Making my voice a little stern, "Are you returning my money or not?"

"I won't. Do what you can," the eunuch replied.

I decided that by hook or by crook I was going to retrieve my money.

I had noticed that she had hidden a small purse in the blouse, because the right chest was mocking at me. I jumped, and in one swift movement flicked the purse, passed it into Dubey, saying, "Brother, run."

And he ran, as if running for life, and disappeared in no time. The eunuch's face lost all its colour, as if she had been deprived of all fortune. What followed were blows, abuses and kicks. I was no kitten in these matters; always the torch-bearer, when physical blows were exchanged in my home area. I had taken beatings all my life, and didn't have a single straight bone in me. The face was already twisted to a 130 degree angle. The body had nothing but bones. Anybody hitting me would end up with sores on his hands!

Translated from the Urdu by
Suresh Kohli

CONTRIBUTORS

Birendra Kumar Bhattacharya (1924–97) is a towering name in modern Assamese literature, universally acclaimed for his 1979 novel, *Mrityunjay*. His masterpiece for which he won the Sahitya Akademi award in 1961, *Irayuungon*, has also been hailed as a masterpiece of Indian literature. One of the earliest winners of the Jnanpith award he authored 22 novels, 30 songs and several volumes of short stories, apart from essays and literary journals.

Manik Bandopadhyay (1908–56) authored 36 novels and 177 short stories in Bengali, including the classic *Padma Nadir Majhi* (Boat Ride on the Padma River) that was also made into an acclaimed film. His work was inspired both by Freudian and Marxist philosophies, dealing with lives of the ordinary and, probing the human mind—all in a career span of 27 years.

Samaresh Basu (1924–88) adopted two nom-de-plumes—Kalkut and Bhramar—wrote 200 short stories and 100 novels; two of which were banned, for a short spell, on charges of obscenity. Also called "the most representative story writer of Bengal's suburban life," drawing substantially from his own life, Basu lived and observed experiences 'half urban, half rural' of life in Kolkata.

Padma Sachdev (b. 1940) is a poet, novelist and a short story writer in the Dogri language, who also writes in Hindi. Her works have been translated into several other Indian languages and also into English: some of these include a collection of short stories, *Where Has My Gulla Gone*, and autobiography *A Drop in the Ocean*.

Manohar Malgaonkar (1913–2010), an author of 24 fiction and non-fiction books, is renowned for using the socio-historical milieu of those times (pre-and-post independence) to form the backdrop of novels like *The Princes, Bend in the Ganges, Combat of Shadows, Distant Drums,* among others. His contribution is seminal and salutary, based on British times. often drawing on his own experiences and observations while serving in the Army. RK Narayan is believed to have described Malgoankar as his "favourite Indian novelist in English."

RK Narayan (1906–2001), together with Raja Rao and Mulk Raj Anand formed an alliance that compelled the English to take writing from India seriously. Almost all of Narayan's works are set in a small fictional South Indian town called Malgudi. Simple narratives with humour that do not miss out on insights into the lives of his characters make his writings eminently readable. 15 novels, six collections of short stories, eight works of non-fiction and three books of reflections on Hindu mythology, complete the author's repertoire.

Gulabdas Broker (1909–2006) is one of the finest exponents of short fiction in Gujarati and known for an insightful depiction of the life of the middle-class; the inner world of an individual, including man-woman relationships, in an otherwise orthodox society.

Aabid Surti (b. 1935) is a multifaceted personality: cartoonist, painter, journalist, environmental activist, playwright, film script writer and an author of 80 books, including 45 novels and 10 story collections – full of satire and dark humour – in Gujarati and Hindi; many of which have fetched him national honours.

Nirmal Verma (1929–2005) is amongst the pioneers of *Nai Kahani* or the 'New Story Movement' in Hindi and the author of five novels, eight short story collections and nine non-fiction books. Verma's works are charged with vivid themes, techniques and economy of expression. In his own words, "My work essentially deals with situations arising out of troubled relationships amongst members of the same family or strained man-woman ties."

Bhisham Sahni (1915–03) was amongst the most prolific writers in the post-independence era with novels, short stories and plays in Hindi dealing with the marginalised sections of the society. He was also a teacher (English literature), translator, polygot—even an actor. *Tamas*, his magnum opus of sorts, reflecting the tragedy of partition and its aftermath, won universal appreciation for its bold but sensitive handling of the subject. It was also made into a television serial. His biography of his brother, actor Balraj Sahni, and autobiography, *Aaj ke Ateet* (Parts of the Present) are some of his other works; apart from seven novels, six plays and more than a 100 stories.

Masti Venkatesha Iyengar (1891–1986), fourth amongst the eight Jnanpith writers in Kannada, Iyengar has been acclaimed mainly as a short story writer, using the pen name of "Srinivasa". He authored 137 books, including 17 in English. His stories were underlined with pathos, underplayed satire and dealt with the working classes and till today remain unparalleled.

Amin Kamil (b. 1924) is primarily a poet and playwright, who has also published a novel and volumes of short stories dealing with life in rural areas of the valley; marked by a judicious mix of irony, humour and socio-political commentary. *Kokar Jung* or *The Cock Fight*, written in the mid-60s, is among his most popular works.

Paul Zacharia (b. 1945) is a controversial name in the annals of modern Malayalam fiction. A severe critic of orthodoxy in life, his radical views and unconventional approach lends an exclusivity to his writing that is unknown in Kerala fiction. Often centre-stage for his socially and politically committed views, Zacharia lives and works in Thiruvantapuram.

Manoj Das (b. 1934) is a multi-award winner in Oriya and English and has been teaching English at Sri Aurobindo Ashram, Puducherry. Talking about his works, distinguished English master, Graham Greene once observed: "I have read the stories of Manoj Das with great pleasure. He will certainly take a place on my shelves besides Narayan. I imagine Orissa is far from Malgudi, but there is the same quality in his stories with perhaps an added mystery."

Gopinath Mohanty (1914–1991) is regarded as the second

greatest writer in Oriya fiction and a winner of almost all literary awards and distinctions. His 24 novels and 10 collections of short stories are known for their portrayal and interpretation of various aspects of human existence, especially insights into the vibrant rural and tribal life in Orissa.

Ajeet Cour (b. 1934) is a strong, bold feminist writer in the Punjabi language, who was born in Lahore. Her shorter fiction, in particular, emphasises the unequal place of women in multiple relationships. She has authored 20 collections of short stories, two novels, three novelettes and a controversial autobiography, *Khanabadosh,* besides newspaper writings on socio-religious issues.

Sant Singh Sekhon (1908–1997) is the author of five collections of short stories, two novels and five books of literary criticism, the most pioneering work being *Punjabi Boli Da Itihas* (History of the Punjabi language). He advocated strong social activism; highlighting questions and dilemmas facing the characters using a subtly philosophical refrain.

Popati Hiranandani (1924–2005) is a poet, short story writer, novelist, essayist, literary critic, biographer, and even has an autobiography in Sindhi called *Huhinje Hayatia Ja Sona Roopa verse* (Golden Silver Pages of My Life) in which she observed "A woman is made to suffer not on account of any vice in her character but because of her virtues." The autobiography has been described as, profound and energising and gives a remarkable insight into Sindhi society and the social and political upheavals following the partition of India.

Ashokamitran (b. 1931 as Jagadisa Thagarajan) is a distinguished Tamil novelist and short story writer renowned for his use of subtle satire and undercurrents of sharp humour, dealing with the life of what's generally called the lower rungs of society. Many feel his depiction of life in Secunderabad (his birth place) and Chennai (his *karmabhoomi*) is unparalled. Author of eight novels, 15 novellas and more than 200 short stories. 'Happy New Gear' was authored in the mid-1960s.

Yaddanapudi Sulochana Rani (b. 1939) is a popular fiction writer, many of whose works have been successfully made into Telegu films. She has published 70 novels and two selections of short stories for which she has won many literary and film-related awards. Her works have also been translated into Malayalam and Kannada. Her work largely deals with the complexities and paradoxes in middle-class families.

Ismat Chughtai (1915–91) has been regarded as a feminist and a stormy petrel of modern Urdu literature. Although a product of elitist India, she drew her characters from the underdogs; the marginalised sections of society. She also wrote stories and scripts for several Hindi films—including *Junoon* and *Garm Hawa*—apart from producing and directing a film herself. Amongst her most prominent works is the short story *Lihaaf* (*Quilt*) for which she was dragged to Lahore High Court on charges of promoting lesbianism. She ultimately won the case.

Sagar Sarhadi (b. 1933) playwright, short story writer and script-writer for films like *Kabhi Kabhie, Silsila, Chandni* and director of critically acclaimed films like *Bazaar*, has been associated with the now defunct Progressive Writers' Movement. His short stories generally deal with street fighters and oppressed and sexually victimized women in the infamous bylanes of Mumbai.